Intersectional Feminist Criminology

Intersectional Feminist Criminology

A CRITICAL COMPANION TO THEORY AND RESEARCH

Venezia Michalsen

UNIVERSITY OF CALIFORNIA PRESS

University of California Press
Oakland, California

© 2025 by Venezia Michalsen

All rights reserved.

Library of Congress Cataloging-in-Publication Data

Names: Michalsen, Venezia, author
Title: Intersectional feminist criminology : a critical companion to theory and research / Venezia Michalsen.
Description: Oakland, California : University of California Press, [2025] | Includes bibliographical references and index.
Identifiers: LCCN 2024054952 (print) | LCCN 2024054953 (ebook) | ISBN 9780520380288 (cloth) | ISBN 9780520380295 (paperback) | ISBN 9780520380301 (ebook)
Subjects: LCSH: Feminist criminology
Classification: LCC HV6020 .M64 2025 (print) | LCC HV6020 (ebook) | DDC 364.082—dc23/eng/20250403
LC record available at https://lccn.loc.gov/2024054952
LC ebook record available at https://lccn.loc.gov/2024054953

Manufactured in the United States of America

GPSR Authorized Representative: Easy Access System Europe,
Mustamäe tee 50, 10621 Tallinn, Estonia,
gpsr.requests@easproject.com

34 33 32 31 30 29 28 27 26 25
10 9 8 7 6 5 4 3 2 1

To my son, Bowie, for more reasons than I could ever count.
I love you.

Contents

Acknowledgments ix

Introduction: Change Your Lens! 1

PART I   "THIS BRIDGE CALLED MY BACK":
RESEARCH METHODS AND CRIMINOLOGICAL
THEORIES   5

1. Research Methods   13
2. Classical and Neo-classical Theories   31
3. Biological and Positivist Theories   44
4. Psychological Theories   56
5. Social Process and Social Development Theories   66
6. Social Structure Theories   83
7. Theories of Victimology   100
8. Critical Criminology   116

PART II	"OUR BODIES, OURSELVES": TYPES OF CRIMES	127
9.	Crimes against People	131
10.	Crimes against Property	145
11.	White-Collar and Environmental Crimes	155
12.	Public Order Crimes	170
PART III	"THE MASTER'S TOOLS": THE CRIMINAL JUSTICE SYSTEM	189
13.	Reforming Police, Courts, and Corrections	193
14.	Abolition	212
	Notes	227
	Bibliography	245
	Index	291

Acknowledgments

My husband, David Caban, made this book possible with his partnership in life, love, and parenting. David, your insights, encouragement, problem-solving, sense of humor, flexibility, and co-parenting allowed me to put my entire self into this work, and I am forever grateful. I love you. My son, Bowie, is always in my heart and mind as I do my work for so many reasons. Bowie, your fierce love, intellect, and analytical swiftness make you so very special, and I am so proud of how hard you have worked toward your best self every day.

I could also never have done this without the rest of my family. To my parents, you instilled feminism, anti-racism, critical thinking, and hard work into me from as early as I can remember. This book is what it is because of you both. To Ravenna, Seth, Adelaide, Charles, and Pocket, I am so grateful to you for the joy that you bring to my life, especially my sister Ravenna, who has always made sure I keep my intellectual arguments sharp. To Don, Sue, Gabby, and Donna, the expanse of your love and kindness adds so much joy to my life. I am so glad you are my family.

I have been beyond blessed to count so many brilliant, kind, revolutionary, and hardworking people among my colleagues and mentors, many of whom are also very dear friends. I am particularly grateful for the work and partnership of, among others, and listed alphabetically, Beverly Astwood, Kia and David Burden, Lynn Chancer, Todd Clear, Norma Connolly, Anupa Fabian, Jeanne Flavin, Janet Garcia-Hallett, Ann Jacobs, Mike Jacobson, Yolanda Johnson-Peterkin, Samantha Jones, Delores Jones-Brown, Amber Kelly, Aileen Keyes, Tanya Krupat, Karolina Ksiazek, Francesca Laguardia, Mickey Lambert, Charona Lewis, Diane Lewis, Mary Loftus, Nickie Phillips, Hillary Potter, Jewu Richardson, Dina Rose, Amy Smoyer, Natalie Sokoloff, Bianca Tylek, and Jason Williams. I am also so very grateful for the help of so many people who gave their time and energy to making sure that I had the time and energy to do this work, including Lauren Beirne (and Emily and Sardine!), Beth Houley, Esther Park, Lenny Pettitte, Kate Willette, Emily Ziemba, and the many incredible members of Team Bowie.

My forever love and admiration goes to my beloved, incredible friends who have steadied with me as I have crossed yawning abysses and who have celebrated with me the highest of joys: Shannon Ballard, Jacqueline Beirne, Amanda Bertana, Kia Burden, Nina Callaway, Sharon Clayman, Alejandra Fernandez, Kat Fleming, Jenn Heckathorn-Deguzman, Felicia Lewis, Makeda Mays-Green, Bhavana Nancherla, Anuli Njoku, Stephanie Odom, Eliza O'Rourke, Daniela Pila, Diane Purvin, Holly Rider, Robin Ritterman, Alison Satake, Aoife West, and Dawn Wiest.

I love my job. I believe so strongly in the power and importance of public education, and I am grateful to my university, my College of Arts and Sciences, and my sociology department. Most of all, however, I am grateful to my students, who teach me not only in our discussions but as I witness their incredible resilience, grit, and love as they continue to show up every day despite incredible challenges.

Finally, I am so lucky to have a wonderful editor in Maura Roessner and partners in Sam Warren, Susan Silver, Stephanie Summerhays, and the people working at UC Press. I am so very glad that we found one another. I am also so very grateful to the reviewers, who truly moved me with the quality and thoughtfulness of their reviews of drafts of this work. This is what work should be: collaborative, communicative, and centered on social justice.

Introduction

CHANGE YOUR LENS!

Traditional criminological theories tend to ask what is wrong with people that made them break the law. Did they make a bad choice, have a brain injury, or grow up with inadequate parenting, for example? Critical criminology, on the other hand, asks who decided that something should be a crime (and that something else should not), how they benefit from that distinction, and who they keep out of power by creating such rules. Most broadly, critical criminology sheds light on the impact of inequality and power on such things as who breaks the law, why they break the law, who *makes* those laws, and the history and workings of the criminal legal system that responds to those broken laws. While someone taking a class in the mid-twenty-first century may see these concepts as normal, they have been neglected by traditional criminology for most of its existence. Critical criminology is a diverse field, which not only maintains connections to its Marxist roots but has branched out into many different subfields, such as Black feminist criminology, convict criminology, and green criminology.

HOW TO USE THIS BOOK

This book is designed as a supplemental text to a criminology textbook or as a text for a class you take after you have taken an introduction to criminology class. You will *not* get the foundational understanding of the theories and practices critiqued in this book. I have skipped these on purpose so that I, and therefore you, can focus on its unique critical criminological perspective. The book is divided into three parts in a way that mirrors most traditional criminology textbooks: criminological theories, types of crimes, and the criminal legal system. In a traditional criminology textbook, the first part usually reviews the many criminological theories. I follow this same format, but I offer you a critical lens with which to understand the material, providing additional information to which your textbook likely does not refer. In addition, I provide an intersectional perspective that includes the experiences of people from marginalized identities.

Critical criminology likely got one chapter in your traditional criminology textbook. This book, on the other hand, infuses a critical perspective into every page of the text so that you are encouraged to rethink the long-worn paths on which your academic career has led you until now. For example, where your criminology textbook likely refers to *minorities*, I will use the term *minoritized*. The difference of just a few letters is very important, for using the word *minoritized* more accurately reflects the power inherent in creating and defining a group of people as lesser: "Referring to Black and Brown people as racial and ethnic 'minorities'

CRITICAL THINKING BREAK 1

Is there something about you that has been defined as "minority"? How does it change your perception of yourself and others as "minoritized" (implying that someone did it *to you*)? Such questions may make you feel uncomfortable—that is okay! Growth and learning happen in uncomfortable places. When you need to, take a break for a glass of water or a breath of fresh air and then get back to reading.

misleads and misdirects attention from racial oppression. The word 'minority' implies that Black and Brown people are fewer in quantity or lesser in quality compared to the white 'majority.' Worldwide, darker-skinned populations outnumber fair-skinned (i.e., white) people and will become the quantitative majority in the United States within 20 years. Further, the reason darker-phenotyped American individuals currently exist in smaller numbers relative to white Americans results from white supremacist policies of abduction and enslavement, restrictive immigration, educational and employment deprivation, reproductive control, carceral discrimination, and healthcare exclusion."[1]

WHO I AM

You will see that I refer to myself in the first person throughout this book. This may be unfamiliar to you, but it is intentional on my part. I ask you to question the concept of *objectivity*, or the very idea that there is a singular knowledge that is measurable and discoverable. On the other hand, I ask you to consider the *standpoint* of the researchers producing and analyzing that knowledge. What experiences and identities are they bringing to their choices about the subject of the research, their methodology, their analysis, and their conclusions? For example, I am a white cisgender woman, the mother of an autistic preteen boy, the wife of an army veteran, and a state university professor with a PhD, who grew up in the northeastern United States. Instead of trying to shed these identities, I choose to welcome them into my work. I recognize that my standpoint impacts the way that I understand and present knowledge. In this book I am asking you to ask similar questions of your textbook, which likely comes from a more objective perspective, and of yourself: Who are you? How does your standpoint impact how you interpret the field of criminology?

Let's do this!

PART I   "This Bridge Called My Back"

RESEARCH METHODS AND CRIMINOLOGICAL THEORIES

WHAT ARE CRIMINOLOGICAL THEORIES?

Most broadly, criminology is the scientific study of crime. In the first part of the twentieth century, Edwin Sutherland defined criminology more specifically as the study of lawmaking, lawbreaking, and the response to lawbreaking.[1] A theory is a way to explain how concepts are related; criminological theories, for the sake of this book, are different ways that experts explain what leads to crime. Criminological theories are generally broken into six categories:

1. Classical and neo-classical theories, which focus on choice
2. Biological theories, which focus on the body
3. Psychological theories, which focus on the mind and mental illness
4. Social structural theories, which focus on the social and economic arrangements between social groups
5. Social process theories, which focus on learning and group membership
6. Critical theories, which hand you a new lens through which to look at how the powerful criminalize the survival strategies of the less powerful

Traditional criminology textbooks focus on the theories of individual and collective shortcomings that cause people to break the law: often five chapters of the mainstream theories ask, What's wrong with those criminals? Not only have many of these theoretical traditions stalled, but most fail to account for larger structural components, and almost all of them fail to explain one of the two most prominent facts in crime research: the gender gap. "Criminologists use the term 'gender gap' to refer to differences in the rate, seriousness, and frequency of men's and women's crime participation. Indeed, whether crime is measured by arrest, self-report, or victimization data, one pattern is clear: men and boys participate at a rate five to ten times higher than women and girls do. Furthermore, studies consistently find gender differences in the frequency and seriousness of criminal involvement, with men participating more often, and in more serious crimes than women."[2] You may have noticed that this quote refers to gender as a binary, whereas gender is more accurately referred to as a spectrum. However, criminology and the criminal legal system almost always adhere to the binary, so this book usually has to refer to only men and women. On the other hand, critical theorists ask not why they broke the law but rather who made the law and why.

In 2001 feminist criminologist Jeanne Flavin wrote "Feminism for the Mainstream Criminologist: An Invitation," outlining the ways in which the broader field of criminology could learn from feminism, from its research methods to its theories. Over a decade later, in 2013, feminist criminologists Meda Chesney-Lind and Merry Morash put out a call in the journal *Critical Criminology* for the field of criminology as a whole to *center* gender and social justice: "Feminism and feminist theory offers all of criminology incredible intellectual vitality and a recommitment to go beyond the collecting and disseminating of knowledge to seeking a just, equitable, and healthy world for all." Kim Cook, a few years later, rhetorically asked, "Has Criminology Awakened from Its 'Androcentric Slumber?'" Black feminist criminologist Hillary Potter showed the ways in which criminology would benefit from an intersectional approach that centers people's identities (such as race, gender, queerness, and disability) and the ways in which those identities shape their experiences, especially when it comes to the criminal legal system.

Jennifer Musto likewise called for criminology to be "transed," embracing trans frameworks, including transgender, transnational, and transformative feminist perspectives: "Just as transing gender includes a movement away from culturally contained gender categories—a move where the crossing of gender also signals 'going beyond' constructed binary gender categories that contain it—transing critical criminology entails another boundary crossing of sorts—in this instance, a conceptual crossing geared toward opening up space for the cultivation of theories and frameworks to address carceral developments, including its expansion in feminist directions."[3] In this book I seek to amplify these strong but often lonely voices, showing you from a pedagogical standpoint what you are missing when you read a criminology textbook without a critical eye.

In this part of the book, I require that you take a look at each of these old categories of theories with new eyes, encouraging a sense of wonder at the ways in which, for example, racist stereotypes, adherence to traditional gender roles, and ableist and anti-queer biases have for many years constrained criminological thinking and the ways in which a critical perspective in general problematizes all of our traditional criminological ways of thinking. All these theories are problematic in their own right, but they have also been what criminologist John Laub labeled "translational," which "aims to break down barriers between basic and applied research by creating a dynamic interface between research and practice. This process is a two-way street—scientists discover new tools/ideas for use in the field and evaluate their impact. In turn, practitioners offer novel observations from the field that stimulate basic investigations. This is the knowledge creation process."[4] However, such translation happened in the wrong way: they have often led to policies that have not only failed all of our communities but have continued to perpetuate the worst of American traditions. The critical perspective in criminology asks us to step outside of the box in which we have gotten comfortable, where we ask what is wrong with someone who commits crime, and look instead at the larger systems that set certain people up for success and others up for prison.

HOW TO BE CRITICAL AS YOU READ

Abigail Henson, Thuy-Trinh Nguyen, and Ajima Olaghere proposed an "undoing" of prominent theories by inverting them—from the original focus on deficits to theories that center race, racism, and acts of resistance in the face of oppression.[5] In the following chapters I challenge you to view your regular textbook with a critical eye, as Henson, Nguyen and Olaghere suggest. For whom have these theories always worked? Whom are they most likely to ensnare? As with history, white men dominate criminology because they write it.[6]

The Origin of the Name of This Part

In 1981 Cherríe Moraga and Gloria E. Anzaldúa first published *This Bridge Called My Back: Writings by Radical Women of Color*, a groundbreaking anthology of essays, poems, stories, and artwork. One important thread of the work was that feminism could not be about just shared womanhood, because the challenges facing white women are very different from those of women of color. This concept is now often conceptualized as intersectionality, thanks to feminist legal scholar Kimberlé Crenshaw, who based the concept in Black feminist theory and critical race theory. The concept of the "bridge" comes from the poem titled "The Bridge Poem," by Kate Rushin, in which she expresses exhaustion and anger at being used by others for their own benefit, while she is harmed instead of being herself and meeting her own needs.[7]

I extend this metaphor to remind you that traditional criminological theories, focused primarily on men's crime, walk on the bridges of feminism created by scholars such as Moraga, Anzaldúa and Crenshaw. This idea is also important when it comes to men's crime and rehabilitation, which is also often done breaking the backs of women either as victims or as the people who hold it down when they are inside or coming out of incarceration. If you were to look more closely at the bridge on which these theorists are walking, whose backs would you see? Would you see your own? What if the bridge were more important and interesting than the walkers, and if that bridge became "the bridge to my own power"?[8] Look at the methods; look at the ideas; look at the focus. How can you shift your perspective to question these long-standing ideas and make us all better?

Whereas regular introductory textbooks dedicate a single chapter to critical perspectives; small sidebars to gender, disability, race, and queerness; and a section of the glossary to translational criminology, this book centers those topics, showing the ways in which we must all recognize that they are the true bones of this discipline. This section starts with theories. Get ready to change your lens and get uncomfortable; it's the best way to learn!

1 Research Methods

In her now classic article, "Feminism for the Mainstream Criminologist: An Invitation," Jeanne Flavin prioritizes the ways in which feminism may be centered in criminological epistemology and in research methodology and methods. Hillary Potter, the founder of Black feminist criminology, expands on this in her book *Intersectionality and Criminology: Disrupting and Revolutionizing Studies of Crime*, where she writes that we must follow the traditions of feminist criminology and critical race theory to center people of color and that we must take an intersectional approach in criminological research. Where research methods in any social science are presented as objective, this chapter reminds students to accept Flavin's invitation and to disrupt like Potter, taking a critical perspective to even the data and methods of criminological research, and introduces students to critical research methodologies.

CRIME SEEMS EASY TO MEASURE: UCR AND NIBRS

Your criminology textbook likely starts its chapter on how we know what we know about crime with a description of the Uniform Crime Reports

(UCR), which is the most widely used measure of crime in the United States. The FBI collects reports from thousands of the police departments in the United States about the number of crimes that came to their attention over the previous year, either by reports from complainants or victims or as the result of police investigation. The data are only from police departments that volunteer to submit data; as of 2021, only half of the eighteen thousand policing agencies in the country submitted data for the full year, and only 63 percent submitted at least partial data.[1]

The annual report put out by the FBI with those data is titled *Crime in the United States*. Your textbook likely explains that one of the main limitations of the UCR is that it measures only the crime that comes to the attention of the police (certainly not every time someone breaks the law). However, there are other reasons why it is a very flawed measure of crime. For example, it is also only a report of "serious," labeled "index" crimes: murder, assault, burglary, forcible rape, robbery, aggravated assault, larceny-theft, motor vehicle theft, and arson. In addition the UCR requires classification according to the Hierarchy Rule, which states that "when more than one Part I offense is classified, the law enforcement agency must locate the offense that is highest on the hierarchy list and score that offense involved and not the other offense(s) in the multiple-offense situation."[2] This means that the UCR, though marketed and used by media, politicians, and the public alike as *the* measure of crime trends, is anything but that. For example, the data on simple versus aggravated assault tend to be taken as a good way to measure severity, and aggravated assaults are included in the UCR, while simple assaults are not. However, there are many factors that go into whether a victimization is called simple or aggravated, such as whether a weapon was present, how different police officers interpret the event, whether there is pressure from supervisors to downgrade or upgrade the charge, or whether a local department is trying to get funding. These individual decisions pile up into changes in trends that may have nothing to do with how much crime is happening. For example, from 2019 to 2020, the UCR numbers showed a 12 percent increase in aggravated assaults, whereas the National Crime Victimization Survey (explained later) showed a 21 percent decrease in the same offense.[3]

The National Incident-Based Reporting System (NIBRS) was created as the next generation of the UCR to generate more detailed information than is available from the UCR, including more categories of crimes, where and when the offense occurred, victim information on the harm caused by the crime, and information about the people arrested (when there are any). While the NIBRS data are richer than those in the UCR, the accuracy of the findings must be questioned: most importantly, the NIBRS still covers only a fraction of the country compared to the UCR, meaning that it underrepresents large parts of the United States (especially areas with larger populations). Police department submission of data plunged once the submission site changed to NIBRS.[4]

So if the UCR is only a reflection of the volume of crime that comes to the attention of the police, and the NIBRS cannot be used as a representation of the entire country, then why are they published as the ultimate measure of crime in the United States? There are millions of crimes that are not reported to the police, so they are not counted in these reports. In addition there are many reasons why people do not report crime to the police, many of which are impacted by factors such as gender, race, disability, and queerness and many of which are particularly well explained by the reporting of sexual victimization, notoriously underreported.

CRITICAL THINKING BREAK 2

Jock Young, one of the most celebrated critical criminologists, coined the term *datasaurs*, also known as *empiricus abstractus*. The datasaur "is a creature with a very small head, a long neck, a huge belly and a little tail. His head has only a smattering of theory, he knows that he must move constantly but is not sure where he is going, he rarely looks at any detail of the actual terrain on which he travels, his neck peers upwards as he moves from grant to grant, from database to database, his belly is huge and distended with the intricate intestine of regression analysis, he eats ravenously but rarely thinks about the actual process of statistical digestion, [and] his tail is small, slight and inconclusive."[1] What do you think Young is trying to say about criminological research methods with this definition of his neologism?

1. Young, *Criminological Imagination*, 15.

Shame

Karen Weiss specifically investigates the impact of shame on whether people report sexual victimization to the police.[5] Although shame is not particular to sexual victimization, feelings of disgust, shame, and self-blame are particularly common when someone has been sexually assaulted. Weiss argues that society's expectations that women act in "feminine" ways mean that when women are raped, they may blame themselves for their victimization—for going places alone or for getting drunk—or they may be ashamed of being "damaged goods" after the assault.[6] But not only women are raped: male victims feel shame for not living up to the idea of what it means to be a "real man"—strong, powerful, self-sufficient, and impenetrable.[7] They may also be accused of being gay in a homophobic world, and men who do not want to be perceived as gay or feminine may experience particular shame when they are victimized and be especially less likely to report.

Fear of the Criminal Legal Process

One of the most underreported crimes is rape, and one of the reasons is that reports of rape rarely translate into convictions, and the criminal legal system has long failed to address the needs of victims of sexual violence.[8] There is even a well-known concept of *secondary victimization,* in which the behavior and procedures of police, prosecutors, and others within the investigative and prosecutorial process exacerbate the trauma of sexual violence. Specifically, procedures often require repeated retelling of the experience and sometimes cross-examination, with victims having to face the person who victimized them. Police reports often show that police themselves endorse rape myths.[9] In New York City Black and Brown women who know their attacker make up the vast majority of the 8,600 sex crimes reported each year. In 2022 seventeen of these survivors and two of their mothers said that their treatment by the New York Police Department (NYPD) was "negligent and sexist," in a letter to the Department of Justice.[10] With all these additional impacts, combined with dismal rates of accountability for such victimization, it is a wonder that anyone reports at all.

Survivor Credibility

Survivors of sexual assault may not go to the police because they do not think they will be believed, especially if they do not fit common ideas of what victims should look like (e.g., not wearing particular clothing) or how they should have behaved during the assault (e.g., fought back). These concerns are particularly salient for sexual and gender minorities, who "are likely to challenge at least one, and in some instances, all 'perfect victim' stereotypes and police perceptions of legitimacy." For example, bisexual people may be stereotyped to be hypersexual, which may lead police officers to engage in victim blaming.[11]

Perceptions of Police Legitimacy

When the police engage in use of force, particularly when those incidents are controversial, it can engender distrust of the police that suppresses reporting with different impacts depending on race. In 2022, Keller Sheppard and Jacob Stowell found that not only did neighborhood crime reporting decrease following fatal police use of force but reporting was particularly stifled in primarily African American and Latinx neighborhoods and in neighborhoods with high levels of concentrated disadvantage compared to predominantly white neighborhoods and neighborhoods with more advantage.[12] The impact of perceived police legitimacy is particularly impactful for victims of hate crimes, which are especially underreported.[13]

Data Problems

Not all problems with police data are due to people not reporting. For example, when police officers stopped "proactive policing" of small-level offenses, large-level offenses went down according to civilian complaints about crimes as serious as burglary and felony assault.[14] Police officers and departments themselves may also not record crimes that come to their attention: John Eterno, Arvind Verma, and Eli Silverman detail a number of ways in which police officers have been shown to manipulate crime data, including data from whistleblowers who, for example, recounted supervisors instructing entire shifts of officers to not take robbery reports if victims were unwilling to come back to the station house. They also reviewed New York City hospital data that showed a 90 percent increase in hospital visits for assault (and a 129 percent increase in firearm assault visits!) during a time when the NYPD reported a substantial decline. One of the main problems, especially with the NYPD, is the lack of transparency, which means that researchers and even former federal prosecutors assigned by the police commissioner himself are unable to get the data they need to assess the accuracy of crime reporting. Eterno, Verma, and Silverman surveyed 1,770 retired New York City police officers and found that they reported extensive manipulation of crime reports because of a set of core variables including time of retirement, pressure from management to keep crime numbers down, and decreasing pressure from management to accurately report crime and follow rules.[15]

NATIONAL CRIME VICTIMIZATION SURVEY

So if police reports of crime are such a limited measure, then how can we get a more accurate measure of how much crime is happening and whether it is changing over time? One way that the United States has tried to address this is with the use of the National Crime Victimization Survey (NCVS). Annually since 1972, the NCVS has gone straight to sixty thousand U.S. households to ask about victimization and whether victims reported their experience to the police. While the NCVS does not include homicide, arson, and commercial crimes or crimes against children aged eleven or younger, people in institutions, and homeless people (all of which are included in the UCR, if those crimes come to the attention of police), it includes simple assault and sexual assault, which are excluded in the UCR. The NCVS also records background information on victims that allows for more analysis about patterns by such factors as age, gender, marital status, and race. As you might imagine, the NCVS does uncover more victimization than is reported in the UCR, theoretically shining a light on the "dark figure" of crime, which refers to the portion of criminal activity that goes unreported to or undetected by police.[16] In fact, in 2017 over five million more crimes were reported in the NCVS than in the UCR for every single crime category.

While the NCVS is clearly an improvement over the UCR as a measure of victimization, Walter DeKeseredy warns that the data are only as useful as those doing the analysis (or what Dawn Currie and Jock Young call, "so what? Criminology" or "voodoo criminology," respectively, to indicate the meaninglessness of the numbers in explaining lawbreaking).[17] He challenges researchers who conduct research on relatively minor issues, presented in an unintelligible fashion, with their own career advancement in mind, using these large surveys repeatedly because getting a grant is so difficult and time-consuming that they are not able or willing to collect their own data. Indeed, the NCVS itself includes "incident narratives" mostly ignored by researchers, but Karen Weiss found they can include some fruitful information about sexual assault, such as survivors' excuses and justification for their own victimization.[18] DeKeseredy challenges us as researchers and students to be fully aware of the limitations of big surveys, knowing that they are here to stay.

BEYOND THE BIG SURVEYS

While the large surveys such as the UCR, NCVS, and surveys of people in prison by the Bureau of Justice Statistics are the main source of so-called crime data, they are not the only way that we know about people who break the law and about our criminal legal system. There are countless peer-reviewed articles about every facet of the field of criminology, many of which are based on primary data collection. For these studies it is just as important to bring the same critical mindset: Who chose the research topic? Was the research done with human subjects? If so, how were people chosen to participate? Who decided what the questions would be, how they would be asked, and whether they were multiple choice or open-ended? Did they give the respondents money for their participation? Did they give respondents an informed consent form before they participated and a debriefing session after the study was over? Did the researchers disappear after the research was done and respondents had no idea where those data went, or did they come back to update respondents on their findings?

One example of creative ways to measure crime is the Veil of Darkness (VOD) hypothesis, which suggests that racial bias in traffic stops can be

> **CRITICAL THINKING BREAK 3**
>
> Before research findings are published in academic journals, they are reviewed by the authors' peers at those journals. Peer review helps the publisher decide whether to reject an article, suggest that it be revised and resubmitted, or accept the article for publication. Peer review is usually done in a double-blind process in which neither the authors nor the reviewers know who the others are. However, we know that women are underrepresented in the peer-review process.[1] How might you take a critical perspective to peer review? For example, being a peer reviewer is not paid—might women, mothers, and Black and Brown academics be less able to participate, which might result in bias against studies about women or critical perspectives?
>
> 1. Helmer et al., "Gender Bias."

determined by comparing the race of drivers stopped during the day (when police can see their race) versus at night (when police cannot see their race). This has allowed researchers to show evidence of racial profiling, because cops who can see drivers' race are more likely to stop Black drivers in similarly situated stops. The most recent versions of the VOD hypothesis even consider that daylight driving may mean that Black drivers are more careful than their white counterparts because they anticipate racial profiling.[19] Car insurance companies, likewise, are often better judges of motor vehicle theft and damage, emergency rooms of assault and abuse, and glass-replacement companies of vandalism, car accidents, and shootings.

One of the most discussed distinctions in research methods is between qualitative and quantitative methodologies. Both the UCR and the NCVS use quantitative research, defined by data that are "quantifiable," or turned into numbers for statistical analysis. It is often defined in contrast with qualitative research (a contrast which Toby Jayaratne and Abigail Stewart describe as "sterile and based on false polarization").[20] Qualitative research is incredibly varied, from participant observation to interviews, with small numbers of participants interviewed in deep depth to large numbers of people asked open-ended questions.

Qualitative research should not be defined simply as "not quantitative" but rather by its strengths and features.[21] Patrik Aspers and Ugo Corte, in their aptly titled article "What Is Qualitative in Qualitative Research," define it as "an iterative process in which improved understanding to the scientific community is achieved by making new significant distinctions resulting from getting closer to the phenomenon studied."[22] More specifically, it is a combination of creating new knowledge by either questioning what we think we know or coining new concepts and then producing the outcome, which adds new knowledge to the scholarly community. In general, qualitative research does not reduce its material to numbers and variables in a way that serves to distance themselves from its data.

Indeed, instead of creating a dichotomy between qualitative and quantitative data collection, Aspers and Corte delightfully muddy the waters, finding in their research that many quantitative researchers do engage in some qualitative methods, such as when they are developing research questions, variables, and hypotheses. They write, "The categories of 'qualitative' and 'quantitative,' unfortunately, often cover up practices, and it may lead to 'camps' of researchers opposing one another.... Our results open up for an interaction not characterized by differences, but by different emphasis, and similarities."[23] This is a theme you will see repeatedly throughout this book: forcing a black-and-white dichotomy on a real world that is almost always full of grays.

WHAT DOES IT MEAN TO BE A FEMINIST RESEARCHER?

Epistemology is the investigation of what distinguishes justified beliefs from opinions and can be approached in myriad ways to get to knowledge, particularly from a critical perspective. Whereas many people view feminism as a monolith, there are many differing viewpoints within feminism that show up throughout this book. Many people may describe a feminist methodology as a qualitative methodology, but there is no reason for this distinction. Feminist researchers use many different types of research methods, as do traditional researchers, who are by default androcentric (male-centered), so there is no reason to assume that qualitative research is qualitative and vice versa.

When it comes to epistemology and research, Flavin outlines three types of feminist epistemologies:

- **Feminist empiricism:** This approach accepts the value and legitimacy of the scientific method but emphasizes the methodological problems with ignoring women or misrepresenting their experiences.
- **Feminist standpoint theories:** This far less conservative approach questions the possibility of scientific objectivity (can we really know anything?) by working from the assumption that knowledge is socially constructed and, therefore, that the perspective of the researcher influences what is known. The work, then, becomes constructing knowledge from the perspective of the people being studied in ways that avoid the distortions often imposed by the powerful seeking to preserve their power.
- **Feminist postmodernism:** This even less conservative approach critiques standpoint theorists by suggesting that, in fact, perhaps nothing is truly knowable because there are multiple truths. While it may seem overwhelming or bleak, many taking this perspective emphasize that this means that we all have a responsibility to work collectively "to do our best to make judgments that make the world a good place to be" for everyone, even if it is anything but simple to know anything.[24]

The Invisible Researcher

One of the most important ways in which we must bring a feminist perspective to research methods is by making something that is absent, present. In most criminological research, the person doing the research is either presented as neutral or is completely invisible. As Susan Miller and Cynthia Burack put it so beautifully, we must engage in a project of "illuminating the myth of the neutral researcher."[25] This is particularly harmful to women and other minoritized groups because it prioritizes as godlike the perspective of the mostly white, cis-gender men who have dominated criminology since its inception, including the questions that are asked, how they are asked, who asks them, who interprets what the answers mean, how the answers are summarized, and to whom and how those conclusions are shared.

Imagine that you are in a research study, being asked about anything from when you have broken the law or when you have been victimized. Your interviewer would have told you beforehand that you might find some questions difficult, and perhaps they would have offered you resources if you felt troubled during and after the interview. Imagine further that you turned the tables on the interviewer, asking them about whether they smoked weed or if someone had hurt them. Almost every researcher would shut those questions down and insist that the questions must only go one way.

However, feminist researchers are often concerned with the ways in which the researchers' own lived experience and history (perhaps better named *herstory* or *theirstory*) are related to and impact the research itself and how the research impacts the researchers in ways that cannot be simply ignored. This may mean that if researchers are committed to reflexivity, they may disclose their own experiences and emotions to research subjects and in their writings. These lenses for how we view the observation, creation, and examination of knowledge are vitally important as you navigate through the chapters of your criminology textbook and as you use this companion volume. But the importance of gender does not exist in a vacuum: it intersects in myriad ways with other personal factors, such as race, disability, and queerness, that are dramatically impacted by structural factors such as misogyny, racism, ableism, and homophobia. The work of critical race theorists allows us to add the critical examination of the impact of race on data collection and analysis to our toolbox.

CRITICAL RACE RESEARCH METHODS AND METHODOLOGIES

Just as feminist researchers have sought to bring a critical eye to so-called objective research in their disciplines, including criminology, critical race theorists have been doing the same with particular attention to the treatment of race. Critical race theory (CRT) began in the late 1980s to early 1990s as a socio-legal theoretical framework. It worked to challenge the ways in which "race-neutral" policies and practices perpetuated white supremacy within the law by contextualizing them in their historical context. This has shown the ways in which race and racism are and have historically been defining characteristics of U.S. society. For example, we can simply accept that drug laws exist to keep people safe, or we can look at *why* they came to be and realize that there was a concerted effort to criminalize particular drugs to imprison Black people. CRT pulls the rug out from under "color blindness" by insisting and showing that it has merely been a way for dominant groups to maintain their power.

Much like feminist research methodologies, CRT is vitally important to research methods broadly because it questions the very nature of what we know and how we know it. In addition it prioritizes the use of qualitative data collection that prioritizes the experiential knowledge of Black and Brown people (in the form, for example, of stories, dialogues, and personal testimonies) as a counternarrative to the racial progress narratives usually told by white scholars. Finally, CRT was explicitly conceived as a way to achieve social justice by linking theory with practice, scholarship, teaching, and the community.[26]

By centering race and racism in all parts of the research process, the focus of CRT on qualitative methods was a way to put together data outside of "official" and "objective" sources that CRT showed are in fact soaked in the racist past and present of the country. If we think back to the UCR, if crime measures are based simply on police activity, which has been shown to be deeply impacted by racism, then to get to truer knowledge about lawbreaking, we must seek other sources of data. CRT has been quite impactful in the field of research in education, where, for example, findings about the impacts of structural racism in education and employment flew in the face of official research connecting education to employment as a panacea for poor Black and Brown youth in Toronto, Ontario.[27]

Likewise, in their interviews of Black women navigating reentry under the watchful eye of state and social institutions, Jason Williams, Zoe Spencer, and Sean Wilson combined CRT into their analysis with a storytelling emphasis in the results.[28] By foregrounding Black women's stories, the authors show the ways in which they lived lives where reentry was just as criminalizing as breaking the law, with a particular focus on the ways in which the surveillance of reentering women's mothering is particularly traumatizing but also the ways in which these resilient women survive. Specifically, the authors foreground women's words about their preincarceration, carceral, and post-incarceration trauma, their mothering, and their recovery and resilience. All these themes, importantly, are contextualized within the U.S. history of separating Black women from their children during slavery, continued today by so-called child welfare agencies and the prison system alike and the especially tangled web of racialized stigma and challenges faced by Black women in reentry. What CRT gives us is the added context of the impact of structural racism in the analysis of these women's experiences in reentry.

STORYTELLING AND COUNTER-STORYTELLING

Counter-storytelling, a way to magnify the stories, experiences, narratives, and truths of underprivileged communities, is a major tenet of CRT. Whereas general storytelling focuses on experiences and lives from the gaze of the dominant culture in everything from movies and media to academia and textbooks, counter-storytelling centers on community voices' ability to create the narratives that define *their* experiences and lives. Counter-storytelling assumes that people are experts of their own lives and can therefore best tell their stories. In her investigation of the ways in which the law and research on pregnancy have justified prioritizing fetal pain over the pain and danger of pregnancy and labor by downplaying the details of pregnancy, Francesca Laguardia emphasizes the importance of counter-storytelling for pregnant and parenting women.[29]

Overwhelmingly, the law has erased the impact of pregnancy, labor, and parenting on women in a way that dehumanizes and deprioritizes women except as vessels for birthing children. If pregnant and parenting women's stories were foregrounded, the overwhelmingly painful and often permanent terrible impacts of pregnancy (called equivalent to torture by Human Rights Watch) would be not just spoken but heard over the loud chorus of voices arguing for the prioritization of fetal pain. Indeed, counter-storytelling may mean that the world is not so black and white, such as is provided by program evaluation research focused on outcomes that are valued by the program and the researchers. In her article, "'Trying to Get Free': A Theoretical Centering of Black Women's Post-carceral Narratives of Systemic Unfreedom," Geniece Crawford Mondé outlines the ways in which such research masks the usually nonlinear nature of women's journeys.[30] These evaluation measures center the institutions, rather than the individuals, in a way that serves to justify the maintenance of these structures rather than directing the funds outside of existing programs and structures.[31] So, yes, it is messier. But not only is it more valid, but it centers on the people who are supposedly the focus already.

POWER AND PARTICIPATORY ACTION RESEARCH

One of the characteristics that *is* particular to both feminist and CRT methods is the common insistence that gender and power, and how they interact with each other, must be considered central in research.[32] As we examine research from the very beginning—even simply deciding on whom to focus, research questions, and hypotheses (let alone when one person gets to ask the questions and pay someone else for their answers and leaves that "subject" having extracted their data, all but oblivious to potential aftereffects)—power emerges. One of the ways that this attention to power has played out is with a questioning of the very idea of research subjects with an objective researcher. Rather, we want to work to engage people as active subjects in all stages of the research process.[33]

Imagine that you have a particular experience or identity, such as that you or a parent have been incarcerated (or both!), and a researcher comes to talk to you about it. Their questions betray that they don't know much about what it means to live the life you live. You answer their questions, but you want so much to tell them the questions they should have asked. This is the idea behind participatory action research (PAR), in which researchers work to break down the hierarchical relationships built into traditional research methodologies. Deeply feminist and critical, the foundation of PAR is the power of collaboration and action in a way that provides insights into the key questions to be asked and a credible interpretation of findings.[34] In their now classic review of the history of PAR, Michelle Fine and her colleagues (most of whom were incarcerated while they co-authored the article) show the ways in which Kurt Lewin began the tradition of action in research, asserting, "no action without research; no research without action," a statement in opposition to the traditional ideas of the two as quite separate. Fine and her colleagues also describe PAR as having grown significantly in the early 2000s with feminist and critical influences to foreground not just the inextricable nature of research with action but also the participation *with*, not only *for*, the community in ways that work explicitly to break down the hierarchies seemingly baked into research with human beings.[35]

Now, even if researchers struggle with the idea of giving up their power to the people they are researching, perhaps they can question how they so often ask questions about the criminalized "others" who so often do not look like them. For well over thirty years, a small number of criminologists have turned the focus on themselves, highlighting the very small number of Black criminology faculty.[36] The positive impact of Black teachers has long been the focus of research on teacher impacts on Black and Brown students, as has the difficulty retaining such teachers due to lack of opportunity and to far more negative experiences and challenges faced by Black teachers.[37]

The same is true for researchers—as Williams, Spencer, and Wilson point out in their article about Black mothers in reentry. Aside from scholarly expertise, Black researchers with "deep cultural understanding and connection with participants' racial-cultural backgrounds . . . gives us additional analytical ability consistent with acquired positionality discourses (in our theoretical frames) to more deeply and forthrightly analyze narratives collected, which is a key component of rapport."[38] Fine and her colleagues explicitly forefront and honor the important contributions of "insider knowledge": "Insiders carry knowledge, critique, and a line of vision that is not automatically accessible to outsiders. . . . First, prison staff and administrators, as well as inmates, simply know things that outsiders do not—formal and informal procedures, lines of authority, practices and their consequences, for instance. Second, insiders understand the profound connections between discrete features of a community that outsiders might erroneously see as separate and divisible."[39] Understanding life at the intersections, as Sumi Cho, Kimberlé Crenshaw, and Leslie McCall have so beautifully articulated, is critical to the sustenance of an organization and can be perversely misunderstood by researchers who work to extract "variables" from the tightly woven fabrics of organizational life.[40] Third, these insiders understand the power and politics of privilege, privacy, surveillance, and vulnerability.[41] If insider voices are appropriately valued, the work of researchers with the benefit of academic training is synergistic with the knowledge that can only be known to insiders.

ETHICS AND INSTITUTIONAL REVIEW BOARDS

An Institutional Review Board (IRB) is a group of experts whose responsibility it is to review research plans before they are conducted, with a particular focus on research with human subjects. The role of an IRB is to ensure, both before the research begins and periodically as it continues, that the researchers are taking the appropriate measures to protect the rights and welfare of the people enrolled in the study as respondents (often called *subjects* in a way that betrays their lack of power in the research process). There are several ways in which IRBs ensure such protection, including the requirement of, for example, informed consent forms (given to respondents before the research begins so they understand any risks and benefits) and formalized protocols for the storage of data that can be traced back to subjects. Arguably, IRBs are particularly important for research done in the field of criminology, given that people are often asked questions about lawbreaking behavior for which they could get in trouble and that respondents are often imprisoned or under community supervision, so they are not as free as others to make uncoerced decisions. Much research on crime focuses on poor people, for whom a small monetary reward for participation in research may be enticing, even with the risks of participating, such as the risk of reexperiencing trauma so common among formerly incarcerated people.

The assessment of the ethics of a research study using human subjects is mostly a project of determining whether the project poses "minimal risk" to the participants. Minimal risk, when it comes to research, according to the regulations governing research with humans, means that the probability and magnitude of harm or discomfort anticipated in the research are not greater in and of themselves than those ordinarily encountered in daily life or during the performance of routine physical or psychological examinations or tests.[42]

Apart from the potential of the risks of research being unevenly borne by disadvantaged people, there is also the risk that particular people's voices are not be heard in research because they are unreasonably considered "protected." One of the groups of people considered to be a "protected population" is pregnant people. In their review of the exclusion of pregnant people from research, Amina White and colleagues found that pregnant people are often excluded from research even when it poses minimal risk of harm to the fetus because of researchers' own reluctance unrelated to risk, including concerns around scientific validity, ambivalence about inclusion, or habitual IRB practices.[43] The fact that these people are far more often excluded from research only extends the historical exclusion of women from research. Some ethics specialists suggest that IRBs have an important role in encouraging researchers to increase the enrollment of underrepresented groups in research, particularly racial and ethnic minorities, young people, and the elderly.

Protected populations in human subjects research include the following:

1. Pregnant women, human fetuses, and neonates: "Because research may pose additional and/or unknown risks to pregnant women, human fetuses and neonates, the regulations require additional safeguards in research."

2. Children: "[This includes] persons who have not attained the legal age for consent to treatments or procedures involved in the research, under the applicable law of the jurisdiction in which the research will be conducted."

3. Prisoners: "Because prisoners may not be free to make a truly voluntary and uncoerced decision regarding whether or not to participate in research, the regulations require additional safeguards for the protection of prisoners."[44]

CRITICAL THINKING BREAK 4

What are the pros and cons of excluding certain people from research?

CONCLUSION

As you read through the rest of this book (and especially your criminology textbook), I challenge you to take this chapter with you: question at all times where information came from, who asked the questions, how they asked them, how they analyzed and reported their findings, who answered the questions, and how others, such as the media, took those findings and reported them again before the information reached you.

2 Classical and Neo-classical Theories

Classical theories are some of the oldest ways to think about crime, based on the centuries-long philosophical focus of white men on men's thoughts and behavior. Classical criminology emerged within the context of the Enlightenment, with its focus on reason, in contrast to the previous system of Christian ethics, with its corruption, cruelty, superstition, and arbitrary application of punishment for crimes, believed to be rooted in demonic possession. In the tradition of John Locke and Voltaire, whose ideas of morality were completely different from the previous era, this classical criminology focused on moving toward increased legitimacy for the state and rule of law, based on ideas of free will, the social contract, and rationality. Your textbook will likely spend many pages covering Cesare Beccaria (1738-94) and Jeremy Bentham (1748-1832), who are considered to be the founders of the classical school and who focused on the role of *choice* in criminal behavior and how laws can help people steer their choices toward compliance with the law using punishment and rewards.

The focus on choice waned but then reemerged again in the form of neo-classical criminology in the 1970s. The resulting theories were softer around the edges—neither pure free will nor pure determinism—but still focused on using policy to nudge people away from committing crimes. As you will see through these next theory chapters, these theories can be very interesting! We must peel back the veneer to realize that most criminological theories are conceptualized, researched, analyzed, and applied in a way that acknowledges only the experiences of white, abled, straight, cisgendered men, and the policies in turn are applied in ways that fail in the pursuit of justice and accountability. Deterrence, rational choice, routine activities: these remain some of the most forefront theories in criminology, but the ways in which structures respond to race, gender, queerness, disability, and other characteristics change the equation are particularly important and under-discussed. In the case of classical and neo-classical theories, the death penalty and the War on Drugs are examples of completely failed and racist applications of theoretical concepts.

DETERRENCE

The concept of deterrence is one of the oldest in criminological and legal theory: that people will weigh the benefits of committing a crime against the swiftness, certainty, and severity of the sanctions. Cesare Beccaria's *On Crimes and Punishment* (1764) is considered the first work of classical criminology, and he outlined the ways in which systems of law could be created as a simple calculus to impact people's decision making. Assuming that people are rational actors in their lives, such systems of punishment may impact people's behavior either *specifically* or *generally*. Specific deterrence is supposed to work by preventing a specific individual from committing a crime again, whereas general deterrence is supposed to work by preventing *others* from committing a crime. These ideas make perfect sense in isolation—would you text and drive if you knew you were fined $500 *every single time* you did it, or if you saw your friends have to pay that fine?

However, even though this is one of the most popular ideas when it comes to crime control, it is far more complicated than simply threaten punishment and people will stop. But this does not stop us from using punishment as a blunt instrument as the basis for almost our entire criminal legal system. Indeed, as Travis Pratt and his colleagues write, "Four decades ago, Jackson Toby . . . could observe that readers of criminology textbooks 'might infer that punishment is a vestigial carryover of a barbaric past and will disappear as humanitarianism and rationality spread.'"[1] Much has changed. Today the criminal justice system is enmeshed in a "culture of control" that has produced a "penal harm movement" and an unprecedented era of "harsh justice."[2] Humanitarian corrections now seem like a quaint ideal in the face of an array of "get tough" policies that have made escalating sentence lengths and burgeoning prison populations enduring realities. These policies not only have strained public budgets but also have exacted a huge human toll while having a questionable (at best) impact on public safety.[3]

Of course, this "get tough" policy agenda reflects broader transformations in U.S. society that have led to the embrace of a conservative ideology that is seeking to dismantle the welfare state and to impose individual responsibility—and, if needed, punishment—on the "wayward poor."[4] They go on to show in their study of deterrence, in which they used meta-analysis, a statistical method that puts together many studies on the same topic and statistically analyzes them all together. They found that all these studies put together showed that the effect of deterrence on crime is small, indicating that crime causation is more complicated than just deterrence. They also specifically found that deterrence theory worked best with white-collar crimes, which are far *less* likely to have punishments than "street crimes," a term often used in criminology that is often seen as a racist dog whistle that actually means crimes by poor/Black/Brown people.

Alex Piquero is one of the foremost contemporary criminologists and has done substantial work to summarize and demystify what we know about deterrence from the research. He and his colleagues have clarified that deterrence research has found that it is less about "does it work or not" and more about *for whom* it works, what they call the "kinds-of-people dimension of sanctions and deterrence."[5] This approach takes into account individual differences such as whether people are married and have jobs, impulsivity, decision-making capacity, and situational differences, such as whether people are under the influence or very emotional at the time. As Abigail Henson, Thuy-Trinh Nguyen, and Ajima Olaghere so clearly put it, despite over two hundred years of research on the ever-so-popular concept, deterrence has yielded very little empirical support as a theory:

swiftness and severity do not appear to work, and, while certainty is effective, it works only when people *know* that it will happen to them, and it must be something they perceive as negative.[6] Rather, punishment can increase criminal behavior because it increases strain, decreases social control, and creates conditions (such as homelessness) that may lead to more criminal behavior in the future. Indeed, the United States is a nation founded on many of these ideas of punishment, yet we lead the world in the incarceration of our citizens, and our recidivism rates hover around 60 percent within three years, and 71 percent within five years.[7]

The so-called War on Drugs was a masterpiece of deterrence theory, increasing penalties for drug crimes dramatically with the goal of reducing crime. As with much of the 1970s and 1980s, the War on Drugs has its roots in the idea that "nothing works" to reduce crime and drug abuse. Declared by President Richard Nixon in 1971 and revamped in the 1980s by President Ronald Reagan, the War on Drugs was made up of three main types of legislation: repeat-offender, truth-in-sentencing, and mandatory-minimum statutes. "Repeat offender laws," often known as

CRITICAL THINKING BREAK 5

There is almost no research on how deterrence is different by race. Now that you have read chapter 1 of this book, why do you think that is? If the components of deterrence—certainty, swiftness, and severity—are more for over-policed and over-punished Black and Brown people, how might that make a calculus different? How does that change the role of choice? When it comes to gender, deterrence research is quiet on the topic of why women have dramatically lower rates of criminal behavior, and there are almost no studies on the role of gender in deterrence. The studies that do exist show "more similarities than differences across gender," which then in turn cannot explain the gender gap.[1] What do you think? Why are gender differences in the effectiveness in deterrence not central in the research?

1. Carmichael et al., "Experiential and Deterrent Effect."

"three-strikes laws," impose stricter penalties on people convicted of multiple criminal offenses.

Truth-in-sentencing laws aim to ensure that people convicted of crimes serve most of their sentence without the possibility of parole or early release. On the other hand, mandatory-minimum sentences are fixed legal penalties that must be given to people convicted of certain crimes. By definition, mitigating factors, individual circumstances, or even judicial discretion do not impact the penalty. This translated to decades of enhanced policing and a dramatically higher use of incarceration to prevent crime, both as a general and specific deterrent. By the principles of classical and neo-classical criminology, these laws were far stricter and far more certain than those in the rehabilitative era of the 1960s. So then why was the War on Drugs one of the most spectacular failures of criminal legal policy in the modern era? Much of the answer has to do with racism. Where the War on Drugs was meant to be an application of specific and general deterrence, it ran into the practicalities of racism in the practical application when applied by police officers overwhelmingly dispatched to Black and Brown neighborhoods.

Another theory that formed a part of the web of the War on Drugs was the "broken-windows theory." George Kelling and James Wilson's 1982 article outlines their hypothesis, pointing their white, male fingers at physical manifestations of disorder, such as broken windows, abandoned buildings, cars, litter, and "marginal shops." Such disorder left unaddressed, they argued, would lead to "untended" behavior and the breakdown of community controls and, finally, to more serious crime.[8] This is one of the most popular theories among students as they enter criminology classes, for it easily demonizes the poor "other" and has a very clear, police-oriented solution. Jeremy Travis argues that the broken-windows theory can have a non-punitive focus: "But the core idea of broken windows—that the government should respond to people's concerns around issues of safety and well-being—is very strong to me. So what does that mean? That means the government should respond when there's somebody who's mentally ill. Government should respond to vacant lots. Government should respond to issues of excessive noise. Addressing those concerns will lead to a better quality of life for the community—an improved sense of well-being and feelings of safety—which is, by itself, a positive outcome."[9]

But this is not what happened. Broken-windows policing quickly emerged as police departments around the country started focusing on policies such as "stop, question, and frisk" (SQF), which overwhelmingly criminalized young Black and Brown men simply for existing in poor neighborhoods. Any such theory cannot exist in a vacuum—it exists in the everyday actions of police officers with huge discretion and very little training on the characteristics that are arguably the most dramatic parts of the application of theories such as broken windows.

The practice of SQF in New York City is traditionally credited with causing dramatic crime drops in the popular media. However, David Weisburd and colleagues found the claims of deterrent effect to be tenuous because SQF is only one part of a "multipronged 'regime' of crime control that includes many other forms of proactive policing and surveillance" and because SQF may not just deter potential crime but may also deter victims.[10] Racial profiling is the discriminatory act of police in which someone is suspected or targeted of criminal behavior because of their race, ethnicity, religion, or national origin rather than because of their own behavior. SQF was so marred by racial profiling that a judge ruled in 2013 that the program was carried out in an unconstitutional manner because the people stopped were overwhelmingly Black and Brown people, and the stops led to very few arrests or weapons.[11]

But the negative impacts of racial profiling policies such as SQF extends even further into the realm of public health: Cato Laurencin and Joanne Walker found that it increased violent confrontations with police in ways that increased the chance of injury or death, police escalation through micro- or macro-aggressions, sub-lethal police contacts, and the adverse health impacts of the stress, trauma, and anxiety of the constant possibility of harm by the police.[12] Moreover, Weston Morrow, Michael White, and Henry Fradella found that SQF encounters with Black and Brown people were far more likely to lead to non-weapon force by police officers than police encounters with white people, leading to a "double jeopardy," whereby people of color must endure both unconstitutional stops and were more likely to be harmed during those stops.[13] And, if that were not enough, where white people know that Black people are the focus of racial profiling, there is more likely to be a "reverse deterrent" effect, where white

> **CRITICAL THINKING BREAK 6**
>
> Before we move on to rational choice theory, have you been thinking critically? What types of crimes do deterrence and the death penalty focus on? Where are the white-collar crimes or the white arrestees? If there are such patterns, do you believe they are all attributable to choice? What about choices by researchers might be impacting these findings?

people engage in more rule-breaking behavior because they know they can get away with it.[14]

THE DEATH PENALTY

One of the most common justifications for the death penalty is that it serves as a deterrent for the most heinous crimes. The overwhelming research findings, however, show that not only is the death penalty a failure as a deterrent but also that murder rates actually *decline* after a country abolishes the death penalty. Dane Archer and Rosemary Gartner found that abolition of the death penalty was followed by *decreases* in the homicide rate among places around the world, from Italy to Helsinki.[15] Nonetheless, the populations on death row in the United States continue to grow and are overwhelmingly poor, non-white, and disabled.

RATIONAL CHOICE THEORY

Deterrence assumes people are rational and want to avoid pain and punishment, and therefore punishment will deter crime. Accordingly, Derek Cornish and Ronald Clarke's rational choice theory looks specifically at individuals' reasoning processes as they weigh the pros and cons of breaking the law.[16] As implied in the *neo* part of neo-classical criminology's name, rational choice theory moves away from the simple prediction that harsher penalties lead to less crime and toward a more nuanced understanding that takes individuals into account. Specifically, newer theories do not assume complete rationality and add in individual awareness of and perceptions of the relative costs and benefits of criminal behavior and how much they are impacted by impulsivity and self-control, personal and observed experiences with crime and punishment, attachments to prosocial institutions, perceptions of other costs of punishment such as shame and respect, and environmental constraints.[17] No longer a simple equation, the elements in an individual's calculus might be anything from the shame of imprisonment to the monetary loss of losing a job due to arrest, from the thrill of getting away with something to the money gained from selling stolen goods. Rational choice theorists consider the heterogeneous ways in which different people might respond differently to rewards and punishments associated with criminal behavior. Consistent criticisms have been that rationality may apply with financial decisions and maybe property crimes, but maybe not big emotional crimes like violent crimes.

But what about women? We already know that gender is one of the strongest correlations with crime, with women committing dramatically less crime, both violent and non-violent, than men. By learning about how women perform their calculus, we may be able to apply what we learn to men's behavior. Rational choice theorists have looked at this in three different ways:

1. Whether women tend to perceive higher risks and lower rewards for breaking the law
2. Whether men and women are differentially affected by utility calculations
3. A combination of the two[18]

Research findings have shown that these differences may be due to women's socialization while they are growing up and higher supervision, which means they think they are being watched more and so are more accountable. Boys are more rewarded for masculinity and its associated aggression and risk-taking. Men may underestimate risk because they are focused on reaffirming their masculinity, and therefore women see crime as less thrilling, with more potential for sanctions. The evidence shows greater fear of formal sanctions among women, but there isn't good research on differences in perceptions of informal sanction risks. Gender differences in perceptions of rewards have been assessed in only two studies, which found nothing, back in 1997 and 1999.

What about morals? Are women particularly impacted by moral codes, which would override the impact of rewards and punishments? We have no idea from rational choice research. Finally, what about the fact that women have higher stakes in conformity, associate with fewer deviant peers, and are generally more religious? But we don't know because no one has looked at these issues. Katharina Neissl and her colleagues' study found that women still expected the same sanctions as men but seemed to perceive fewer rewards of crime. Many feminist scholars have focused on the role of peers.[19] So then what is the role of maintenance of the patriarchy? As masculinity is reaffirmed for men by criminal choices, women do not break the rules because they are more sensitive to changes in the certainty of apprehension and less sensitive to the personal rewards of crime. This is both a direct effect of women invested in conformity and a diffused effect of peers (whose opinions women value more than men do) not encouraging one

CRITICAL THINKING BREAK 7

How does it fit that Black men are so much more likely to be arrested, given that they know that their probability of detection is so much higher? Likewise, if women's likelihood of detection is so much lower, then why does that not increase their lawbreaking behavior? Some research showed that although people may weigh specific risks and specific benefits, they may not balance them rationally. For example, Irving Piliavin and colleagues interviewed people and found they were motivated by the reward aspect of rational choice theory, but they underestimated the cost or the risk of punishment. What might be the role of structural racism, ableism, anti-queerness, and patriarchy, for example, in these calculations?[1]

1. Piliavin et al., "Rational Choice."

another to offend. Men, on the other hand, feel freer to follow impulses, and crime is actually a manifestation of what men feel like they should be doing to be hegemonic men—aggressive and not risk averse.[20]

ROUTINE ACTIVITIES THEORY AND LIFESTYLE APPROACH

At the core of routine activities are three elements: a motivated offender, a suitable crime target, and the absence of a capable guardian against a potential crime. This perspective assumes that there will always be people ready to commit crimes, but where there are no targets or where there are capable guardians, crime will not occur. Within routine activities theory, there is still the assumption of rational decision making on the part of the offender, but the theory focuses on the behavior of victims rather than on people breaking the law. As with most other neo-classical theories, routine activities theory is considered very useful because it has particularly strong implications for policy and practice in the prevention of crime. The focus on situational factors means specific recommendations can be made to increase guardianship, such as installing burglar alarms and increased lighting.

However, as with almost all the theories in this book, almost everyone who investigates routine activities theory includes factors such as race and gender as afterthought control variables rather than as central organizing principles. Routine activities theory, for example, makes rape simple: if a rapist is willing to rape, they will rape, but if there is no opportunity to rape, they will not rape someone.[21] Hillary Potter writes that it is essential to examine the salience of identities and statuses of people in relation to their experiences with crime and victimization.[22] Raleigh Blasdell argues that "gender, race, and class all impact how one is socialized, the process whereby people learn how to behave in accordance to their status, along with how to react to the statuses of others. Gender, race, and class shape the choices people have at their disposal, which subsequently acts to either enhance or limit access to power in the United States. Additionally, gender, race, and class impact opportunities available to individuals in society, which subsequently impacts their routine activities."[23] The implication is that routine activities theory negates the social issues that make some people more likely to break the law and others more vulnerable to victimization (and for many it is both).

The routine activities theory takes for granted the existence of the "motivated offender," the "lack of a capable guardian," and lifestyle choices without critically approaching the structural reasons for their existence. Jillian Turanovic, Travis Pratt, and Alex Piquero problematize the idea, for example, that potential victims could make themselves safer by changing their risky behavioral routines, by looking at victimization, behavior change, and structural disadvantage. They found that structural conditions absolutely matter: "Indeed, those who live their lives in communities plagued by economic deprivation will not only be exposed to greater levels of criminogenic structural conditions, but they will also be subjected to—and will therefore have to be sensitive to—the cultural expectations that emerge in response to those very conditions. What this means in the present context is that victims of crime who live in low wealth communities may be less able to change their risky behavioral routines, even if they really want to."[24]

Criminological research has established that minoritized status in everything from gender to race to queerness to disability are risk factors for crime victimization. Specifically, females are at greater risk for experiencing domestic violence, intimate partner homicide, rape, sex trafficking, and stalking.[25] Beyond this not only are the risks of victimization variable by gender but also an intersectional approach is the most effective at explaining victimization patterns. For example, Black and Latina women who frequently ride public transportation are at increased risk of violent victimization, but this is not true for white women. For white women, on the other hand, frequent time spent shopping is related to violent victimization, but not for Black women. As you may have guessed, the authors suggest that these differences in lifestyle and activities are rooted in structural inequalities across race, ethnicity, and class, such as not having money for a car or living in disadvantaged communities.[26] The experiences of disabled people are even more understudied in criminology than those of women, but Bradford Reyns and Heidi Scherer use a routine activities approach to suggest that disability itself is a risk factor for stalking victimization.[27] In all, we know that victimization is different at the

CRITICAL THINKING BREAK 8

How and why might gender, class, race, queerness, or disability impact routine activities? For example, how might routine activities and lifestyles be impacted by structurally influenced factors such as these?

- Neighborhood design
- Names
- Concentration of intergenerational wealth
- Location of surveillance cameras, cops, and security guards
- Teacher expectations of misbehavior coded by race and disability
- Lack of access to quality education

intersections of gender, race, class, queerness, and disability, and we must look at how personal characteristics and privilege or the lack thereof impacts whether and how people have routines and have access to capable guardianship with limited resources and "unconventional," more rigid schedules.

On the topic of gender, Jordana Navarro and Jana Jasinski found that girls are more likely to be victims of cyberbullying, even when engaged in comparably risky cyber behavior as boys were, such as using chat rooms. The only place where boys were more at risk was on blogs, where it turned out they were acting more feminine. The authors take a "cyberfeminist dystopian perspective" that girls are at a higher risk of cyberbullying because of their relative disadvantage in society.[28] Cyberdystopianists believe that the internet is yet another location for the oppression of women (whereas cybertopianists believe that the internet is a potentially liberating space for women).

CRIME-EVENT CRIMINOLOGY

Also known as environmental criminology, crime-event criminology zooms out from individuals to the spatial and temporal variation in crime events. You might think about it as the ways in which a combination of elements come together, such as how motivated offenders and suitable targets come together in the same place or how time and place converge to make crime events more likely. This allows for crime prevention to happen not by targeting "at risk" individuals but by making targets less available (e.g., by locking them up, labeling them, tracking them, or hiding them) and by increasing guardianship (e.g., with better lighting or more cameras). While some have criticized crime-event criminology for ignoring the structural components of crime, it has also emerged as a theory that can be practically implemented in a way that is not punitive and that centers the prevention of victimization.[29]

CONCLUSION

Where simple theories relying on choice (and therefore deterrence) have clear policy implications, we know from the transition from classical to neo-classical theories in the past century that policy implications are more complicated than carrot-and-stick calculations. Most of the solutions suggested by deterrence models do not take social inequities or social justice into account; the policies and actions suggested by deterrence are such things as implementing hardened targets and locks, traveling in groups, enhancing street lighting, increasing staff, installing burglar alarms, fixing broken things quickly, and setting cab fares. But all these are the symptoms of class disparities, racism, misogyny, ableism, and anti-queerness. True social justice responses can take a deterrence stance if they take inequities in everything from resources to harm, particularly among members of minoritized groups, and address not just individuals but also the systems built on the domination and exploitations of human beings.

3 Biological and Positivist Theories

One of the original ways to think about criminal behavior was that it had roots in people's physical bodies. Your criminology textbook may even have two chapters about the biological theories of crime—one covering "early biological theories" and the other with more contemporary biological theories, often called "positivist" perspectives.

THE BIOLOGY OF RACE

Race is one of the most studied and debated topics in criminology, even though race is not a biological fact but a social construction—a set of meanings attributed to, for example, Black and white racial groups. Racial categories developed throughout history due to particular circumstances and have continued to be reified—turned from abstract ideas into something more real—by the media, government policy, and people who embrace their racial identity or people who reject others' racial identities. Whether taught or not, everyone learns racial categories and the physical attributes that go along with them, even though there is no biological basis to those categories. Rather, there are many reasons why such categories emerged, from political struggles to economic conditions to legal rulings.[1]

For this book it is important that you learn about the many different early theories—that body shape or skull shape or even the length of one's chin was related to crime—because they expose very clearly the racist and misogynist origins of criminology. Cesare Lombroso, for example, is widely considered to be the founding father of positivist criminology, which is based on the idea that information is measured, and the results of these measurements are considered to be objective and independently true. His goal was to use the scientific method to explain criminal behavior, and he concluded that one could observe inherited characteristics in people to determine their propensity to criminal behaviors, such as weak chins, long arms, and sloped foreheads. One of his most influential ideas was that of the "born criminal," whom he considered to be atavistic (or an evolutionary "throwback"). As Tammi Arford and Eric Madfis write, "Lombroso started with the assumption that European males were the most evolutionarily advanced form of the human species and found 'evidence' in accordance with his assumptions. It is no coincidence that the 'primitive' physical features of Africans, African Americans, Asians, Native Americans, Sicilians, and other Southern Italians correlated with the 'born criminal,' who was said to have black hair, dark skin and eyes, and large lips." His theories helped to legitimize eugenics and had an explicit impact on Mussolini's imperialist war against Ethiopia, Nazi actions against Jews and Gypsies, and even the Rwandan genocide because of its roots in colonialism.[2]

Likewise, Franz Joseph Gall originated the field of phrenology in the early 1800s, which claimed (erroneously) that the brain's over- or underdevelopment in certain areas would be indicated in the shape of the skull. By examining the shape of a person's skull, he contended, one could learn about their personal characteristics, including their propensity for criminal behavior. His ideas were very popular in the 1830s and 1840s and were used, for example, to justify slavery in the United States due to African people's skulls showing their "tamableness" that required them to have a master. Likewise, phrenology was used as a justification of the removal of Native Americans from their lands because their skulls indicated that they were slow learners.[3]

Your textbook likely also went into quite a lot of detail about theories relating crime to everything from body type (e.g., Ernest Kretschmer and William Sheldon) to heredity (e.g., Sir Francis Galton or the story of the Kallikak family) and from the moral panic of the XYY supermale to studies of twins, whether raised together or raised apart (e.g., the Minnesota Twin Family Study). In this chapter I present some theories with a critical eye and cover some biological issues that your textbook may not have covered.

BODY MASS INDEX, RACE, AND CRIME

It is likely not in your criminology textbook, but Da'Shaun Harrison, in *Belly of the Beast: The Politics of Anti-fatness as Anti-blackness*, makes an important connection between Quetelet's creation of the body mass index (BMI), which he based on his calculation of the "average man" (or *l'homme moyen*). He began with a cis-gender white man, and, at the peak of the bell curve of the BMI, instead of calling it "normal," he labeled it "ideal." His work later became the basis of, and justification for, eugenics. Harrison makes the comparison between the War on Drugs and the War on Obesity, both of which target Black people and their bodies:

> At the core of the War on Drugs is the Black, and at the core of the War on Obesity—even if not as explicitly so—is the Black fat. Black people make up roughly 13 percent of the American population, but about 51 percent of America's fat population.... The world's obsession with obesity and being overweight is less about health and is more about the cultural and systemic anti-Blackness as anti-fatness that diet, medical, and media industries profit from. Just like with the War on drugs and the crack epidemic, major institutions falsified evidence about the effects of fatness or obesity as a way to criminalize and profit off fat people—especially the Black fat.

When people launch campaigns against "unhealthy," "unsafe," or "dangerous" behaviors, they are often anti-Black at the core, and the BMI is no exception.[4]

THE BIOLOGY AND SOCIAL CONSTRUCTION OF GENDER

The terms *sex* and *gender* are often used interchangeably in casual conversations, but they have very different meanings, and not everyone's sex aligns with their gender identity. *Sex* refers to the biological characteristics of a person, categorized based on reproductive anatomy and physiology such as genitalia, chromosomes, and hormonal profiles. These are typically divided into two categories of male or female because in most cases people are born with either male or female characteristics. Intersex people also exist, who may have a combination of both or atypical sex characteristics.

Gender is a social and cultural construct that covers far more than biological characteristics. Typically, people have been categorized into male and female genders that have a prescribed set of roles, behaviors, attitudes, and expectations that society associates with being a man or a woman, even though they have nothing to do with people's genitalia. Although gender has traditionally been dichotomous, there are a spectrum of gender identities, such as man, woman, non-binary, genderqueer, genderfluid, and more.

Much as racial categories were created without any scientific basis, sex and gender have been conflated and used widely in criminology. Ironically, Lombroso is also known for being one of the first and only criminologists to pay attention to women's criminality. He and his work, however, were deeply misogynistic. He focused most of all on women's predisposition for lying without shame, which he said was caused by their lack of testicles and the fact that they are like children. He also wrote that female criminals were especially cruel and "savage" and were more masculine than women who did not commit crimes.[5]

Recent research has shown that even sex is far more complicated, however, than the dichotomy of male and female sexes. As Gina Rippon argues, dichotomies in either sex or gender do not exist, but there is rather quite a lot of overlap between male and female brains, and any real difference boils down to physical size.[6] Similarly, Rebecca Jordan-Young and Katrina Karkazis debunk the association between testosterone levels and everything from tendency for violence to appetite for risk or sex to physical strength.[7] Nonetheless, gender is socially constructed and reified every moment, so most of these theories must be understood as manifestations of centuries of cemented ideas about biology rather than facts. Indeed, women's bodies ended up as justifications for their lack of intellectual achievement when, in fact, it was reified gender roles that made such work more possible for men such as Freud, Einstein, and Thoreau, who have well-documented support from the women in their lives, from toothbrushes waiting with toothpaste and meals brought to them to a complete lack of childcare responsibilities.

LANGUAGE MATTERS TO PERCEPTION

In her classic article, "The Egg and the Sperm: How Science Has Constructed a Romance Based on Stereotypical Male-Female Roles," in the feminist journal *Signs,* Martin dissects the perception in reproductive biology that the functions of the sperm and the egg mirror traditional gender stereotypes yet have nothing to do with the biological facts. She shows that the common depiction of the egg is one of a passive, weak, and timid "damsel in distress" and of the sperm as the proactive, strong, brave, and masculine "heroic warrior" coming to save the day. The reality is that the sperm does not "penetrate" the egg, but rather the sperm and the egg stick together because of adhesive molecules on their surfaces, and the egg may even select sperm.[8] Lisa Campo-Engelstein and Nadia Johnson found, over twenty years after Martin's article was published, that fertilization in human reproduction continues to be gendered (what they call the "fertilization fairytale") even in science textbooks from the middle school to the medical school level.[9]

GENETICS AND CRIME

The pursuit of the code to the human genome is one of humankind's greatest projects. Among neuro-criminologists, there is a hope that the gene for crime will be discovered. The strongest link between genes and aggression has so far emerged as a gene named monoamine oxidase A (MAOA), which has a role in the presence of neurotransmitters such as dopamine, serotonin, and noradrenaline in the body. Research has shown that people with the low activity form of the MAOA gene (MAOA-L) are hypersensitive, meaning that they react more aggressively to negative experiences. However, this gene expression is mediated by environmental factors, such as whether or not people experienced abuse as children.[10] Similarly, Jasmin Wertz and colleagues found that genetic predictors of educational attainment predicted criminal behavior. They are careful in their discussion to remind readers that environment had a mediating effect, whereby people with lower genetic scores for educational attainment were *also* more likely to grow up in "criminogenic environments" but are steadfast in their focus on genetic risk factors for school problems and in turn crime.[11]

Certainly, we know that crime is heavily concentrated within families: one study found that only 7.8 percent of families accounted for over half (52.3 percent) of suspects.[12] Researchers focused on the intergenerational continuity of crime work to untangle the many threads of familial impact, which could be causal (parental crime causing the crime of children) or spurious (factors that impact both parents and children are what lead to crime) and which could be genetic (inherited) or environmental (such as poverty, family values, or abuse). One way that scholars have done this is through family-based research designs that can control for environmental variables (since they are a family unit, experiencing most things together). Steve Van de Weijer, for example, found continuity of crime across generations. When he quantitatively removed the impact of demographic and socio-economic variables, the strength of that relationship got much weaker (which he attributed to the huge impact of resource inequality, also known as relative deprivation, on crime), but it did not disappear. He concluded that this meant that we cannot rule out a causal effect, separate from environmental factors.[13]

CRITICAL THINKING BREAK 9

How do you think that environment and biology influence crime? Which one do you think plays the biggest role in crime? Why? If you wanted to test your hypothesis, how would you do that?

XYY SYNDROME

XYY syndrome is a genetic condition in which males are born with an extra Y chromosome. They are likely to be particularly tall and have learning disabilities. In the 1960s biochemist Mary Tefler began focusing on XYY as the representation of the "supermale," and the *New York Times* published a three-part series about XYY syndrome. This story focused in particular on a man named Richard Speck, a man working to have his murder conviction overturned because (they erroneously claimed) he was an XYY male.[14] While future studies found no support for the hypothesized relationship between XYY and crime, the damage had been done publicly, characterizing people with the XYY chromosome as criminal supermales and ruining future scientific examination of the XYY characteristic.[15]

THE REAL LINKS BETWEEN BIOLOGY AND CRIME

Since these main categories traditionally thought to be biological are simply social creations, then is there any relationship between biology and crime? Absolutely, but they are more biosocial than purely biological, which means that it is more complicated!

Lead and Crime

Many decades of data show that lead has terrible impacts on many human organ systems, and exposure to lead remains widespread around the world. One of the impacts that has been studied in criminology is that when children are exposed to lead, they are more likely to develop aggressive behaviors, create problems, have impaired cognitive functioning, and exhibit criminal behavior. Lead's impact on people and larger communities is quite profound. One estimate suggests that the reduction of lead exposure in children may be responsible for up to 28 percent of the homicide drop in the United States. Of course, this is not only a biological issue but also a sociological one: lead levels are higher in urban areas, higher among non-Hispanic Black children than among non-Hispanic white children, higher among children living with people who did not have a college education or higher, and poor people, all of whom are more likely to live near polluted areas in aging housing with deteriorating lead-based paint and near heavy traffic or work in lead-related industries.[16]

Trauma

Psychological trauma can develop from a wide range of experiences, including natural disasters, serious accidents, terrorist acts, war and combat, rape and sexual assault, historical trauma, intimate partner violence, and bullying. One may be traumatized through directly experiencing victimization, the threat or experience of serious injury, and the threat of dying; learning of the violent or accidental death of a loved one; or witnessing the death or serious injury of another person.[17] Indeed, historical trauma is cumulative emotional and psychological wounding over the lifespan and across generations, emanating from massive group trauma experiences. The historical trauma response is the constellation of features in reaction to this trauma, often including depression, self-destructive behavior, suicidal thoughts and gestures, anxiety, low self-esteem, anger, and difficulty recognizing and expressing emotions. It may include substance abuse, often an attempt to avoid painful feelings through self-medication.[18]

One of the main ways that researchers study the impact of trauma uses data from the Adverse Childhood Experiences (ACE) project from the 1990s. Research based on the ACE data about negative experiences during childhood such as abuse, neglect, and family and household challenges such as violence or substance use in the home showed significant impacts on long-term physical and behavioral health, and these impacts were *cumulative*. Studies of incarcerated youth show that they are far more likely to report one or more ACEs compared to their peers without criminal legal system involvement. Incarcerated adults, likewise, have especially high ACE scores: 4.3 for men and 5.5 for women, far higher than the scores for their counterparts in the community.[19] The psychological and physiological impacts of trauma are wide-ranging. The official diagnosis of post-traumatic stress disorder (PTSD) includes a long list of potential symptoms, including having intrusive thoughts such as distressing dreams or flashbacks; avoiding reminders of the traumatic event; experiencing memory changes, ongoing fear, horror, anger, guilt, or shame; being unable to experience positive emotions; having angry outbursts; being overly watchful of one's surroundings; and having sleep disruptions.[20]

Most, if not all, of these impacts have biological roots. For example, people with PTSD respond to traumatic triggers with a fight-or-flight response because their childhood experiences resulted in the recalibration of parts of the body's stress-response system, meaning that they are chronically physiologically hyper-aroused. Where trauma left adults struggling to regulate their moods, they often numb those intense feelings with alcohol, drugs, or food. Consider some of the biological impacts of childhood trauma:

- Childhood trauma interferes with normal brain development so that, for example, right-brain development is compromised, resulting in neuron damage and atrophy.
- Childhood trauma can cause long-term changes to the brain, such as smaller brain sizes and smaller corpus callosum, that can impact memory, learning, the ability to regulate affect, and social development.
- Childhood trauma causes long-term changes in the endocrine system, such as causing hyperactivity of the hypothalamic-pituitary-adrenal system, which leads to, among other things, disruptions in cortisol levels, which increases people's vulnerability even to mild stressors.[21]

It is clearly important to understand that biological factors cannot be overruled when it comes to criminology. However, we must be careful to note the complicated nature of biological factors and the paramount importance of the interaction with the environment, because of the very real threat of eugenics.

CRITICAL THINKING BREAK 10

Think like a critical criminologist. Who decides who is inferior?

POLICY IMPLICATIONS OF BIOLOGICAL THEORIES OF CRIME

When you think of eugenics, you likely think of the Holocaust, in which six million Jewish people, along with millions of others, including Romani, Polish, Soviet, queer, and disabled people, were systematically persecuted and murdered by Nazi Germany and its collaborators. The justification for the Holocaust was rooted in the genocidal ideology of Nazi Germany, led by Adolf Hitler and his associates, who believed in an extreme form of racial purity and supremacy, wherein Aryans were a superior race. This meant that they believed that Jewish and other marginalized people were inferior and a threat to their vision of a "pure" Aryan society. The Nazis annihilated these "others" using a network of concentration camps, death camps, and mass shootings, but the first negative eugenic measure passed by the Hitler regime in July 1933 was a forced sterilization law, which targeted people considered "feebleminded" or who were schizophrenic, bipolar, alcoholic, or epileptic.[22]

Despite the horrors of the Holocaust, the sterilization of people considered "inferior" predated (and informed) Nazi Germany, continued after World War II ended, and has particularly impacted Black and Brown people. Adolf Hitler himself said, "There is today one state in which at least weak beginnings toward a better conception [of citizenship] are noticeable. Of course, it is not our model German Republic, but the United States." Indeed, in the United States, beginning in 1909 and continuing for almost a century, California led the country in the number of sterilization procedures performed on men and women, often without their full knowledge and consent, in state institutions. The Progressive-era elites used the emerging science of heredity to justify the use of eugenics to restrict the breeding and growth of those they believed unfit. Perhaps not surprisingly, these presumptions of "unfit" often correlated strongly with negative stereotypes about race, class, and disabled people and used fear of crime and "immorality" to justify these sterilizations, particularly at the "Pacific Colony" for delinquent "morons." Lest you think that someone using such a word is unlikely, this is a direct quote from Judge Edwin J. Han of the juvenile court explaining in 1923 why California critically needed a "colony" designed for "morons": "One half of the children who come before my court are of the moron class. If we are to stop the crime wave that is sweeping our country we must give attention to the source of the stream. In other words it is imperative that we should care for our feeble-minded children. Pacific Colony was established for this purpose and it would be a distinct misfortune if for any reason this institution is not completed."[23]

But these sterilizations based on biological "inferiority" have not stopped. In the United States, between 1997 and 2013, doctors performed 1,400 involuntary sterilizations in California prisons to stamp out the genes they decided were undesirable.[24] One of the doctors performing these sterilizations told a reporter that the $147,460 cost of the procedures was reasonable. "Over a ten-year period, that isn't a huge amount of money, compared to what you save in welfare paying for these unwanted children—as they procreated more."[25] Sterilizations also continued with people detained in Immigration and Customs Enforcement detention centers. In early September 2020, a nurse working at an ICE detention center in Georgia came forward with shocking allegations of medical neglect and abuse, claiming that numerous involuntary hysterectomies (uterus removal surgeries) were performed on detained immigrant women.[26] Reporting on an interview with a formerly incarcerated woman who said that she resisted the pressure to be sterilized, Bill Chappell wrote that there was "pressure that she says came while she was under sedation and strapped to an operating table. 'Being treated like I was less than human produced in me a despair.'" She later added that she sees the state prison officials as "the real repeat offenders."[27]

CONCLUSION

The positivist tradition valorizes the use of measurement and the quantification of criminal behavior using scientific methods. But, as you know by now, researchers have subjective points of view that impact their research questions, participants, measurements, questions, definitions, and in turn results. This is especially true in studies of people with criminal legal system involvement, which automatically overrepresents Black and Brown people, given their overrepresentation in the criminal legal system for reasons independent of their biology. This is so important in studies of "undesirable" characteristics, such as the propensity for criminal behavior, because of the potential policy implications up to and including elimination of people "predisposed" to criminal behavior.

Nikolas Rose writes that we have moved away from the original "biology of control," which insisted that human characteristics were inherited and therefore emblematic of particular sub-groups and also that they were unalterable. Now he suggests that the new biology of control is more subtle, meaning that, once a genetic basis for an undesirable characteristic (such as "criminal predisposition") is found, a variety of interventions can neutralize that "risk," such as psychopharmacology and gene therapy.[28] While it might be too controversial to screen all inhabitants of inner cities, he argues, we may see genetic screening of "disruptive school children" under the guise of ADHD or the requirement of genetic testing for people on probation or parole, employees at risk of being fired, or people interested in insurance. Indeed, Wertz and colleagues' study of genetic predisposition for educational problems indicates that children with such genes, and therefore low self-control and academic difficulties, might be targets for early identification and intervention.[29]

4 Psychological Theories

In mainstream criminology, psychological theories focus on individual people who commit crime and the role of personality, cognition (i.e., ways of thinking), psychodynamics (i.e., how early life experiences shape the development of the self), and learning on those individuals' motivations to engage in criminal or violent behavior. So many psychological theories regarding crime are about men's crime as it relates to their relationships with women, particularly mothers and sexual partners. In this chapter, for example, you will learn less about Sigmund Freud's misogynist theory of penis envy and more about Karen Horney's theory of womb envy. And, for example, where your textbook may focus on such popular concepts of "criminal profilers" and "objective assessments of dangerousness" with little critique, we dig into those practices to their racist and ableist roots.

PENIS ENVY AND WOMB ENVY

Sigmund Freud based his theory of human behavior on the practice of psychoanalysis, which he developed. Freud believed that criminal behavior is maladaptive, or the product of inadequacies of one's personality. Your textbook likely covers Freudian ideas such as the ego, superego, and id and also August Aichorn, a psychoanalyst in the Freudian tradition who believed that crime happened when people were unable to control the impulses of their id. One of the best-known concepts from Freudian theory is penis envy, the belief that little girls are angry at their mothers because they do not have penises and as a result transfer their love to their fathers and can satisfy their desire for a penis by having a male child. Freud did not believe at all that boys had any envy of girls' bodies, as his theories emphasized what girls do not have and what boys do have, which is yet another example of hegemonic masculinity. Several scholars have criticized Freud's myopic focus on the penis without any attention to boys' envy of the female body and its capacity to create and grow life.[1] In fact, Freud himself wrote that "the sexual life of men alone is accessible to our research, that of women is shrouded in mystery" to justify their absence from his theory of sexuality.[2]

German psychoanalyst and psychiatrist Karen Horney, born thirty years after Freud, introduced the concept of "womb envy," for which she was eventually ostracized from the psychoanalytic community. This theory, where men's behavior is due to an envy of women's ability to create and nurture human life, is also known as vagina envy, woman envy, and uterus envy and has been the topic of a number of theorists.[3] While the concept is relatively understudied, more recent publications indicate that common reactions to womb envy are femiphobia and misogyny.

MORAL DEVELOPMENT THEORY

The theory of moral development and its associated six stages is very popular and quite lovely as a model for human development. The model is founded on three levels of moral development: pre-conventional morality, conventional morality, and post-conventional morality, each of which has two stages within them. Along this model people move from a childlike selfishness and avoidance of punishment, where they only act to meets their own interest (stages 1 and 2) to expressing attitudes shared by the larger community (stages 3 and 4) and finally (ideally) to looking beyond societal beliefs toward an ideal version of society with particular rights and values (stages 5 and 6).[4]

Like most theories in criminology, moral development theory was itself developed based on Lawrence Kohlberg's studies of boys and may not apply to women's development at all. This was the suggestion of Carol Gilligan, who theorized that women's unique life experiences impacted their development in ways not considered in Kohlberg's "universal" model of moral development.[5] This means that women have been judged to fail by a standard that does not fit them and that women, unlike men, focus their moral actions on their relationships and responsibilities. She argues, and research has since shown, as you may have seen in your own life, that women focus on care and nurturing, which has traditionally been devalued, making women "inferior" in Kohlberg's stages.[6] Notably, Gilligan's classic book, *In a Different Voice,* does not refer to the gender binary.

Gilligan spoke more recently about how patriarchal societies use shame as a social control of women most of all, who are shamed for not silencing their sexuality, their voices, and their very selves. Male violence, she argues, keeps women ashamed and silent. She suggests as an alternative that including women's voices in, for example, research, reveals the problems of patriarchy, shame, and men's violence. The system is intentional; as Carol Gilligan and Roman Gerodimos point out, "Hierarchy literally means a rule of priests, and in patriarchy, the Hieros, the priest, is a Pater, a father. Patriarchy is a rule of fathers, elevating some men over other men and all men over women."[7]

When it comes to race and moral development theory, Cheryl Moreland and Mark Leach suggest expanding on it by integrating it with racial identity development. Racial identity development was born of the civil rights movement of the 1960s and mirrors moral development quite well:

> Several researchers have suggested that moral development and racial identity development constructs are theoretically linked. The theoretical components of the levels of moral development and the statuses of Black racial identity development appear to share common themes. First, preconventional moral reasoning (Stage 1) and pre-encounter racial identity theorized morality and Blackness, respectively, as external to oneself. Second, preconventional morality (Stage 2) and encounter racial identity emphasize the beginning of awareness of one's individualism. Third, conventional morality

(Stages 3 and 4) and immersion-emersion racial identity underscore an affection with community and shared identity. One's thoughts, beliefs, and actions are to be endorsed by the community. Finally, postconventional morality (Stages 5 and 6) and internalization racial identity encourage more objective, universal thinking and allow the acceptance of individual differences (e.g., race, beliefs, values, and behaviors).[8]

These perspectives suggest moving beyond Kohlberg's original white-male-centered theory to account for the different lives of women and of Black people, respectively. These changes can have a dramatic practical impact. Moral development programs exist in a variety of settings, such as schools, prisons, and counseling centers. By taking racial and gender identities into account, and their emotional impacts, these programs can be far more effective. An example cited by Moreland and Leach is Black students at predominantly white institutions, who may particularly benefit from a moral development theory informed by race, for with racial identity development among Black Americans comes increased involvement in campus organizations and increased retention in school.[9]

EMOTIONAL DYSREGULATION

Emotion *regulation* is defined as an automatic or controlled process by which people manage their emotions, "involving the (a) awareness and understanding of emotions, (b) acceptance of emotions, (c) ability to control impulsive behaviors and behave in accordance with desired goals when experiencing negative emotions, and (d) ability to use situationally appropriate emotion regulation strategies flexibly to modulate emotional responses as desired in order to meet individual goals and situational demands."[10] Emotion *dysregulation* is when people have difficulties with these emotional skills; it is believed to be caused by an invalidating childhood and a biological predisposition to emotional reactivity. Over time this inability to regulate emotions may manifest as behavioral problems that psychologists and criminologists have linked to crimes such as domestic violence.[11]

When it comes to gender, research has shown that aggression happens when men are anxious and afraid of their own emotions: "If men cannot

> **CRITICAL THINKING BREAK 11**
>
> People often confuse causation with correlation, but educational attainment could increase flexibility, flexible people could be better at traditional education, or there could be a "z factor" impacting them both. What makes sense to you?

tolerate or delineate the emotions they are experiencing, then they may be less able to develop appropriate regulation strategies to manage those emotions and may use aggression to terminate their feelings of vulnerability or confusion."[12] Other researchers found that even though females reported higher levels of emotional dysregulation than males, antisocial and risk-taking behaviors were far more likely among males than females. They suggested that, in line with previous research, men and women's behaviors were constrained by socialized gender roles, where men are expected to be aggressive and engage in risk taking, whereas women are expected to act vulnerable and submissive. They also found that the higher someone's educational attainment, the more flexible they were and therefore had fewer problems with emotional dysregulation.[13] Consistent with these findings, Chloe Bliton and her colleagues found that emotional dysregulation difficulties were associated with intimate partner violence in dating relationships.[14]

POST-PARTUM PSYCHOSIS: THE CASE OF ANDREA YATES

In 2001 Andrea Yates and her husband, Rusty, lived in a Houston suburb with their five children, John, Paul, Luke, Mary, and Noah, all born within seven years and all homeschooled by their mother. Andrea Yates suffered from extreme post-partum depression and the much rarer post-partum psychosis, which led to several suicide attempts and hospitalizations after the births of her children. Multiple doctors warned that Yates should not have more children and should not even be left alone with her children. Rusty did not follow this advice, insisting on having more children due to his procreative religious beliefs that focused on having as many children as possible. In March 2001 Andrea Yates waited until her husband left the home and drowned her children in the bathtub, believing that they were "doomed": "It was the seventh deadly sin. My children weren't righteous. They stumbled because I was evil," Melissa Ferguson quoted Yates as saying, "The way I was raising them they could never be saved. . . . Better for someone else to tie a millstone around their neck and cast them in a river than stumble. They were going to perish." She then screamed, "I was so stupid! Couldn't I have killed just one to fulfill the prophecy? Couldn't I have offered Mary?"—a reference to her six-month-old daughter. Then she calmly asked, "Are they in heaven?"[15]

Ferguson, who interviewed Yates several times during her first week in jail, said Yates told her she drowned the children because "they had to die to be saved." To fulfill "the prophecy," Yates told Ferguson, Satan had to be destroyed. "She told me in fragments what the prophecy was, but it didn't make sense," Ferguson testified. Ferguson also testified that Yates believed alternately that she was marked by Satan and that she was Satan— indicating she had changing delusions. Yates, who has been on a suicide watch since her arrest, once asked Ferguson for a razor to shave her head so she could see whether the satanic numbers "666" were on her head. Yates said she could hear Satan behind the jail walls and heard growling noises coming from the hallway. To "calm the beast," she said, she put her plastic food tray in the doorway at a certain angle, Ferguson testified. Yates also said she heard Satan's voice coming through the intercom in her cell. "In all the patients I've treated for major depression with psychotic features, she is one of the sickest I've ever seen," said Ferguson, noting that she had treated six thousand patients when she stopped counting several years ago."[16]

While men are more likely to kill their children (filicide), they are most likely to do so to retaliate against their wives and to regain patriarchal power in the relationship or because physical discipline ended up in the death of their children. Women, on the other hand, most often kill their children for altruistic reasons (e.g., that they have failed as mothers and that their children, therefore, are better off dead). Both fathers and mothers who kill their children are likely to be poor, have mental health problems, and low levels of social support. Desirée West and Bronwen Lichtenstein suggest that Andrea Yates's profile is the embodiment of the mental health problems and social pressures of this altruistic mother who kills her children in the face of failing to be the "perfect mother." They argue that the combination of mental illness, the social and religious pressure on these mothers, and the overwhelming responsibilities of housekeeping, teaching, and caregiving mean that they do not ask for help and that they end up altruistically killing their children to save them.[17] In 2002 Andrea Yates was found guilty of capital murder, but upon re-trial she was found not guilty by reason of insanity and has lived the ensuing many years in psychiatric hospitals.

Andrea Yates's case is one where people might use the common word *hysterical*. The word comes from the Greek root *hystera*, which means "uterus." The word *hysteria* has been used for thousands of years, including by Sigmund Freud, to describe the physical and psychological symptoms of distress due to defects in women's wombs, as it was a diagnosis almost exclusively for women. The word was first used by Hippocrates in the fifth century BCE to describe behaviors caused by having a migratory and restless uterus moving around the body, causing anxiety, tremors, a sense of suffocation, and sometimes even convulsions and paralysis.[18] Freud used it famously in the case of a woman he called "Fräulein Anna O.," whom he considered to be one of the earliest cases of hysteria. Interestingly, "Anna O." herself, whose name was actually Bertha Pappenheim, became a leader in the German Jewish feminist movement in the early twentieth century.[19]

ALGORITHMS AND RISK

One of the main areas of focus when it comes to crime and psychology is on the assessment of risk. Risk assessment tools are used widely in the U.S. justice system in the pre-trial stages to determine an individual's risk to community safety. By implementing uniform measures, the argument goes, decisions about risk can become "objective," avoiding bias in ways that the subjective decisions of judges cannot. Proponents of risk assessments crow that these instruments will result in dramatic reductions in pre-trial detention, a goal shared by advocates for criminal legal system reform, who know that pre-trial detention means a significant increase in

CRITICAL THINKING BREAK 12

In my discussion of algorithms and risk, why did I put the words *objective* and *objectivity* in quotes? Is objectivity truly possible? Use your critical eye. Who wrote the assessment? How did their perspective impact the questions they chose or even the order or the words they used?

the likelihood that a person will plead guilty, be convicted, and receive a long sentence. People in pre-trial detention are still considered innocent under the law and have not been convicted of anything, though they are being held behind bars. But behind the claims of "objectivity" hide so many locations of discretion, where decisions are made by humans with biases, even in something as foundational as defining "risk" at all. "Despite their widespread support, risk assessments are based on a deficient theory of change: they provide neither objectivity nor meaningful criminal justice reform. Risk assessments bear no guarantee of reducing incarceration—instead, they are more likely to legitimize the criminal justice system's carceral logics and policies. Yet because support for risk assessments emerges in part from the socio-technical imaginary that sees all problems as solvable with technology, critiques that articulate the technical limits of risk assessments will likely be met by calls for "better" risk assessments.[20]

One of the main ways that assessments have been made "better" is with the increased use of algorithmic risk assessment, defined as "an automatic rule that uses numerical inputs to produce some result, in this case a prediction relevant to the criminal justice system," which means that they it relies on statistical analyses of large datasets of historical behavior and demographic characteristics of people involved in the criminal legal system.[21] There is substantial concern among researchers and activists that these technology measures will increase incarceration and punitive surveillance, especially among Black and Brown people, and many suggest an abolition of algorithms in the criminal legal system.[22] Indeed, David Garland highlights the expansion of such assessments as one of the managerial crime control techniques used as the United States moves away from a welfare state.[23] The reason for this, Sandra Mayson suggests in her brilliantly titled *Yale Law Review* article, "Bias In, Bias Out," is circular. Because the system, including prediction, is already racist, its predictions will in turn be racist: "Tweaking an algorithm or its input data, or even rejecting actuarial methods, will not redress the racial disparities in crime or arrest risk in a racially stratified world."[24] Technological advances such as these algorithms are increasing throughout the criminal legal system, such as with check-in kiosks, electronic monitoring devices, and video visitation in prison.

PRISONS ARE AMERICA'S LARGEST MENTAL HEALTH PROVIDERS

For those people assessed as too high of a risk and those sentenced to time behind bars, their time incarcerated will be among people overwhelmingly impacted by mental health struggles. Many have argued that one of the many reasons for this is the decades-long deinstitutionalization of U.S. mental health hospitals, where people with psychiatric, intellectual, and developmental disabilities were moved from state institutions and hospitals into the community, often due to closure of those facilities. Such hospitals now house only a tenth of the number of incarcerated people who are also struggling with their mental health. Incarcerated people with mental health challenges are also particularly likely to be suffering from co-occurring substance abuse, and the combination makes them especially likely to engage in and be victimized by violence during their incarceration.[25] Older people, usually emotionally more well in the general population, are particularly likely to suffer from mental health problems when they are incarcerated.[26] People in prison are particularly likely to commit suicide, especially those with a psychiatric diagnosis; have suicidal ideation while imprisoned; and spend time in their cell alone.[27]

In her book *Decarcerating Disability: Deinstitutionalization and Prison Abolition*, Liat Ben-Moshe, on the other hand, argues that deinstitutionalization was *not* the reason why so many people suffering from mental illness are in prisons. Rather, she suggests that we focus instead on the lack of comprehensive community support options that follow people's deinstitutionalization and on the racist criminal justice policies they meet

> **CRITICAL THINKING BREAK 13**
>
> Put those critical glasses on! Should the focus be on making prisons more comfortable for the people caged inside, or is it about making sure no one with mental health problems (or anyone else) is caged in the first place?

upon release. In addition she shows the ways in which prisons are in their nature maddening, disabling, and a form of state violence that maintain their own existence by fomenting deep suffering. Notably, her work connects deinstitutionalization with prison abolition and encourages collaborations among activists in abolition, psychiatric deinstitutionalization, and disability rights.[28] So much of this literature is how to make prison health care better, to reduce the risk of suicide, and to provide better substance abuse treatments. This is like the "gender responsive" movement inside prisons, which makes prisons more trauma-sensitive, for example.[29]

CONCLUSION

Psychological approaches in criminology are based largely on the experiences of white men and must evolve to account for the experiences and behavior of women, Black people, and other minoritized communities. When it comes to mental illness and crime, not only is our criminal legal system overwhelmed with people suffering from mental health problems that cages are ill-equipped to handle but the system itself is built to ensure that Black and Brown people are far more likely to be incarcerated.

5 Social Process and Social Development Theories

Social process theories focus on the interaction between social influences such as the family, employment, and friendships, particularly as it relates when people break the law. One of the themes that you will see clearly in this chapter is *socialization*, or the process by which people learn how they are supposed to behave in society. Social learning theories focus on how we are socialized to accept and engage in lawbreaking behaviors or to reject them.

DIFFERENTIAL ASSOCIATION AND SOCIAL LEARNING THEORY

Social learning theories center the role of learning, which we use for pretty much everything else, in the pathway to criminal behavior. It began with the work of Edwin Sutherland in the 1930s, where he, not coincidentally, was a student and then faculty at the University of Chicago. His focus within the concept of differential association was on the cultural transmission of delinquent values, in which he posited that criminal behavior is learned in interaction with people in intimate personal groups—that is, people learn from their friends not just how to commit crimes but also that crime is something favorable. Later, theorists such as Ronald Akers and Robert Burgess added in the concepts of reinforcements, punishments, and imitation to describe the mechanism by which people are encouraged by others to break the law. Therefore, people break the law when attitudes, values, and rationalizations that normalize criminal behavior have been rewarded more or punished less than definitions that oppose breaking the law. What we know empirically is that association with delinquent peers increases crime, from substance use and vandalism to intimate partner violence and stalking.[1]

So then what if social learning theorists centralized women and girls in a way that examines the ways in which they are socialized to stay out of lawbreaking behavior? There are two ways in which social learning theories simply assume the gendered crime difference rather than centralizing it. First, males are more likely to associate with delinquent peers than females, making the transmission of criminal behaviors less likely, despite the simplicity of that dismissal.[2] Second, decades of research have shown that behaviors considered to be gender-appropriate are rewarded and those that do not fit are punished.[3] Likewise, girls are punished more than boys for criminal behavior because it is considered to be antithetical to the definition of femininity—being passive, nurturing and physically weak— making girls "doubly deviant" when they break the law.[4] Therefore, girls learn more unfavorable definitions for breaking the law than boys, while boys may learn more favorable definitions of breaking the law because of its association with aggression. Boys' far higher association with peers who break the law all contribute to the gender gap.[5]

Researchers who have investigated gender and delinquent peer associations have focused on the fact that even though girls may spend significant time with delinquent peers, gendered socialization (what they call "type scripts") mute the impact of those associations for girls (whose type scripts are related to femininity, considered antithetical to aggression) but encourage it for boys (whose type scripts are related to the aggression, toughness, and status related to masculinity). Likewise, research shows that girls' peer groups focus more on sharing personal problems, feelings of caring and trust, and negative emotions such as depression.[6] Boys, on the other hand, focus with their peers on conflict, status striving, and the belief that boys "couldn't be themselves while with their group."[7] On the flip side, Stacy De Coster suggests that males may have more negative associations with depression than criminal behavior and may anticipate more negative reactions to depression than to criminal behavior; females are the other way around, which may even further explain males' overinvolvement in criminal behavior and females' higher rates of depression.[8]

GENDER AND SOCIALIZATION

Socialization refers to the ways in which people gradually learn the "proper" way to live according to the norms and values of the society in which they live. You will recognize in many of these theories the role of socialization, but, unsurprisingly, they almost completely neglect to consider the arguably paramount importance of gender and racial socialization.

Masculinity

Classic research by Carol Gilligan shows that girls approach morality with an "injunction to care" and an avoidance of harming other people, whereas boys understand morality as involving the right to freely pursue their own self-interest.[9] So then how is this connected to the concept of masculinity? To understand these ideas, it is helpful to take a step back and understand the concepts of *hegemonic masculinity* and *emphasized femininity*. Raewyn Connell introduces these two concepts in *Gender and Power* within an understanding of gender as a social structure itself. She defines hegemonic masculinity as "the configuration of gender practice which embodies the currently accepted answer to the problem of the *legitimacy* of patriarchy which guarantees (or is taken to guarantee) the dominant position of men and the subordination of women."[10]

This type of masculinity is particularly important in its relation to emphasized femininity, which is subordinate, compliant, and accommodating to hegemonic masculinity. The ideas have since been refined (or rather, complicated, in a good way) in collaboration with James Messerschmidt to account for the intersectionality of gender with other social inequalities and to account for the differences in how hegemonic masculinity operates at the local (face-to-face), regional (society-wide) and global (transnational) levels. Messerschmidt has argued that crime and deviance are resources that some men use to signal and attain hegemonic masculinity (and therefore power) as they engage in "doing masculinity" in a way that incorporates differences of class, race and ethnicity, age, sexuality, and bodies. While much research has focused on the ways in which masculinity is linked to violent crime by less powerful men, the "new masculinities" approach reminds us that masculinities are structurally embedded, deeply intersectional, and inextricable from struggles for social power between and within genders.[11]

Kinds of Masculinities

- **Hegemonic masculinity** is "the pattern of practice (i.e., things done, not just a set of role expectations or an identity) that allowed men's dominance over women to continue. Hegemonic masculinity was distinguished from other masculinities, especially subordinated masculinities. Hegemonic masculinity was not assumed to be normal in the statistical sense; only a minority of men might enact it. But it was certainly normative. It embodied the currently most honored way of being a man, it required all other men to position themselves in relation to it, and it ideologically legitimated the global subordination of women to men."
- **Complicit masculinities** "do not actually embody hegemonic masculinity yet through practice realize some of the benefits of unequal gender relations and consequently when practiced help sustain hegemonic masculinity."
- **Subordinate masculinities** "are constructed as lesser than or aberrant and deviant to hegemonic masculinity, such as effeminate men."
- **Marginalized masculinities** "are trivialized and/or discriminated against because of unequal relations external to gender relations, such as class, race, ethnicity, and age."
- **Protest masculinities** "are constructed as compensatory hyper-masculinities that are formed in reaction to social positions lacking economic and political power."[12]

CRITICAL THINKING BREAK 14

Have you ever seen examples of these types of masculinity? How have you seen them change over time?

Ethnic-Racial Socialization

Ethnic-racial socialization (ERS) is the process by which racial and ethnic minoritized families teach their children about race, ethnicity, and racial discrimination. Families are the core of ERS and have a significant role in using socialization to build a strong identity and resiliencies in children, in particular helping them to understand their race, ethnicity, and culture. ERS can be implemented in many ways, such as teaching children about dangers related to racism and discrimination and how to cope with those dangers. The ERS framework outlines the four dominant themes:

1. Cultural socialization, including the transmission of cultural values, customs, traditions, history, and pride
2. Preparation for bias
3. Promotion of mistrust, for example, of other ethnic-racial groups
4. Egalitarianism through a focus on the equality of different ethnic-racial groups[13]

Adriana Umaña-Taylor and Nancy Hill's review of the research shows that the literature on ERS has exploded in the past fifteen years, moving away from a singular focus on the family into neighborhoods, whose effects are far more nuanced than those in the family. They encourage future researchers to examine the role of extended family and fictive kin, groups such as Native Americans, families without documentation, and white people.[14] With all this discussion of connection to others, we move to social bonding theory, which focuses on the ways in which socialization, both formal and informal, produces connections that prevent crime.

SOCIAL BONDING THEORY

Travis Hirschi's book *Causes of Delinquency* focuses on the role of social bonds in whether or not people engage in lawbreaking behavior. Specifically, social bonds are made up of four components: attachment, commitment, involvement, and beliefs. Bonds may be to people (attachment), activities like sports (involvement), jobs or engagement in school (commitment), and how society operates (beliefs). When people are tied into these things (particularly, according to Hirschi, informal connections represented by being worried about what parents might think, for example), they are far less likely to break the law because they are worried about the loss of approval from conventional others.

While your textbook may have explored social bonding theory, it is very important to look at gender in particular when it comes to social bonding, since it is, as usual, central to our understanding of whether people engage in lawbreaking. But most research, particularly that likely centered in your textbook, focuses on the bonds (or lack thereof) of men and boys. Ngaire Naffine and others have asked why, if social control theorists are looking to explain conformity, they would test this hypothesis with men and boys, when women and girls are infinitely more likely to follow the law.[15] Gender socialization has been argued in particular to lead to a different process of social bonding, in which girls have a greater capacity for relational and affective bonding and different types of relational bonding. These bonds exert differential control on girls' delinquency, and girls' socialization is influenced by increased supervision and monitoring, which impacts their openness to risk. Matthew Grindal found that girls reported more cultural socialization, but he primarily looked at the impact of ethnic-racial socialization on young adult delinquency, seeing that ERS can lead to greater social bonds, which in turn reduce delinquency.[16] Where adults used ERS techniques such as cultural socialization and preparation for bias, social bonds were developed that inhibited delinquent behavior.

CRITICAL THINKING BREAK 15

What are your social bonds? To whom do you feel closest? On whom can you rely for support and resources? Do your ties to them impact whether or not you break the law?

GENERAL THEORY OF CRIME

In 1990 Michael Gottfredson and Travis Hirschi proposed what they called the "general theory of crime" (GTC) that confidently states that it could explain everything—from "deviant," gratifying behaviors such as excessive drinking and unprotected sex to clear crimes such as sexual assault (which Gottfredson and Hirschi call "sex without consent") and robbery—by examining a person's level of self-control and related elements of impulsivity and risk taking. More specifically, the theory assumes that such behavior is simply gratifying and that the question is more about why people *don't* break the law and engage in deviant behavior. The root of low self-control, according to GTC, is when parents are not attached to their children and therefore do not exact control over their children's bad behavior. Specifically, those parents who are attached to their children, supervise their children appropriately, and recognize and punish deviant acts ensure that those children develop the self-control they need to resist the easy gratification of misbehavior in childhood and then as adults to be able to delay gratification. The usual critiques of GTC charge that it is tautological, and therefore untestable, for example, in that it does not make sense for crimes such as white-collar crimes, which entail planning antithetical to the core of GTC. But overall the connection between low self-control and crime has been proven relatively consistently over the past few decades.[17]

However, I suspect that you may, at this point, be surprised that Gottfredson and Hirschi had the confidence to propose what they called their general theory of crime focused on impulsivity and self-control without taking intersectionality into account. Almost fifty years after Carol Smart criticized criminological theories for explaining little more than male behavior from a (white) male perspective, you are likely reading about GTC in your criminology textbook.[18] As Susan Miller and Cynthia Burack so succinctly put it, "In this way, the reification of the status quo is neatly established without challenging either the patriarchal structures of social relations and institutions or their concomitant paradigms of social inquiry." In your textbook you will read about GTC as a theory that can explain it all by focusing on low self-control and the role of parenting in teaching children to control their impulses in a way that later impacts whether or not they will engage in criminal behavior. But if we were to introduce intersectionality, would GTC hold up? Decades before your textbook was likely even written, Miller and Burack critiqued GTC for three main problems.[19]

First, GTC tries so hard to be neutral that it chooses to ignore that there is a gendered power imbalance in society that has real implications not just for lawbreaking behavior but also for victimization rates that are dramatically impacted by larger social structures and therefore by gender, race, socioeconomic class, disability, and queerness; it simply cannot explain the differences. As Abigail Henson, Thuy-Trinh Nguyen, and Ajima Olaghere so aptly put it, "The theory places the onus on parents and the institution of school to effectively socialize youth, without considering how the structure of society undermines the function of those domains. . . . It is important to recognize the impact and cause of blocked opportunities, the malleability of individuals' identities, attitudes, and behaviors, as well as the unique response individuals enact when subjected to oppressive conditions." Likewise, Jeanne Flavin demonstrates that in claiming that the general theory of crime is gender-neutral, Gottfredson and Hirschi render their theory useless by, for example, ignoring that most of men's victimization is by strangers, whereas most of women's victimization is by someone they know, and by referring to parenting in a gender-neutral way when parenting is anything but that. Henson, Nguyen and Olaghere suggest, alternatively, a "Socio-structural Induction Theory," which works to explain illegal behavior and the fear of crime without excluding the role of the state, the dominance of certain classes, and macro-social forces. The proposed theory moves away from focusing on the individual and instead looks at the ways in which characteristics behind so-called street crimes, such as impulsivity, risk-taking, and impulsivity, are actually a strength for people struggling under oppressive social structures.[20]

In addition, when GTC points the finger at the role of "ineffective child-rearing" in self-control and therefore crime, it is pointing that finger at women, who are overwhelmingly responsible for childcare. Notably, Gottfredson and Hirschi explicitly deny that their critique is of mothers, but in doing so they completely ignore the reality of childcare responsibilities in the family. This scapegoating means that women are responsible not just for failing to teach self-control and for being absent when they work out of the home but also that they are responsible for socialization, presumably the gender socialization that results in the crime gap. So perhaps GTC *does* centralize women, albeit not explicitly, and, it is implied, particularly single mothers and Black mothers, who not only have the sons who are more likely to be arrested but who are also even more likely to be burdened with poverty, racism, and misogyny than white mothers. In the end the theory then places the blame for (overwhelmingly male) crime on women's failure to mother effectively.

Relatedly, while Gottfredson and Hirschi do include a (brief) focus on rape, they base their analysis on the factually incorrect assumption that most sexual assault is committed by strangers. Their analysis continues to put the blame on women for rape, by suggesting that female potential victims must restrict their freedom of movement and that mothers must do a better job of socializing their male children to have self-control so that they do not rape. Likewise, their (also brief) treatment of intimate partner violence ignores not only the fact that IPV is deeply rooted in larger social structures that value and legitimize male violence as a way to maintain patriarchal control, but also the fact that IPV is not rare and is very often *not* a single, impulsive interaction but often an escalating cycle that only increases in violence, frequency, and injury.

PULLING TOGETHER SELF-CONTROL, PEER IMPACTS, AND GENDER

A few theorists have more recently criticized theories that center low self-control without accounting for gender, at least partly because of gender socialization effects on the impact of peers.[21] Among other things, their studies have found that the difference in self-control by gender is due to a far stronger effect of peer delinquency and therefore offending for boys. They argue that this reflects classic feminist criminology proposals of gendered pathways of offending related to girls' socialization into femininity that so strongly excludes crime and aggression.[22] Further, De Coster also pulls these together:

> Overall, the process leading to law violation and depression can be summarized in the following sequence: social-structural positions influence exposure to stress and deviant responses to stress. Stress exposure and its deviant

responses, including both law violation and depression, subsequently shape social relationships or attachments to conventional and unconventional groups. Attachments to these groups, in turn, affect role-taking in ways that ultimately increase future law violation and depression. Thus, structural positions, stress exposure, social relationships, and the role-taking process are common causes of law violation and depression. However, the content of social relationships, social learning and role-taking may vary systematically across gender, thereby channeling deviance in dissimilar directions for males and females.[23]

LABELING THEORY

Labeling theory focuses on the ways in which people's self-concept may impact whether they break the law. The focus here is the impact of their interaction with institutions of formal control, such as police, courts, and prisons. Specifically, labeling theorists focus on the first contact between people and the criminal legal system that impacts them negatively and makes them think of themselves with a "criminal" label. But that the label then has real-life impacts on their ability to engage in a life without breaking the law, since it makes it harder to get a job, for example.

From a critical perspective, there are a number of important issues to address with labeling theory. First, the focus of labeling theory is on negative labels rather than on "restored" labels. In his work on phenomenological theories of crime and desistance, Shadd Maruna writes about the importance of identity change to whether and how people desist from lawbreaking behavior. Phenomenological criminology is an attempt to understand criminal decision making through an examination of incarcerated or formerly incarcerated people's self project: the self-image they are hoping to uphold, the ends they aim to achieve, and their strategies for creating meaning in their lives. According to this perspective, people who are to desist from lawbreaking behavior must therefore develop a coherent, prosocial identity for themselves. Neal Shover and Walter Gove both suggest that desistance consists of a set of internal changes.[24] While the language each researcher uses to describe these processes is different, the basic idea is that individuals shift away from self-absorption toward caring for others within a context of acceptance of more prosocial values, distinct from the negative label insisted on by labeling theory. The phenomenological examination of desistance therefore focuses not on an individual's behavior but on the meaning that the individual attaches to those experiences. In his examination of desistance, Maruna found much support for the idea that a change in "script" has dramatic effects on the behavior of formerly incarcerated people.[25] A large body of qualitative research on desistance and on substance abuse treatment success also supports this idea of a personal change.

Some desistance literature has focused specifically on the internal changes associated with women's desistance. In their qualitative exploration of female street offenders, one of the few studies to examine women, desistance, and identity change, Ira Sommers, Deborah Baskin, and Jeffrey Fagan applied the phenomenological approach to women's desistance behaviors, finding that specific experiences cause women to reevaluate their identities and move toward the construction of a new identity. They found that identity transformation reinforcement worked both ways: as the women began to feel socially accepted and trusted, their determination to desist was strengthened, as were their social and personal identities as non-criminals. Once a new, more prosocial identity had been created, the authors found that women's strong commitments to their children, new friends, and new educational and vocational skills created new experiences of conventional roles: "In short, the women in the study developed a stake in their new lives that was incompatible with street life."[26] Peggy Giordano, Stephen Cernkovich, and Jennifer Rudolph found that women's transitions were more likely than men's to involve religion.[27] My own research, which seeks to show that women's identity changes related to desistance are due to relationships with children, shows in fact that women's identity changes are due, in fact, to their time spent incarcerated, including conflicting feelings about time lost and invaluable time spent getting to know oneself, no matter how terrible the location.[28]

However, I encourage you to think not just about the ways in which we choose to perceive those who have broken the law and how those labels in turn affect them but even more so about the structures that make the label impossible to lose. Half of labeling theory would not even exist if we were to invest our resources in ensuring that people re-enter the community ready for mental and physical health, a livable income, safe and comfortable housing, and supported relationships, where a "redeemed" label was prioritized over a "criminal" label.

SOCIAL DEVELOPMENT THEORIES

In the 1930s and 1940s Sheldon and Eleanor Glueck studied, for over a decade, a sample of five hundred "delinquent" boys who were sent to reform school in the 1930s and a matched sample of five hundred "nondelinquent" boys on measures of a wide range of physical, psychological, and social factors that might predict crime. In 1986 John Laub was doing research on the lives of the Gluecks, specifically the data on these boys from birth to age thirty-two. According to Laub, "One day, I asked a little white-haired archivist in the Harvard Law School Library what ever happened to the Gluecks' data. . . . 'I'm not sure what you mean by data,' she responded, 'but let me show you what we have in storage in the sub-basement.' There, I discovered 55 boxes of information on 500 delinquent boys who had been sent to reform school in the 1930s. As Rob [Robert Sampson] says in this interview, 'When I first [saw] the raw materials that they had collected, I was frankly stunned. . . . You almost had to go up on a ladder to get to the top.' To say that the Glueck data was "rich" is a grand understatement. In addition to scores of official administrative records on a variety of topics, we found notes that the Gluecks made when they visited these kids' houses—what the conditions were like, were the screens falling off the doors? We found notes of interviews they had conducted with the kids' neighbors and teachers. We found psychiatric assessments of the boys, a series of intelligence tests, and physical exams." John Laub and Robert Sampson and their team then followed up on those same boys, now in their late sixties. From there the life course theory emerged as one of the most popular criminological theories.[29]

Life Course Theory

The relationship between age and crime rivals only the relationship between gender and crime for the most well-established in criminology. For almost everyone, crime emerges in the teenage years, peaks before the age of twenty-one, and declines quickly after that. In their study of age-graded social control, which turned into the longest life-course study of criminal behavior ever conducted, Laub and Sampson found that even people who continue breaking the law after most people desist can stop committing crimes after experiencing significant "turning points" in life.[30]

Significant turning points in Laub and Sampson's research were getting married, joining the military, and starting a job. These new bonds are not just important in themselves, but they also serve as a moment of change in how people view themselves. They mean that new people are monitoring, and they change routine activities in a way that increases routine. Your criminology textbook will likely spend many pages describing the different versions of life course criminology and the profound implications that the many publications and their findings have for policy in the criminal legal system. What you will likely not see, however, is any emphasis on the fact that the data that Laub and Sampson used were almost exclusively from boys and the men they became at the time of follow-up studies.

While life course theorists have overwhelmingly focused their attention on the Gluecks' data on boys, they also collected and analyzed significant data on girls. In their book *Five Hundred Delinquent Women*, they outline the methods and findings from their women's reformatory study, which includes detailed case history data on the women in the study, including retrospective information on their childhood, adolescent, and early adult backgrounds; reformatory experiences; and post-reformatory adjustment to work and family, as well as their offending behavior during a five-year post-parole follow-up period.[31] Incredibly, these data (originally collected in paper format) were stored on microfiche at the Henry A. Murray Research Center of Radcliffe College and were not even converted to an automated format until the early 2000s, when Lisa Broidy and Elizabeth Cauffman's team printed the data, entered it by hand into a computerized database, and re-analyzed it to very little fanfare, comparatively.

The "Good Woman"

Not only are women missing as subjects of desistance research, but they are most often missing even from research on men's desistance when women themselves are named as the hook for change. If, for example, a man who has continued breaking the law long past when his peers desisted, finally stops when he marries who Laub and Sampson call a "good woman," then the lack of focus on who *she* is and what *she* is doing is further proof of criminology's seemingly unending "androcentric slumber."[32] If women are not only so able to resist engaging in criminal behavior but also so pivotal to men's desistance, life course theorists' insistence on ignoring women makes even less sense.

We already know from research about heterosexual relationships more generally that women invest more emotional work in their intimate relationships than men.[33] When it comes to women's relationships with men desisting from crime, Lauren Hall and Lyndsey Harris have suggested that the emotional work and emotional capital women provide is even more impactful than in the general population. They created the concept of "Desistance Emotional Work" that covers the emotional work and capital that women give to men and the impact it has on them, which they found to include, for example, "emotional work particularly around guilt and hope; caregiving; parenting; practical and financial desistance support such as transport and prison visitation; and identity and agency change often as dictated by the socio-structural, as well as the desistance-related, context."[34] Given that millions of women are in relationships with desisting men and that they hold such an important role in that process, more research on this topic should be a priority.

Women's Desistance

When it comes to women's own desistance, researchers have begun to include data on women into their projects. Elizabeth Cauffman, Kathryn Monahan, and April Gile Thomas, for example, found that women whose criminal "careers" continued through adulthood (only 7 percent of "serious female offenders") had different underlying factors than their male counterparts. The women who persisted had more exposure to violence, more struggles with mental health, and more adversity in their interpersonal relationships than the women who desisted.[35] Other researchers have built on this idea by examining categories of when in their lives women start engaging in crime: early-onset, adolescent-onset, and adult-onset groups. They found that a large percentage of women offenders started engaging in criminal behavior as adults. These women were distinct from early-onset women, who were more likely to have experienced childhood sexual abuse, engaged in sexual precocity, were lacking in bonds during childhood, and had low levels of supervision. Women in the adult-onset group, on the other hand, did not have these risks, nor the negative impacts (such as low levels of social capital or limited work experience) of more extensive histories of criminal behavior.[36]

EMPLOYMENT

Much of the research into the link between employment and crime for men concludes that unemployment increases the likelihood of criminal behavior and that employment and job stability increase desistance behaviors.[37] This connection has had mixed support in research on formerly incarcerated women. Certainly, female rates of offending have been found to correspond with increases in women's financial instability.[38] However, Christopher Uggen and Candace Kruttschnitt's research found mixed support for the connection between employment and recidivism: specifically, that women's work history was not related to self-reported desistance behavior but was related to official arrest histories. Related to opportunities for employment, Uggen and Kruttschnitt also found significant effects of education on criminal involvement.[39] Anita Grace has suggested that women's paid work is qualitatively different from men's because women have dramatically more domestic work responsibilities and face higher rates of poverty, trauma, mental health, and addiction.[40] Work often brings with it relationships with co-workers, employers, customers, and others, which present an impactful path towards women's desistance.[41]

Separate from employment (which may not always be gainful enough to impact poverty), Kristy Holtfreter, Michael Reisig, and Merry Morash found that, for women, poverty is significantly related to re-arrest and supervision violation and that state-sponsored support to counteract the effects of poverty (e.g., childcare, public housing and job training) reduces poverty's effect on women's recidivism.[42] While such findings are encouraging in that they indicate a relatively discrete domain that can be addressed by social programming, we must remember that women and their children are disproportionately poor in the United States and that female offenders are overwhelmingly likely to come from poor, inner-city neighborhoods.[43]

MARRIAGE

Substantial research has shown that marriage plays a strong role in encouraging desistance in males.[44] This may start even before the wedding itself, as the desistance process may start even before the transition to marriage, and "good" marriages have been shown to have a cumulative effect on desistance, slowly increasing its preventing effect.[45] Likewise, broken marriages have been shown to increase the possibility of offending.[46]

Stephanie Covington argues that typically women's primary motivation is to build a connection to others and that "to create change in their lives, incarcerated women need to experience relationships that do not repeat their histories of loss, neglect, and abuse."[47] As such, she suggests that any programming for incarcerated women should include relationship and mutuality as core elements to encourage psychological well-being and feelings of empowerment. Relationships such as those with a marriage partner may therefore be particularly effective for women's desistance.[48] However, while men's marriages are often to prosocial women, female offenders' marriages (and other romantic relationships) are likely to involve domestic violence, making the potential relationship between marriage and desistance particularly complicated for women.[49] In turn, research has generally shown that marriage does not impact women's desistance as much as it does for men.[50]

CHILDREN

Given that most incarcerated women are mothers, it seems obvious that the role of becoming a mother or reunifying with children upon reentry should be studied as a potential turning point. While research has shown that parenthood does not have a role in men's desistance, it does have a role in women's desistance, though the stress of parenting, usually done alone, poor, and traumatized, can outweigh the importance of children as a reason for desistance.[51]

PATHWAYS THEORY

As you have now seen over and over again, so-called traditional criminological theories are rightfully criticized by feminist criminologists as male-centered and inadequate to explain why women and girls break the law (or do not). This recent enrichment of life course theory with more inclusive samples provides empirical support for one of the most prominent feminist criminological theories: pathways theory.[52] This is a perspective that focuses on the way that women and girls uniquely enter into lawbreaking behavior. Specifically, it outlines a pathway where girls are victimized in the home as children and end up breaking the law by engaging in criminalized survival strategies, such as running away from home and drug use.

One of the most important studies to know when it comes to the study of pathways theory is the work of Kathleen Daly, who describes five unique pathways for women in criminal court. These include "harmed and harming" people with histories of abuse and neglect and of behavior problems as children; "street women," who ran away from home as the result of childhood abuse and whose survival strategies, such as sex work and drug use, have been criminalized; "battered women," whose male abusive partner was the reason for her involvement in the criminal legal system; "drug-addicted women," whose drug use and selling had resulted in criminal legal system involvement; and a final "other" category, whom she hypothesized engaged in lawbreaking as the result of greed.[53]

CONCLUSION

After three chapters focused on the very personal reasons why people commit crime, this chapter on social process and social developmental theories should have felt very sociological, for good reason. Socialization is a powerful process that impacts us over our entire lives, and mainstream theories should account for intersectionality far more than they do, as you have seen in this chapter. The next chapter examines social structural theories, also rooted in the field of sociology, and also enriched by the use of a critical lens.

6 Social Structure Theories

In this chapter we review the theories under the umbrella of social structural theories in criminology. By this point it will not surprise you that these theories have overwhelmingly focused their attention on poor Black and Brown men's crime, while ignoring the substantial crime that occurs among white men, both wealthy and poor; glossing over their failure to explain women's low rates of crime; and failing to account for impacts on marginalized communities.

The social structural perspective is rooted in the field of sociology, which shifts the focus from the individual to social responsibility for criminal behavior. When sociology began as a discipline in the early 1900s, it was within a time of great societal change, away from an agrarian society toward industrialism, and the simultaneous development of major urban centers, which all in turn led to huge population growth. Crime came along with all these changes, particularly in these new urban areas. When so-called mainstream criminologists look at the concept of *structure*, they are referring to the ways in which society may play in either the encouragement or impeding of lawbreaking behavior, what social factors lead individuals to break the law, and what parts of society relate to the crime rates of particular neighborhoods, cities, or countries. You should notice that, while this is a dramatically different approach from what we have been looking at—choices, biology, and psychology—it is still a focus not only on poor people's crime but also on people who break the law rather than the people who make the laws that define who is a "criminal." They also fail almost completely to take gender and many other intersections into account and largely conflate poverty with being Black and Brown. I start this chapter with French philosopher Émile Durkheim, where modern sociology and in turn mainstream criminological theories originated.

DURKHEIM, ANOMIE, AND THE "OTHER"

Émile Durkheim is one of the founders of sociology, whose focus on social problems is a part of the bedrock of sociological approaches to crime. Some of the concepts will seem familiar from the neo-classical approach: that crime is functional and that humans are by nature selfish and greedy. However, Durkheim added structural context, such as the impact of societal change and the functions of social groups. He suggested that, when a society changes and in turn norms and values are in flux, that imbalance is called *anomie*, translated as "normlessness," which makes people uncomfortable. Such discomfort and lack of norms spur the tendency for people to act in a deviant way. Durkheim's used industrialization, the resulting need for cheap labor, and the influx of immigrants as examples of such an anomic time. As a solution, Durkheim proposed that when people came together in social cohesion or group solidarity, their shared values could either prevent or generate deviant activity.

Particularly important for the work we are doing in this book, Durkheim identified two types of solidarity: mechanical and organic. Mechanical solidarity has common beliefs within society because the individual members are like one another. Organic solidarity, on the other hand, is more complex, emphasizes people's *interdependence* on one another in a community, and is far stronger than mechanical solidarity. Indeed, if we look at the ways in which economic values have penetrated non-economic institutions such as family and education, Durkheim would have argued that community values and social bonds are in turn weakened, which leads to self-serving behaviors such as crime.

SOCIAL DISORGANIZATION THEORY

From the roots of Durkheim's ideas about anomie, social integration, and social control grew the tree of social disorganization theory. The city of Chicago in the 1940s was fertile ground for sociological theories, which grew from the first sociology department at the University of Chicago: industrialization, immigration, and urbanization all came together, and crime ballooned. The original work by Clifford Robe Shaw and Henry Donald McKay focused on racial and ethnic heterogeneity, residential mobility, and relative deprivation.[1] The concept of relative deprivation is attributed to Robert Merton and his strain theory. Relative deprivation is an actual or perceived lack of essential resources (such as food, money, rights, status, safety, and prestige) that have become the norm among particular socioeconomic groups. Such disparities are at the root of social movements such as the civil rights movement in the United States and the marriage equality movement for marriage rights for queer people. The social disorganization theory was reimagined in the 1980s to extend measurements of social disorganization to include concepts like immigrant concentrations and household composition and mediating factors such as social ties and collective efficacy.

Prominent criminologists from Shaun Gabbidon to Nikki Jones to Hillary Potter have worked to remind us that W. E. B. Du Bois's work should be centered not just in sociology but also in criminology, and he should be considered a founding father of both. When it comes to criminology, Gabbidon suggests an "Atlanta School" in the same tradition as the Chicago School. While at Atlanta University, Du Bois used a variety of research methods to study "crime among Negroes." His research in Philadelphia led to publication of the book *The Philadelphia Negro*, in which he argues that crime is less a deficiency of Black people and more a result of racial discrimination and a designed lack of opportunity.[2] But because of his race, and perhaps also because of a twenty-year departure from academia, Du Bois is excluded from the academic field of criminology.

Following this path, the work of Abigail Henson, Thuy-Trinh Nguyen, and Ajima Olaghere lay the inadequacies of social disorganization theory bare, writing that for too long scholars have taken a deficits approach:

academics have been focused on these neighborhoods as sick and crime as a symptom, without looking at who is pumping in the poison. They argue, "Social disorganization theory is better conceived as a theory of consequence that explains the impact of structural inequality, racial/ethnic discrimination, and racial/ethnic inequities. What criminologists measure are the behavioral responses to structural stressors with crime as the main outcome of interest.... Conflating place ecology with race/ethnicity, gender, and social status treats people as disorganized." Rather, they suggest "Critical Environmental Adaptation Theory," which flips the focus from the problems of such neighborhoods to the adaptations that the people of these neighborhoods have made in the face of the purposeful historical disruption and destruction of communities. The deliberate legal, social, and economic exclusion that resulted, they argue, has meant incredible adaptations such as community enclaves, investment in informal economies, and other creative adaptations to economic strain.[3]

Similarly, in "Motherwork under the State: The Maternal Labor of Formerly Incarcerated Black Women," Susila Gurusami shows the ways that formerly incarcerated mothers have survived by creatively adapting to the constant threat of Child "Welfare" Services surveillance by creating mothering strategies to keep them and their children safe and together:

- **Collective motherwork:** The ways in which mothers rely on one another to share child care responsibilities, resources, and information.
- **Hypervigilant motherwork:** May be seen as "hovering," where moms keep children close by to keep them safe from those who may harm them, whether individuals or the state through removal.
- **Crisis motherwork:** When women are in crisis situations where they were immediately threatened with losing custody of a child, at risk of reunification not occurring, or reincarceration and had to very quickly gather their resources and react in a way that sometimes meant that they had to abandon commitments such as employment.[4]

Critical criminologist Michael Hallett goes even further, arguing that social disorganization is in fact a "market opportunity." He quotes Angela Davis as she writes about the political economy of prisons, which, he suggests, "relies on racialized assumptions of criminality—such as images of Black welfare mothers reproducing criminal children—and on racist practices in arrest, conviction, and sentencing patterns." Indeed, where prisons used to be profitable because they provided labor (having come directly from slavery—a la Michelle Alexander), now they are wildly profitable for everything from laundry to phone calls to commissaries.[5]

You may be wondering why the focus of the translational criminologists is on strengthening institutions of social control rather than on how the so-called disorganized structures are actually working quite well, not for the so-called criminals but for the people who profit off of criminalized poverty and Black and Brown people. The resources that the prison industrial complex pillages from Black and Brown communities are even harder to build back because it is not only taking money but depleting both social capital and human capital. Social capital "'refers to the social skills and resources needed to effect positive change in neighborhood life' and involves a neighborhood's ability to create 'capability through socially structured relations between individuals in groups.'" Human capital, likewise, is "the human skill and resources individuals have to function effectively, such as reading, writing, and reasoning ability. Human capital is the capital individuals acquire through education and training for productive purposes."[6]

Where we see social disorganization in communities, we also see limited social and human capital and in turn crime and incarceration. Dina Rose and Todd Clear took it to the next step and showed how taxpayer dollars are shifted from building social institutions (e.g., schools, tuition support, summer jobs), social capital, and human capital toward funding the prisons that only continue to siphon more money from communities into corporate coffers.[7] In fact, everything from short jail stints to long prison terms serve to break down the very community and family bonds identified by social disorganization theory to prevent crime, and as a result we see dismal rates of return to incarceration, where most of those returning are doing so on parole violations.[8] So then if we are to take a social disorganization perspective on crime, the very prisons built in the name of preventing crime must be dismantled, with funding diverted to strengthening not the bars of separation but the informal and formal institutions of connection and stability in not just our wealthy communities but also those beset by poverty. We must also break down the many ways in which the criminalization of poverty has been codified and the many formal and informal ways in which poverty, and the ways in which it intersects with race, are continued over generations, such as redlining, isolating housing projects, and the Ban the Box campaign.

Ban the Box

Have you ever applied for a job or a place to live and had to answer a question about whether you have a criminal record? A campaign started by All of Us or None, an organization fighting for the rights of incarcerated and formerly incarcerated people and their families, the Ban the Box campaign works to stop employers and housing providers from asking about an applicant's criminal conviction records until after that person has been found "otherwise qualified." According to the campaign itself, as of 2024, "Over 45 cities and counties, including New York City, Boston, Philadelphia, Atlanta, Chicago, Detroit, Seattle, and San Francisco, have removed the question regarding conviction history from their employment applications. Seven states, Hawaiʻi, California, Colorado, New Mexico, Minnesota, Massachusetts, and Connecticut have changed their hiring practices in public employment to reduce discrimination based on arrest or conviction records. Some cities and counties and the state of Massachusetts have also required their vendors and private employers to adopt these fair-hiring policies. In some areas private employers are also voluntarily adopting Ban the Box hiring policies."[9] For example, in 2019 Colorado passed a Ban the Box law as a part of the Colorado Chance to Compete Act, which prohibits private employers from asking about applicants' criminal background in their initial application for employment and from advertising a job that bars people with criminal histories from applying.[10]

Redlining

The historical practice of redlining is named for a term used in a government housing program that began in the early twentieth century:

> To stabilize housing markets and homeownership following the Great Depression, the federal government established the Home Owners' Loan

Corporation (HOLC)—which offered refinancing assistance to struggling homeowners, purchasing their mortgages and reissuing amortized mortgages with longer repayment timelines—as well as the Federal Housing Administration (FHA)—which underwrote mortgage risk to increase banks' comfort with mortgage lending. In consultation with local financial and real estate informants, these agencies conducted widespread neighborhood appraisals of investment risk in the form of color-coded "residential security" maps, typically ranking neighborhoods from "A," best, to "D," hazardous. The practice of ranking neighborhoods as hazardous and credit-unworthy is referred to as "redlining," after the color assigned to "D" grade neighborhoods on these maps.[11]

However, the neighborhoods outlined in red—*redlined*—on these maps were overwhelmingly populated by Black people, which meant that no matter their personal qualifications for loans, Black people were denied access to credit because of where they lived. Even though redlining was outlawed in 1968, its implications live on in the absence of generational wealth in those communities and also in the characteristics of the neighborhoods, which are more likely to be polluted, have less green space, and have lower maternal and neonatal health.[12]

The African American Redress Network (AARN), which engages in local-level reparation efforts with a focus on Black land loss, has helped intervene in two communities—Evanston, Illinois, and Brown Grove, Virginia—communities that were purposefully racially segregated with zoning ordinances and redlining. AARN works to remediate the current-day impacts of these policies on housing, schools, services, and more and to fight for reparations to interrupt these racist legacies.[13] Interestingly, digital redlining is a newer concept, in which century-old redlining tools are modernized using broadband accessibility, biases in mortgage lending, and more.[14]

The Prison Industrial Complex

Critical Resistance defines the prison industrial complex (PIC) as

> the overlapping interests of government and industry that use surveillance, policing, and imprisonment as solutions to economic, social and political problems. Through its reach and impact, the PIC helps and maintains the

authority of people who get their power through racial, economic and other privileges. There are many ways this power is collected and maintained through the PIC, including creating mass media images that keep alive stereotypes of people of color, poor people, queer people, immigrants, youth, and other oppressed communities as criminal, delinquent, or deviant. This power is also maintained by earning huge profits for private companies that deal with prisons and police forces; helping earn political gains for "tough on crime" politicians; increasing the influence of prison guard and police unions; and eliminating social and political dissent by oppressed communities that make demands for self-determination and reorganization of power in the US.[15]

Profiteers have found many ways to leverage incarceration to profit from the caging of human beings. Within the corrections industry, this includes charging exorbitant rates for items bought in the commissary or vending machines and for phone calls or emails to loved ones, adding surcharges to money transfer services to incarcerated people, and paying almost nothing for labor done by incarcerated people, among many others.[16] This for-profit prison system is inherently exploitative as it capitalizes on increased criminalization and the use of so-called correctional facilities.

STRAIN THEORY

Strain theory emerged in the 1930s with the writing of Robert K. Merton. Rooted in Durkheim's concept of anomie, Merton's strain theory focuses on the idea that where economic success is prioritized, crime is more likely. When wealth is an important cultural goal, the people who do not have the means to achieve it feel strain. He suggests that there are four ways that people respond to that strain: ritualism, retreatism, rebellion, and innovation. While Merton's strain theory was a very important development in criminology, it is rife with problems. While the difficulties of poor people should be highlighted, the connection to crime just doesn't hold up. From a critical perspective, these should be quite obvious. Merton's strain theory explains crime only by poor people, so it completely fails to explain, for example, white-collar crime and the fact that poverty rates and crime rates do not vary together over time. It also fails to explain the fact that different people respond to strain in different ways, and it has no explanation at all for why women, who are far more likely to be poor, engage in criminal behavior far less than men.

Rather than fade away, however, strain theory got an overhaul by Robert Agnew in 1992 with the proposal of general strain theory (GST). Instead of focusing on just money, GST sees strain as originating from negative emotions such as fear, depression, frustration, and especially anger, which then lead to some sort of coping, including crime. He categorized the sources of strain into three areas:

1. The threatened or actual experience of not achieving a highly valued goal, such as not getting a promotion and as a result writing rumors that get someone fired
2. The loss of a valued person or thing, such as the death of a loved one, which leads to someone trying to get revenge illegally
3. The presence of a negative stimulus, such as bullying that leads to someone skipping school

In addition Agnew further clarified that strains that are high in magnitude (i.e., severe, harmful, threatening), that are seen as unjust, and that are linked with low social control and where crime is incentivized are more likely to lead to crime. There are particular strains that meet all four of these criteria, such as parental rejection, excessive discipline, child abuse, and criminal victimization and are therefore especially likely to be criminogenic.[17] The most obvious improvement of GST over Merton's strain theory is that it no longer explains crime by only poor people, because it is not limited to the discrepancy between economic means and ends. It covers everything from the fear of losing a job to the impacts of living in a violent home to worries about having failed a college course.

More recent GST research has focused on the ways in which race and strain intersect. Larger structural factors such as poverty and unemployment have an impact on strain in a way that is different by race.[18] Racial micro-aggressions also have a dramatic impact: "Racial microaggressions are brief and commonplace daily verbal, behavior, or environmental indignities, whether intentional or unintentional, that communicate hostile, derogatory, or negative slights and insults toward people of color. Perpetrators of microaggressions are often unaware that they engage in such communications when they interact with racial/ethnic minorities."[19] Stacy De Coster and Maxine Thompson, for example, looked at the impact of racialized micro-aggressions, which have already been shown to increase negative emotions such as anger, shame, fear, and anxiety, on crime. Indeed, Agnew himself focused on the importance of stressful experiences that people perceive as undeserved, harmful, unfair, and ongoing, which are particularly likely to lead to anger and are also particularly likely when it comes to racial injustices. De Coster and Thompson found that Black students' higher rates of delinquent behaviors are accompanied with dramatic stress from pervasive race-based micro-aggressions.[20]

So then what does GST have to say about the fact that women, who arguably have more strain than men, do not commit crimes at anywhere near the rate of men? GST is one of the few major theories that attempts to explain the gender ratio problem (that women are underrepresented for most criminal behaviors). In 1997 Lisa Broidy and Robert Agnew sought to explore the ways in which GST can (unlike most other criminological theories) explain the gender differences in criminal behavior and the distinctive characteristics of women's crime. Specifically, they explored the ways in which gender differences might predict differences in reactions to strain (and therefore crime). They and others have found that women may actually experience more strain and anger than males, but several gender differences impact the fact that women are far less likely to break the law. For example, they found evidence that men and women may conceptualize fairness differently (i.e., men focus on whether or not material things are fairly distributed), while women focus more on personal relationships and fair procedures.[21]

Much like De Coster and Thompson found with Black and Brown youth, others have found that women are likely to experience certain types of gender-specific strain such as gender-based discrimination, behavioral restrictions, more extensive demands from family members (especially for Black women), and greater exposure to certain types of criminal victimization such as sexual abuse, sexual assaults, rape, and intimate partner violence.[22] These ideas mesh well with feminist pathways theory, which focuses on the role of childhood victimization in the pathways of girls and women into law breaking behavior by including a focus on how victimization and oppression may impact deviant behaviors.[23] On the other hand, men may experience more problems in relationships with peers and may be more vulnerable to financial strain.[24]

Black feminist activist Taylar Nuevelle writes and speaks about the "trauma to prison pipeline" that she herself experienced. She is the director of the Who Speaks for Me? project, which centers the childhood trauma experiences of queer Black and Brown women and the ways in which those experiences led them to criminalization.[25] "When I say 'Who speaks for me?,' it means when I'm incarcerated or too depressed or beaten down, I may need someone to share my story. But when I'm able to share my story myself, those allies and accomplices can come along and help me. At the end of it, it really is about healing from the trauma that was untreated that led to the incarceration because we have a system that's built upon preying upon those that are most marginalized, over-sentencing them, and then punishing them for identities that aren't agreed with."[26]

When it comes to the importance of anger to whether crime results from strain, the emotional experiences of women have been found to be more complex, joining other emotions such as guilt, sadness, and depression.[27] In turn women's responses to strain are likely to turn inward, such as in the form of eating disorders and self-harm.[28] Nicole Piquero and her colleagues' research into women's responses to strain focused on inner-directed strain, and it is important to note that such behaviors are not necessarily preferable to outer-directed strain, though the harmful impact is dramatically different. The role of gendered socialization also plays a part in this web, for women are likely to have more social support than men.[29] Specifically for Black Americans, research has shown that, while Black men and women both experienced anger in response to strain, Black women were more likely to experience depression and anxiety, but high levels of religiosity helped Black women with distress, in turn impacting criminal behaviors, which are dramatically lower.[30] On the other hand, men may be more likely both to have more deviant friends and to feel the expression of anger and competition as a valued trait of masculinity.[31]

This combination in women of depression and anger seems to be centrally important to the ability of strain theory to account for the behavior of women. Gendered strain theory suggests that depression tempers the impact of anger on delinquency among women, whereas others focus on societal expectation impacts on gender differences in the *expression* of emotions, which means that, for example, depression exacerbates the effect of anger on delinquency among males.[32] What if we focused on the women behind bars? They have a particularly high concentration of needs because women are able to internalize and manage strain more effectively than men and therefore do not end up behind bars until their pile of challenges has gotten very high. This has meant that incarcerated women are particularly likely, for example, to be accused of malingering, have a very complicated constellation of needs, and have correctional officers fighting against working with women even with monetary incentives. Such a dichotomy also lays bare that men's crime in the face of opportunity blockage is seen as functional, while women's crime is seen as weakness. I also explore the many harmful (though not criminal!) ways in which women express strain, from substance abuse to self harm, from abusive relationships to mental health challenges. So then what's the takeaway? Societal expectations of women means that even though they have as much anger as men, they are expected to keep everything under control. Plus they have friends who help them manage, whereas men have criminal friends, so they just don't manage their anger the way women do and then they commit crimes that, by the way, we already associate with masculinity.

BLACK FEMINIST CRIMINOLOGY

While not all Black and Brown people are poor, socially disorganized neighborhoods with associated higher crime are far more likely to be overwhelmingly populated by Black and Brown people, victims of disadvantage by design. In addition, being Black and Brown means higher strain due to racism, such as in micro-aggressions. Women are subject to more strain (including that due to living under patriarchy) but deal with it in the combination of depression and anger and the resulting internalized harm. So while gendering these theories helps us understand women's emotions, it still means overwhelmingly centering the priorities and experiences of middle-class white women, while neglecting to look at the particular experiences of Black and Brown people.[33]

Black feminist criminology encourages us to complicate our understanding of individual experiences by looking at the intersections and by studying the lives of Black women with a lens that recognizes that unique lens of Black womanhood.[34] Particularly important for this chapter, Black feminist criminology recognizes that Black women face multiple structural sites of oppression and that their identities are multiplicative, intersecting, and fluid.[35] Imagine a web: trauma that begins with abuse, then moves to juvenile criminalization, fragile relationships with gender-based violence, and intimate partner violence (a victimization most common among Black women), which leads to lawbreaking and staying in abusive relationships because of poverty.[36] This web is both personal and structural and leads to imprisonment.[37] As Wendy Middlemiss notes, poverty not only impacts the tangible economic status of a family but also takes a toll on the emotional bonds strained under its weight.[38] This in turn can impact relational dynamics in historically marginalized communities.[39] So then, if we are going to look at structural factors, we must centralize Black women, who are so uniquely impacted by them.

SUBCULTURAL THEORIES OF CRIME

As social disorganization and anomie theories came together, the subcultural theoretical perspective emerged. Unsurprisingly, these theories focused on poor people and have overwhelmingly neglected gender.

Focal Concerns

While Walter B. Miller's theory of focal concerns explicitly focuses on the "lower class," one of the more recent avenues of research grounded in this theory has expanded his ideas to many other groups, though you may not see it in your regular criminology textbooks.[40] In fact, over half a century after Miller proposed it, the focal concerns theory has become the primary perspective when it comes to decision making among members of the court, with a particular focus on judges. The focal concerns used in this framework include the court actors' interest in the blameworthiness of the suspect (the individual's level of potential responsibility in committing the crime and making sure the punishment fits the crime), protection of the community (an assessment of the accused's future behavior and determining if they would be a danger to society), and practical constraints and consequences that affect system case-processing efficacy.[41]

Others have suggested the addition of other concepts, such as "salvageability," in which they found race to impact decision making so that Black people were significantly less likely to be referred to rehabilitative programming as opposed to traditional punishment, even if that referral would be an upward departure from a guidelines-conforming sentence.[42] However, even when focal concerns are clearly powerful, race and gender are still overwhelmingly impactful. For example, in a study of police decision making in stop-and-frisk situations, some research found that focal concerns theory failed to remove evidence of racial bias alone and the effect of racial and gender bias considered together.[43] The race of the citizen alone, or in conjunction with the gender of the citizen, shows that these demographics still matter when it comes to police decision making in stop-and-frisk situations based on reasonable suspicion.

When it comes to intimate partner violence and sexual assault decision-making research, crime seriousness, weapon use, and criminal history have emerged as additional concerns. There is also the contrast between stereotypical views of "real rapes" and "genuine victims," as opposed to nontraditional women or women who engage in some type of risk-taking behavior and who are less likely to be viewed by court actors as victims deserving of protection under the law.[44] Eryn Nicole O'Neal and Cassia Spohn focused specifically on court actor and police officer decision making in cases of intimate partner sexual assault, which is defined as a sexual assault incident involving a suspect and victim who are married, cohabitating, dating, legally, separated or divorced, or who have children together.[45] This is a particularly important area because research tends to dichotomize sexual assault and intimate partner violence and examine them individually, but intimate partner sexual assault is relatively common—between 7 percent and 14 percent of women who marry or cohabitate will be sexually assaulted by their partners on at least one occasion.[46] O'Neal and Spohn found that focal concerns played an important role in the entire decision making process, from police officers making arrest decisions to prosecutors making charging decisions. Importantly, they also focused on the need for police officers to treat non-stranger rape as "real rape" to facilitate victim cooperation, which in turn impacts focal concerns and decision making in the criminal legal system process (in addition to victim healing, of paramount importance).[47]

In fact, O'Neal and Spohn did additional work with Kimberly Kaiser to flip the focal concerns approach to victim decision making about whether or not they decided to participate with the criminal legal process after being sexually assaulted.[48] Sexual assault is one of the most underreported crimes. For example, Patricia Godeke Tjaden and Nancy Thoenne analyzed the results of the National Violence against Women Survey and found that only 19.1 percent of women who were raped since their eighteenth birthday reported the crime; a similar survey in Canada found that only 6 percent of sexual assaults were reported to the police, despite being so common.[49] Given the importance of victim cooperation to the successful prosecution of sexual assault and intimate partner violence cases and the difficulty of securing victim cooperation throughout the criminal legal system process, Kaiser, O'Neal, and Spohn innovatively used three victim focal concerns—crime seriousness, costs of cooperation, and likelihood of conviction—to examine why victims decide to cooperate. They found that focal concerns indeed impacted victim participation, which has direct implications for the ways in which police and other criminal legal system professionals can impact victim cooperation in sexual assault cases, such as establishing empathetic rapport.

CRITICAL THINKING BREAK 16

Scholars such as Rodney Kingsnorth and Randall Macintosh have suggested that rational choice theory works best for understanding victim decision making, saying that victims use a "complex decision-making process" in which they weigh the costs and benefits of cooperation.[1] Which theoretical application makes more sense to you: focal concerns or rational choice?

---

1. Kingsnorth & Macintosh, "Domestic Violence," 322.

Differential Opportunity

Richard Cloward and Lloyd Ohlin's theory of differential opportunity will sound very similar to Merton's strain theory in that it focuses on the importance of wealth to "delinquent" youth and that crime happens among these kids when access to such wealth is structurally blocked. Indeed, it is considered to be a classic modification of Merton's theory in which they focused, however, on the fact that opportunities for crime are far more available in some neighborhoods where there are, for example, well-organized operations for drug distribution. In other neighborhoods conditions have deteriorated enough so that not only "legitimate" social control agencies fall apart but also organizations for criminal behavior (here you will also recognize social disorganization theory).[50] Differential *opportunity*, therefore, refers to the availability of both legal and illegal opportunities for success, and where illegal opportunities exist in the absence of access to wealth, gangs will emerge.

By now you will be familiar with the observation that this theory does not account at all for the gender gap in who commits crime and applies only to poor people. But what if differential opportunities are different for men and women not just because of poverty but also because misogyny impacts women's opportunities in "legitimate" work, where women earn seventy-five cents to a man's dollar and are limited in almost every way when it comes to access, promotion, and compensation? Sarah Becker's research looks at the gender gap with a focus on the sex-segregated character of offending, in which women are shown to commit less crime than men, and their crimes are usually less serious, violent, and profitable. In her 2011 article with Jill McCorkel, they found that women are represented across a broader array of crimes when they co-offend with men, compared to when they co-offend with women or work alone. Specifically, women are several times more likely to be involved in gender atypical offenses like robbery, drug trafficking, burglary, homicide, gambling, kidnapping, and weapons offenses when they have at least one male co-offender compared to when they work alone or in a same-sex group. They attribute this in part to the fact that men have more access to resources that are more accessible to men, such as illegal drugs to sell, and the ability to intimidate a target.[51]

CONCLUSION

I find that social structure theories of criminology are more satisfying in their understanding of larger social structures such as poverty and racism. As you have seen in this chapter, however, research from these theoretical perspectives generally continues to travel the well-worn paths we have seen criminologists follow in each chapter of this book so far.

7 Theories of Victimology

Victimology is, unsurprisingly, the study of victims. Not all criminology textbooks explore theories of victimization, but it is a growing and evolving field, worthy of examination. This is true particularly because of highly stereotyped media and popular conceptions of victims and because lawmakers and criminal justice workers often use victims to justify "tough on crime" decisions, even when those decisions do not serve them.

TRIGGER WARNING

Before we begin the substance of this chapter, please think about whether your professor gave you something they called a "trigger warning" before you began this topic (or another one that can be difficult to learn about). They may have called it a "content advisory" or even "a note about course content," to be a clear break from the now-controversial term "trigger warning." The debate about content notifications has long been a passionate one: on one side are people looking to protect students (and others) with trauma histories from having upsetting responses to difficult material so that they can engage in learning without re-traumatization. On the other side are those who believe that content notifications are a way that students are being coddled and encourage students to be lazy and avoid work in a way that undermines academic integrity.[1]

I will give you the content notification that I give my students for most of my classes: the material that you will read in this chapter (and in much of this book) describes harm that you may have experienced or that people in your life may have experienced, and that may make you feel bad in a way that makes you less able to learn well. If you find something difficult to read, take a break! Take a breath, take a sip of water, give yourself a hug, or do something else that makes you feel good. When you feel taken care of and fortified, you will be more able to learn than if you feel distressed.[2]

VICTIM PRECIPITATION THEORY

Victim precipitation theory is the first theory of victimization, which held that victims' traits and behaviors have a role in their own harm from crime and maltreatment, such as their style of speech or dress or their actions or inactions. Proposed in the 1940s by criminologist Hans von Hentig and defense attorney Benjamin Mendelsohn, this theory fell out of favor quickly because it very explicitly blamed many victims for their own victimization, even creating a typology of victims that ranged from "completely innocent" victims (such as children) to "voluntary victims" to victims who are "the most guilty."[3]

In their footsteps criminologist Menachem Amir created a typology of forcible rape, including "victim precipitated forcible rape": "those rape situations in which the victim actually, or so it was deemed, agreed to sexual relations but retracted before the actual act or did not react strongly enough when the suggestion was made by the offender(s). The term applies also to cases in risky or vulnerable situations, marred with sexuality, especially when the victim uses what could be interpreted as indecency in language and gestures." Amir deemed that the people who raped them were "less guilty."[4] By the 1970s and 1980s, criminology turned its back on victim precipitation, as Lilia Cortina, Verónica Caridad Rabelo, and

Kathryn Holland wrote, "lambast[ing] it for logical inadequacies, questionable evidence, unfounded assumptions, untestable hypotheses, and unwarranted generalizations."[5] For example, if a victim precipitates her own victimization, then wouldn't every woman drinking alone lead to a crime?

When one focuses on individual victim behavior, the implications are to change how people act to ensure that they are not victimized. This favors personal "failings" but ignores the structural factors, such as misogyny and patriarchy, which are the true larger causes of crime, particularly against women. Indeed, victim precipitation explanations are largely used to explain crimes by men against women, as Michelle Meloy and Susan Miller express it: "Why is it that we tend to sympathize with someone who is mugged, burglarized, or injured by a drunk driver, yet victims of male-on-female violence often experience victim blaming and self-blame?"[6] In other words, we focus on the ways in which rape victims "ask for it" in ways that we do not for other crimes, and by doing so we remove the agency from the people who did harm, which in turn may mean they are not seen as accountable for their actions.

We know that rape myths are, after all, myths. This does not mean they do not impact criminal legal system responses to sexual assault, however. Research has shown that incorrect beliefs about victim precipitation impact police, prosecutors, and juries, even meaning, for example, that police did not submit thousands of rape kits for forensic analysis because of their beliefs about victim culpability in their own assaults.[7] This in turn stops victims from even reporting their victimization to anyone, including to police.

Interestingly, victim precipitation has recently enjoyed renewed attention in the organizational sciences, where theorists have been trying to use victim characteristics to explain workplace mistreatment, including sexual harassment. Researchers who reviewed the data from many studies on the same topic (called a meta-analysis), however, confirm what criminology found decades ago—that the relationships between victim traits and mistreatment are weak or nonsignificant and that researchers and practitioners should instead focus on understanding the role of the environment and the people who commit the offenses.[8]

DEVIANT PLACES THEORY

In the 1980s Rodney Stark chose to research crime in a way that focused on "kinds of places" rather than the traditional study of "kinds of people." In the tradition of social disorganization theory, Stark believed that certain places and the "criminal traits" of those places caused increased probability of victimization, due to population density, poverty, mixed use, transience, and dilapidation, which all in turn led to moral cynicism, increased opportunities for crime and deviance, increased motivation to commit crime, and diminished control.[9] With the public, popular media, and criminology all myopically focused on crime and victimization in urban areas, we can see how such a hypothesis might become very popular. However, the way that these data are collected may be obfuscating the realities. For example, Barry Ruback and Kim Menard found rates of sexual victimization are higher in rural counties. They suggest that this may be due to the opposite of one of Stark's main characteristics (density)—that dispersion of people means that most interactions between people happen between people who know one another.[10] Most sexual assaults happen between people who know one another and are in turn less likely to be reported to the police, which may increase the likelihood of normalizing the behavior and therefore increasing reoffending. They also hypothesize that the lower rape-reporting rates in rural areas may be due to more limited ability to communicate with supportive others because of lack of public transportation and lack of funding for victim support.

VICTIMS' RIGHTS MOVEMENT AND PUNISHMENT

The victims' rights movement was born out of the 1960s, where vibrant radical social movements met law-and-order politics, which sought to redefine participation in the anti-Vietnam war and Black Power movements as a crime. As with most law-and-order initiatives, this met with support from, as Carrie Rentschler puts it, "a small constituency that tends to be the least victimized groups of people within a population." In turn this politicization meant that the "victim perspective" reflected a political need more than the actual perspective of people who had experienced victimization, and, indeed, "victims rights" became the platform from which the constitutional protections of criminal defendants were attacked. This continued for many years to come: "The image of rightless victims juxtaposed against the image of rights-bearing pathological street criminals fed the moral tale of crime common in news reporting.... Narrating this wrong as an imbalance of constitutional rights presents a powerful, easy-to-identify, moralistic and highly mobilizing frame. According to victims' rights, we can 'fix' the problems created by these inequalities by passing legislation that guarantees rights to people as victims within the criminal justice system."[11]

Indeed, the crime victims' movement was an unlikely mix of feminists, liberal reformers, right-wing think tanks, the gun lobby, and Republican and Democrat politicians, all interested in services to victims and in punishment for those considered to be responsible. In fact, the Law Enforcement Assistance Administration (LEAA) was central to the development of this movement, though its primary function at the time was to respond to the "urban" riots and anti-Vietnam war protests and to funnel federal resources into local police departments for "crime control" purposes. Indeed, Mark Fishman shows the ways in which the LEAA manufactured fear of crime waves against the elderly in New York City, for example (even though crimes had not increased) to manufacture a victim perspective on crime and in turn act as publicity for police, who wanted to be seen as a coalition with victims.[12] More explicitly: the recognized movement has been largely a movement of middle- and upper-class white people who are focused on victims and reinforce myths about victimization and the image of the ideal victim.

Victims themselves in victims' rights activism, doing what Rentschler defines as "collective grief work," are used extensively to do the political and commercial work of activists, journalists, and politicians and have themselves evolved using those techniques to represent their own causes.[13] In the early 1970s, the victims' rights movement had some major accomplishments, including the institutionalization of state-level victim compensation programs, the development of annual publicity events, and the institutionalization of victimology in the academic and professional spheres. Also at this time multiple victim organizations began, including the National Organization for Victim Assistance (NOVA; formed out of the LEAA conference in 1975), the National Coalition against Sexual Assault, and the National Coalition against Domestic Violence. As victims and their families realized, however, that the criminal legal system was failing to meet victims' needs, a parallel grassroots movement developed to create victim service organizations to increase awareness of victims, their families, and their experiences. This movement fought for attention as the police-centered movement had powerful spokespeople, such as Ronald Reagan, who focused on federal victim-centered policy initiatives in the 1980s in a way that consolidated the movement as a battle between victims' rights and defendants' rights.[14] Since the late 1980s, the victims' rights movement has focused mainly on codifying victims' rights into law in the form of constitutional amendments and victims' bills of rights in the states.

VICTIM COMPENSATION AND RESTITUTION PROGRAMS

The first of the victim compensation funds began in California, where trauma was translated into medical, psychological, and economic costs so that victims, or families of victims, could be compensated for those losses. These services spread through the country and now include such things as medical costs, mental health counseling, crime scene cleaning, funeral and burial costs, and lost wages or loss of support.

The Victim Witness Protection Act of 1982 authorized restitution to victims as part of a sentence. Since then restitution has emerged as "both a blessing and a curse," where restitution is not ordered in every case (even when it is mandated), often goes unpaid, and ends up confusing both those who owe (about whether they are supposed to pay and how much, given the many fines and fees applied in the aftermath of a crime) and victims (about if they are even entitled to such funds). However, the funds can be useful to victims.[15] Barry Ruback, Andrew Gladfelter, and Brendan Lantz found that people who owed restitution were far more likely to pay it if they were provided with information about, for example, how much they owed and were thanked for payments made.[16] There are a number of ways different states are working to identify who owes restitution, how much they owe, to whom it is owed, and how it is collected and disbursed, which is a process that requires cooperation and data sharing between a number of different entities in the criminal legal system. The Restitution Resource Center, coordinated by the Council of State Governments, is available as a resource to states looking to improve their ability to achieve these goals. Likewise, when restitution is paid to victims, they are more willing to report crimes in the future. But it is important that victims not only get money.[17] Rather, they must also be "made whole" by the delivery of actual procedural, informational, and interpersonal justice from the criminal legal system.[18]

RESTORATIVE JUSTICE AND VICTIMS

We revisit the concept of restorative justice in later chapters of this book, but its role in victims' healing and, well, restoration, is an important one for this chapter as well. The traditional criminal legal system's approach to "justice" in the United States is adversarial and offender-oriented, and there is widespread victim and victim advocate dissatisfaction with the process and the outcomes of this approach. Gerald Hotaling and Eva Schlesinger Buzawa found that almost half of victim-survivors were dissatisfied with all aspects of their experience with the criminal justice system, and another 27 percent were dissatisfied with the prosecution of their cases in court.[19]

Restorative justice approaches offer a solutions-based process that focuses on healing (rather than retribution) and reconciliation (rather than punishment) in a way that prioritizes victims' voices. Traditionally, restorative methods such as family group conferencing, healing circles, and community reparations have been used for property crime cases and cases involving juvenile offenders and have not been used in cases of severe violence or gendered violence such as domestic violence, in particular, due to power imbalances. However, more recently, people have been exploring the possibility of adapting the practices of restorative justice to violent crimes, and gendered crimes in particular. Dartmouth, for example, is offering it for sexual assault and Title IX cases. Research on the effectiveness of such practices and the satisfaction of victims (and others) in the process is only in its infancy, but what researchers have found is that restorative processes are appropriate only when there is not a concern of ongoing danger to the victim by the perpetrator, so there may be categories of batterers with whom restorative justice will not work, such as those who have antisocial tendencies and those who are emotionally volatile.[20] We must examine and implement alternatives that both keep victims safe and provide more healing and closure than the current system, which leaves so many people unwilling to report, and most of those who do, deeply unsatisfied.

PRISON ABOLITION AND VICTIMS' RIGHTS

Mariame Kaba is a champion of, among other things, prison abolition and victims' rights, two topics that many may see as in direct contradiction with each other, given the decades of very public alliances between police and victims' rights organizations. Her focus on "transforming harm" takes on, directly, the assumed fact that we must punish people to repair harm. She and her collaborators focus, rather, on the topics of transformative justice, abolition, community accountability, healing justice, restorative justice, and carceral feminisms in a way that imagines a world where healing and accountability can take place within supportive communities without the coercive control of oppressive systems born out of slavery and the oppression of women and other racial and gender minorities.[21]

THE IDEAL VICTIM

The idea behind the "ideal" victim is that some victims are perceived to be more legitimate when they meet a series of requirements, such as being "weaker than the offender, acting virtuously, unknown to the offender, and blameless of the harms *she* experiences." These representations and opinions are correlated with ideal victims being affluent, white, and female and *not* poor, male, and Black or Brown. The ideal victim image has been used to create fear of crime that, in turn, has justified many punitive laws such as Megan's Law and Amber Alerts and has even been shown to mean that judges and juries give more severe punishments when victims are considered more "worthy" and are white and female.[22]

For example, in 1993 twelve-year-old Polly Klaas was hosting a sleepover at her home when Richard Allen Davis broke in, threatened the girls with a knife, tied them up, put hoods on their heads, took Polly, and disappeared. As adults, Polly Klass's sisters, Jess and Annie Nichol, released a statement in 2021 about the punitive laws passed, literally, in their sister's name: "Over the last 26 years, three-strikes laws have significantly contributed to mass incarceration in the United States and have exacerbated the systemic racism inherent in our justice system. As Polly's sisters, it is difficult to fathom how these laws became our sister's legacy. The beauty of Polly's life shouldn't be overshadowed by this pervasive injustice." Annie underscored later in an interview the role of race in the criminal legal system and added, "I don't want Polly's legacy to be purely about punishment and vengeance. I want it to be about healing and actual justice."[23]

THE VICTIM-OFFENDER OVERLAP

While popular representations of victims and offenders are pictured as a dichotomy, where innocent, ideal victims are the opposite of their evil victimizers, the victim-offender overlap refutes this, showing that most of those who offend have previously been victimized (often seriously and frequently), and many of those who have been victimized have also committed crime or will in the future. As Mark Berg and Carrie Mulford put it, "Victims and offenders are not necessarily distinct groups; rather, the same people rotate between each role with regularity."[24] This overlap is one of the most relevant facts about crime in the field, and research has consistently shown that it remains true in a wide variety of settings—from pre-schools to prisons, from low- to high-poverty neighborhoods (though the relationship does vary in strength), and even within people's experiences of intimate partner violence. This means that unless we address victims' needs, many are likely to become the people who cause more harm and who are harmed, repeatedly.

However, many years of research have still not uncovered the conditions that produce the overlap, though several very interesting studies have uncovered different aspects. For example, Michael Gottfredson found a correlation between victimization and traffic accidents, which can be considered a proxy for risky behavior, and Janet Lauritsen, John Laub, and Robert Sampson found that associations with deviant peers and certain elements of social bonds—variables commonly considered to be causes of crime—were also predictive of victimization.[25] Mark Berg and Christopher Schreck upend criminology's traditional focus on offenders, suggesting instead that the victim-offender overlap is so consistent that it should be centered in theory and policy. They argue that interventions such as early childhood programs could reduce both criminal offending and victimization later in life by teaching children "lasting self-restraint and appreciation of the immediate and long-term consequences of decisions."[26] This means that future editions of your textbook will be more reflective of the research not only to have more information about victims but to reflect the overlap in every chapter of the book, rather than passively suggesting that victims and offenders are two separate categories of people.

You will see some of the facts of this overlap in the theoretical perspectives here and in the rest of this book, including differential exposure perspectives such as routine activities and lifestyle theories; cultural perspectives that take such factors as honor and respect (where victims become offenders because of norms that justify retaliation) into account; theories which prioritize individual differences such as biological characteristics; psychological processes; cognitive abilities; and situational perspectives. Overall, the research shows that early childhood programs can improve long-term judgment and restraint in ways that can reduce both later victimization and offending.[27]

ROUTINE ACTIVITIES AND LIFESTYLE THEORIES

While lifestyle and routine activities theories are often paired together, they have an important difference that has implications for victimology. Remember from earlier in this book that routine activities theory says that crime happens when three factors come together: a motivated offender, a vulnerable and attractive target, and the absence of a capable guardian.

Lifestyle theory, first conceptualized in the 1970s, is very similar, but focuses on the probability of victimization given particular behaviors. Michael Hindelang conceptualized high-risk times, places, and people in a way that created probabilities for how risky behaviors (such as stealing things or using drugs) elevate people's risk for victimization.[28] As with many criminological theories, these ideas lend themselves far more to personal victimization than to crimes like hacking into the computers of a giant retailer to steal people's credit card information.[29]

VICTIMIZATION AND DISABLED PEOPLE

While disabled people are often vilified as dangerous and violent, they are in fact far more likely to be victims than to be people who victimize: they are more likely to be abused, to be abused more frequently for longer periods, and to be unable to access the criminal legal system and less able to easily access support services, such as health care and victims' services.[30] Physical and sexual abuse are twice as likely among children with disabilities, and disabled people are victims of nearly one million non-fatal, violent crimes every year, including rape, sexual assault, aggravated and simple physical assault, and robbery. Disabled people are also more likely to experience several less common forms of abuse, such as manipulation of medications or refusal of essential assistance or withholding of access to assistive equipment and technology, including communications devices.[31]

Adaptive technology refers to special versions of already existing technologies or tools that provide enhancements or different ways of interacting so that disabled people may accomplish a specific task, such as adjustable tables and computers with voice output. A subset of adaptive technology is assistive technology, which refers to any low-, mid-, or high-tech tool or device that helps people with disabilities perform tasks, such as communication, mobility, and working, with greater ease and independence. There are many ways in which these devices are often abused, such as monitoring or intercepting communications, misusing the devices to impersonate or harass disabled people, or breaking, tampering with, or denying access to the devices by removal or bodily injury. Efforts to empower disabled people to have more protection against abuse or to report abuse include a focus on how people with disabilities can incorporate assistive technology into their safety planning, such as using code phrases or safe words; turning off locators; using headphones for programs that speak; and having extra chargers for when they decide to leave an abusive situation.[32]

There are many reasons why disabled people are more likely to be victimized. Disabled people, for example, may have limited communication abilities or cognitive difficulties, making it difficult to report abuse. Disabled people may also live in places like group homes or with small circles of caretakers, where abuse can happen and be hidden more easily, where there is limited access to people who can help, and where the victim is dependent on the people around them for their very survival. Disabled people may also be seen by abusers as weak, vulnerable, unable to report their abuse, or as less human than others, making abuse even more likely.

VICTIMIZATION AND QUEER PEOPLE

The year 2017 was when the National Crime Victimization Survey (NCVS) first included information on the sexuality and gender identity of respondents. These data uncovered that LGBTQIA+ people are nearly four times as likely to experience violent victimization than their non-LGBTQIA+ counterparts (71.1 per 1,000 people compared to 19.2 per 1,000 people for non-LGBTQIA+ people), including rape, sexual assault, and aggravated or simple assault, and their victimization is more likely to be at the hands of both someone well known to them *and* a stranger.[33]

VICTIMIZATION OF PEOPLE IN PRISON

Victimization is a truly common occurrence in prison facilities. Sexual victimization among incarcerated women is particularly common, where women experience it in a variety of ways, from sexual harassment to coercive sexual fondling and molestation during strip searches to pressured or forced sex with prison staff. Reporting such victimizations is already constrained outside of prison walls; behind them it is especially unlikely, given individual, institutional, and cultural factors and the fact that perpetrators are often staff: "Given the oppressive environment of prison, the authoritarian power of correctional officials, and the women inmates' lack of agency over their bodies, women victims of sexual assaults in prisons may have even lower reporting rates than women victims of sexual assaults in free society."[34]

The victim-offender overlap is no more obvious than in prisons and jails. Caged people report significantly higher levels of childhood abuse and maltreatment before their incarceration and the subsequent adjustment problems, including mental health struggles, behavioral problems, and victimization before and during incarceration, although these numbers are likely vastly low because of underreporting. Likewise, victimization during incarceration is difficult because of fears of the ramifications of reporting. Studies show anywhere from 4 percent of people incarcerated in state and federal prisons filing official reports to 38 percent of men and 37 percent of women self-reporting physical or sexual victimization by staff or other incarcerated people. Physical or sexual victimization prior to prison has also been identified as one of the strongest and most consistent predictors of victimization during incarceration. Interestingly, people in prison with histories of victimization are also more likely to engage in misconduct, having trouble with "maladjustment" while incarcerated, and be sanctioned more severely for institutional rule violations. This may be because victim blaming leads to higher sanctions, because victims are perceived by staff as a greater risk to prison safety and order, or because staff are unaware of histories but react instead to behavior influenced by trauma.[35]

Not only are transgender and gender diverse (TGD) people disproportionately incarcerated in the United States relative to the general population, but they are also particularly likely to have experienced victimization throughout their lives, often due to the stigma of having a gender identity or expression outside of socially constructed gender norms. This means that discrimination can lead to lawbreaking because, for example, employment and housing access may be limited, which may lead to sex work for survival, which is especially likely to lead to incarceration among transgender women. Likewise, victimization can lead to the use of illegal drugs to cope, which can lead to involvement with the prison system. Once TGD people are imprisoned, they are typically housed according to their genitalia, meaning that TGD individuals who have not had gender-affirming "lower" surgery are usually placed in facilities that do not match their gender identity or expression. In turn they are at particularly high risk for experiencing verbal, physical, and sexual assault by other incarcerated people and jail and prison staff.[36] These findings are similar to those for other marginalized populations behind bars, such as women, youth, disabled people, and Black and Brown people. The concept of the "TGD Oppression-to-Incarceration framework" has helped conceptualize this pathway: "The high burden of incarceration among TGD people is theorized to be driven by discrimination, violence, and other forms of victimization."[37]

Victimization during incarceration is so prevalent that a 2003 law, titled the Prison Rape Elimination Act, requires that the Bureau of Justice Statistics collect data with the goal of detecting, reporting, and preventing prison rape, partially by increasing the accountability of correctional staff if they fail to prevent rapes in their facilities. But direct victimization is not the only risk behind the prison walls, for even people are not directly victimized during their prison stay, they are exposed to extreme violence, with people reporting that they have witnessed frequent, brutal acts of violence, including stabbings, attacks with scalding substances, multi-person assaults, and murder in a way that was unavoidable and traumatizing. They may witness or have to clean up blood after an attack or murder, for example.[38]

VICTIMIZATION OF PEOPLE IN THE MILITARY

While the media pays quite a lot of attention to victimization by strangers, you know by now that people are most likely to be harmed by people they know—and often love. Much as such assaults are often ignored, the epidemic of victimization of people in the military is likewise often avoided, despite how often it happens and its dire impacts. In the armed services, only 16.5 percent are women, but more than half report experiencing harassment, and one in four report experiencing sexual assault during their time in the military.[39] Men also report sexual harassment and assault, but at significantly lower rates than women, even though there are so many male military survivors, given the gender imbalance in the ranks.

The impacts of these assaults can be profound: one study found that 29 percent of servicewomen and female veterans who had experienced sexual assault were currently contemplating suicide, and women are overrepresented in the numbers of military personnel who complete suicide.[40] Over a third of women who reported their assaults also experienced retaliation afterward, and they are also twice as likely as other women veterans to become homeless.[41] In her 2023 book *Hardship Duty: Women's Experiences with Sexual Harassment, Sexual Assault, and Discrimination in the US Military*, Stephanie Bonnes presents findings from her interviews of fifty U.S. servicewomen and concludes that the military as an *organization* prioritizes masculinity and denigrates femininity in a way that encourages harassment and abuse among servicemembers. Bonnes shows the ways in which such an organizational culture eclipses any policies designed to address victimization, which means that survivors are further victimized by the process meant to address the harm visited on them.[42]

A case of military victimization that got media attention was the story of Vanessa Guillen, who was murdered in the armory at Fort Hood, Texas, by a fellow soldier, Aaron David Robinson. Her death led to an investigation that found "a permissive environment for sexual assault and sexual harassment at Fort Hood" because Guillen had complained of sexual harassment before her murder.[43] Under the Uniform Code of Military Justice, when soldiers report being victimized while in the military, commanders decide whether their experience is investigated and prosecuted rather than police, as it would be in the civilian world, if the accused person was in active duty at the time of the incident. More specifically, "of the more than 6,200 sexual assault reports from 2020, only 0.8 percent (50 cases) resulted in sex-offense convictions."[44] This means that there are countless stories of victims who either choose not to report or who report and whose cases are not pursued.

Over the years political attempts at reform—including Senator Kirsten Gillibrand of New York introducing the Military Justice Improvement and Increasing Prevention Act—have mostly failed, except for some small improvements, such as allowing victims to request a transfer to a new unit or installation and the addition of special victims' counsels (who are overwhelmed with work), who provide victims with information, resources, and support. More recently, however, in late 2021 President Joe Biden signed the I Am Vanessa Guillén Act into law as a part of the National Defense Authorization Act, which took effect in January 2024. This act criminalizes sexual harassment under the Uniform Code of Military Justice, removes the decision to prosecute sexual misconduct cases from service members' chains of command, and directs commanders to request independent investigations of formal complaints from victims and to forward the complaints to their next superior officers in the chain of command who are authorized to convene general courts-martial. Organizations such as the Service Women's Action Network support, connect, and advocate for women who have served or are currently serving in the military and have been instrumental in, among other campaigns, addressing military sexual victimization of women.

CONCLUSION

The topic of victimology, as I hope you have seen in this chapter, is long overdue for a larger spotlight in the field of criminology. In particular, victimology would benefit greatly from a critical lens, which allows us to examine victims' experiences from a different perspective and which might uncover different populations of victims, such as victims of corporate and environmental crime, heretofore unexamined because of our narrow focus on street crimes.

We now come to the end of our review of mainstream (or, more accurately, "malestream") criminology and some of the many ways in which it falls short.[45] We will now move to critical criminological theories, which you should by this point recognize. In particular, you should notice, again, that all the theories we have been reviewing focus most of all on what is wrong with individual people to explain why they break the law. Both the explanations and the implied solutions all center the need for individuals and smaller institutions to make changes, rather than focusing on how our larger social structures and institutions (capitalism, policing, the prison industrial complex, and hegemonic masculinity, for example) not only perpetuate the structural conditions that lead to lawbreaking but also make the laws (and fail to make others) that define "criminal" and "noncriminal" alike.

8 Critical Criminology

In their inquiry about the social engineering practices of the powerful, including the use of social stratification and criminal codes, Abigail Henson, Thuy-Trinh Nguyen, and Ajima Olaghere wrote, "Most researchers' critical gaze remains hyper-focused on the individual as 'criminal' and examines engagement in illegalized behaviors through the prism of individual decision-making and psychological deficit or pathology without examining the structural facilitators of social conflict." They found in 2023 that a search for "deterrence," "social disorganization," and "self-control" in the abstracts of three of the top criminology journals in the previous five years yielded between six and eleven mentions per journal. They found zero to one mentions of critical criminological terms (they chose "conflict theory," "relative deprivation," and "feminist") in those same journals in the same period.[1] Despite the recent focus on abolition and defunding, criminology is behind the times. By now you are well versed in critical approaches to the mainstream theories of criminology; in this chapter you will learn about the specific critical theories that frame these approaches.

Critical criminology is a group of theories that see the major roots of crime to be unequal socioeconomic, racial and ethnic, and gender relations that control our society. There are many subsections that we review here, but the core of all of them comes back to the unequal distribution of power and material resources.[2] As Kenneth Sebastian León puts it, "Critical criminology—broadly defined—reflects a commitment to punching upward hegemonic forms of power that shape criminological and criminal justice phenomena."[3] The schools of thought in critical criminology are commonly thought to be radical, left realist, postmodern, cultural, feminist, Black feminist, queer, masculinity, peacemaking, and survivor and convict.

RADICAL CRIMINOLOGY

Birthed at the University of California at Berkeley in the 1970s, radical criminology is an explicitly Marxist paradigm for studying social control and the role of power and domination in the criminal legal system. Radical criminology focuses on class struggle: capitalism precipitates and defines crime in the interest of the powerful, to maintain their power and control the working class. The solution to the crime problem, therefore, is the overthrow of capitalist systems, eliminating class conflict and the unequal distribution of resources.[4] U.S. critical criminology today has branched out from its Marxist roots, and, though it still holds that the powerful create laws to maintain their power and keep it from the powerless, the focus is now more on having a general critical orientation within criminological scholarship.[5]

LEFT REALIST CRIMINOLOGY

This area of criminology developed in the early 1980s, centered on the work of Jock Young, who aimed "above all else ... to develop a radical crime control strategy for the working class communities in Britain which, taking the brunt of post-Fordist de-industrialisation, were faced with rising crime and socio-economic deprivation."[6] Rather than idealizing working-class crime as a form of rebellion, Young reminded "left idealist" criminologists to get out of their armchairs and into the streets with the "left realists," where most "working-class crime" was against other working-class people, weakening their communities as they were already suffering from deindustrialization. This is a difficult line to walk: criminology "must neither succumb to hysteria nor relapse into a critical denial of the severity of crime as a problem. It must be fiercely skeptical of official statistics and control institutions without taking the posture of a blanket rejection of all figures or, indeed, the very possibility of reform."[7]

POSTMODERN CRIMINOLOGY

Postmodern criminology emerged in the 1990s, arguing that we should question, well, pretty much everything, for even the very language we are taught supports dominant views of the world, whether we know it or not. As Bruce Arrigo and Thomas Bernard explain it, "Postmodern criminology examines the relationship between human agency and language in the creation of meaning, identity, truth, justice, power, and knowledge." This means that postmodern criminologists believe that there do not exist any foundational truths, which means that the people who control the creation of language can control the definitions of law and crime. Alternatively, postmodern criminology suggests replacement discourses, which are "ways of communicating that embody both one's meaning and one's desire at the same time . . . [which] substitute methods of control with languages of possibility."[8]

CULTURAL CRIMINOLOGY

In the 1990s and 2000s, cultural criminology emerged as "the placing of crime and its control in the context of culture; that is, viewing both crime and the agencies of control as cultural products—as creative constructs."[9] The focus of cultural criminology is, as you might guess, crime as it is presented in popular culture, especially mass media. It merges the fields of criminology and cultural studies to examine the ways in which crime and criminals are presented to audiences: "From this view, the study of crime necessitates not simply the examination of individual criminals and criminal events, not even the straightforward examination of media 'coverage' of criminals and criminal events, but rather a journey into the spectacle and carnival of crime, a walk down an infinite hall of mirrors where images created and consumed by criminals, criminal subcultures, control agents, media institutions, and audiences bounce endlessly one off the other."[10] You may see in cultural criminology all the critical criminologies that came before, from radical to postmodern.

FEMINIST CRIMINOLOGY

Feminist theories are far more diverse than you might imagine from popular opinion; while they all recognize the oppression of women, they differ in what they believe are the causes of, and therefore solutions to, that oppression. You may be most familiar with what is called *radical feminism*, which focuses on the ways in which patriarchy creates a power differential between men and women, which causes men to use violence such as rape and domestic violence to control women's labor, sexuality, and reproduction. However, feminism has many distinct categories, some of which are very different from, and in conflict with, other types:

- **Radical feminism** states that by eliminating gender differences in power and opportunities, men will no longer be able to dominate women, and society can be transformed. Radical feminism has had a huge impact on feminist criminology, particularly that involving men's abuse of women.[11] Likewise, Lisa Maher and Kathleen Daly's research on women in the drug market shows that men kept women out of positions of power (because they were "weak" or "not bad enough"), meaning that they had less access to capital and had to supplement their income with less lucrative jobs such as sex work.[12]

- **Liberal feminism** suggests that gender oppression would be reduced or eliminated by altering the way in which girls and boys are socialized and by reforming laws and their implementation, for example, by eliminating bias in the sentencing of women and men and between racial groups.

- **Socialist feminism** makes an important contribution to understanding that not just gender but also class results in oppression, by integrating Marxist analyses with theories of gender relations. As Barbara Ehrenreich so engagingly puts it, "You are a woman in a capitalist society. You get pissed off: about the job, the bills, your husband (or ex), about the kids' school, the housework, being pretty, not being pretty, being looked at, not being looked at (and either way, not listened to), etc. If you think about all these things and how they fit together and what has to be changed, and then you look around for some words to hold all these thoughts together in abbreviated form, you'd almost have to come up with 'socialist feminism.'"[13] To end gender oppression, socialist feminists believe, capitalism must change.

- **Multicultural feminism** "takes as its starting point the cultural consequences of the worldwide movements and dislocations of people associated with the development of 'global' or 'transnational' capitalism" and, like **intersectional feminism,** explains the nature of gender differences by looking at the ways in which characteristics such as race, age, queerness, legal status, and myriad other differences intersect with gender.[14] *Intersectionality* is a term coined by Kimberlé Crenshaw: "We tend to talk about race inequality as separate from inequality based on gender, class, sexuality or immigrant status. What's often missing is how some people are subject to all of these, and the experience is not just the sum of its parts."[15]

- **Black feminist theory** "sprang from the shared belief that black women are inherently valuable, that our liberation is a necessity not as an adjunct to somebody else's but because of our need as human persons for autonomy. . . . The mere names of the pejorative stereotypes attributed to black women (e.g., mammy, matriarch, Sapphire, whore, bulldagger), let alone cataloguing the cruel, often murderous, treatment we receive, indicates how little value has been placed upon our lives during four centuries of bondage in the Western hemisphere. We realize that the only people who care enough about us to work consistently for our liberation is us."[16] Early (first- and second-wave) feminism was dominated by white women and their concerns (e.g., the right to vote and work), drowning out the very different concerns of Black women on plantations, such as fighting against rape, forced pregnancy, and separation from children.[17] Black feminists center the experiences of Black women and the places where race and gender intersect and change each other.

- **Postmodern feminist theory** focuses on the ways in which gender is determined by culture and society, with a particular focus on the role of language and mass media in teaching and maintaining men's domination over women.

- **Global and postcolonial feminisms** emphasize the differences between women's experiences around the world with a particular focus on the role of colonialist violence on women and on the ways in which mainstream feminist movements have ignored intersectionality to the detriment of Black and Brown women and women in low-income countries (often referred to with the hierarchical term *developing countries*).

One of the most popular challenges to the fact that women commit less crime than men is that women do not get in trouble because police and judges let them off because they are women. This "chivalry thesis" proposes that when workers in the criminal legal system are confronted with women breaking the law, particularly those who conform to traditional female roles of wife and mother, they treat them with more leniency than their male counterparts. But what does the research show? Lin Liu and colleagues found that female offenders do not always have shorter incarcerations than their male counterparts and that they are more likely to be treated with leniency when their crimes conform to female stereotypical behavior (such as shoplifting).[18] This finding fits with earlier research, which shows lighter sentences when female offenders are white, married mothers committing nonviolent crimes.[19]

The field of feminist criminology has grown for the past sixty years, although, as Frances Heidensohn writes, the reasons for its origin remain areas for development:

- In most mainstream criminology, women and girls were invisible and ignored; where they did appear their lives and experiences were distorted and stereotyped.
- The notable differences between men and women in recorded crime rates—the "gender gap"—was not questioned or explored, leaving much of conventional theory weakened and inadequate.
- A major program of research on women and crime was needed to catch up with decades of neglect.
- An important outcome would be the learning of valuable lessons for criminal justice policy for both sexes.[20]

In recent years feminist criminology has been reflecting on its history, and many feminist criminologists have been focused on enhancing the discipline's approach to diversity and inclusivity. For example, Jace Valcore

CRITICAL THINKING BREAK 17

The Division of Feminist Criminology, formerly known as the Division on Women and Crime, is a subsection of the American Society of Criminology, one of the world's pre-eminent organizations of criminologists. Why do you think the name changed in 2022, after a vote from the membership?

and colleagues debunk the myth that the criminal legal system can keep women safe (remember carceral feminism) and remind us that trans people, particularly Black and Brown trans women, are far more likely to be victimized than to victimize someone.[21]

BLACK FEMINIST CRIMINOLOGY

You may have noticed that Heidensohn's concerns in 1968 did not mention the importance of intersectionality, particularly when it comes to crime and gender. Hillary Potter, at the University of Colorado at Boulder, developed a Black feminist criminology as an expansion of feminist criminology, using Black feminist theory and critical race feminist theory.[22] This framework challenges mainstream feminist criminology's damaging gender essentialism, which insists on a universal "women's experience" that is unaltered by people's other identities, such as race and class: "Black women experience sexual and patriarchal oppression by Black men but at the same time struggle alongside them against racial oppression."[23] Black feminist criminology reminds us that Black women do not just experience more oppression, but rather their oppression is qualitatively different because of the ways in which their identities intersect as a whole more than the sum of their parts so that experiences such as battering are different for Black women because of influences such as social structure, community, family, and identity.[24] Feminism and feminist criminology are not about just gender awareness but a centering of the female experience and action. Men's patriarchal control of everything from street drug sales to boardroom fraud means not that women should lean *in* to men's crime but that women should lean *out* to avoid such crimes and their larger structural harm on a societal level.

QUEER CRIMINOLOGY

The field of queer theory emerged in the late twentieth century, which was later integrated into criminology as *queer criminology*. Much as feminist criminology encourages the inclusion of gender into traditional criminology, queer criminology points to the absence of data on the experiences of LGBTQIA+ people in theory and research, despite the literature's focus on queerness as deviance.[25] By expanding the field to incorporate queerness since the early 2010s, queer criminologists have examined everything from "reducing invisibility of sexual and gender identities, bias crimes, gay and lesbian intimate partner violence, queer offending, gay gangs, relationships between queer populations and the police, perceptions of lesbian and gay police officers, incarcerated queer populations, queer issues in criminal justice education, global persecution of queer people, attention to issues related to queer youth including bullying, homelessness, delinquency, dating violence, and attention to theoretical and definitional queer criminological considerations."[26]

MASCULINITIES AND CRIME

Even though we have known for hundreds, if not thousands, of years that men commit most of the lawbreaking behavior, the field of masculinity and crime is only recently gaining academic attention. The field of masculinity and crime has focused quite a lot on the role of male patriarchal power as the roots of violence and discrimination.[27] Raewyn Connell's work theorizing gender relations focuses on men's power over women, power differentials between groups of men, and the fact that these power dynamics shift over time. Hegemonic masculinity, for example, is the dominant masculinity, but it shifts over time so that the "ideal man" looks one way in one decade and may be quite different in another, but they always have power, and their way of thinking is always seen as the current version of "common sense."[28]

As you may recall from chapter 5, James Messerschmidt has been a prominent scholar of masculinity and crime for decades. He has used Connell's concept of hegemonic masculinity to advance the field of criminology most recently by conducting and analyzing life histories of adolescent girls and boys. His findings connect later sexual violence with in-school bullying; reflexivity (i.e., when you consider *yourself* in relation to your experiences, asking, "How did that experience or interaction make me feel?" or "How will I respond to this social circumstance?"); embodiment (i.e., the ways in which you *physically* reflect identities, such as engaging in sexual assault as a way to reflect one's hegemonic masculinity); and dominant and hegemonic masculinities.[29] Other scholars have focused, for example, on the pleasure and status associated with lawbreaking behavior.[30] As always, critical scholars have reminded us to examine the ways in which high levels of street crime are related to social structures and to not neglect the crimes of powerful men.[31]

PEACEMAKING CRIMINOLOGY

Richard Quinney and Hal Pepinsky founded peacemaking criminology in the 1990s. They, like the critical criminologists about whom we have already learned, view crime as a social construction of the powerful. They created peacemaking criminology as a way to focus on how we respond to crime, "from a moral imperative on through classifying crime, selecting sanctions and defining due process, to including parties affected, to making responses socially just, to nonviolence."[32] Peacemaking criminology connects the violence of war with the violence of our both crime *and* official responses to crime within the criminal legal system. Peacemaking criminologists, on the other hand, suggest non-violent solutions to the suffering that crime creates. It may not surprise you that it is inspired by Buddhism's focus on kindness, compassion, and empathy.

Some scholars have suggested that peacemaking criminology is a wonderful idea in concept, but that it is not yet very useful in practice.[33] In 2003 Kieran McEvoy suggested that peacemaking criminology might be more practically effective if it focused on places where violence is currently occurring, such as in Belfast or in Baltimore.[34] This is so that its theoretical framework can be usefully applied to make change, particularly in communication with the field of human rights and especially in a way that the impact of peacemaking interventions can be measured.

SURVIVOR AND CONVICT CRIMINOLOGY

Kimberly Cook, herself a survivor of domestic and sexual violence, and her colleagues advocated for the creation of survivor criminology in 2016 as a way for criminologists themselves to acknowledge personal experiences with trauma:

> Feminist criminologists, to varying individual degrees, are committed to conducting research that helps to push the policy arena farther along toward human rights without apologizing for the portion of feminist work that is politically relevant as well as empirically researched. Arguably, many of us in feminist criminology are already "survivors" and thus already engage in "survivor criminology." After all, our lives are deeply influenced by the same sexism, racism, classism, and homophobia that has influenced the field in which we work; to ignore that our personal experiences are also political would require us to amputate a significant part of our analytical capacity, a specious separation that I am not willing, like many other feminists, to endure.[35]

Another relatively new field under the umbrella of critical criminology, convict criminology prioritizes the voices and standpoints of people who self-identify as having histories of criminalization or with the criminal legal system.[36] Convict criminologists are graduate students and professors, often with histories of incarceration, "who believe that convict voices have been ignored, minimized, or misinterpreted in scholarly research on jails, prisons, convicts, correctional officers, and associated policies and practices that affect these individuals."[37] One of the most important contributions of convict criminologists is that they offer inductive, experiential voices to complement the deductive exclusively scholarly approaches to experiences of the criminal legal system. There is a division of convict criminology as a part of the American Society of Criminology, the pre-eminent organization of criminologists in the United States, and convict criminology has the *Journal of Prisoners on Prisons* as their official publication.

These organizations, it must be noted, have been criticized for being filled with overwhelmingly white, cis-gender, straight men.[38] A feminist convict criminology has emerged in recent years to counteract this fact, including a panel at the 2019 meeting of the American Society of Criminology titled "Convict Criminology from a Feminist Perspective," on which formerly incarcerated female panelists presented their papers. Alison Cox and Michelle Malkin recommend that, for convict criminology to be more inclusive, it can increase its focus on the experiences of women in the criminal legal system, especially with an intersectional lens.[39]

CONCLUSION

Imaginative criminology is defined as one that "eschews administrative criminology's quest for evidence of the already-known in favor of imagining the new, it is one manifestation of the broader critical criminology. Unlike administrative criminology [right realism], which involves a reflexive journey into an official past, imaginative criminology embarks on an uncharted voyage into an unofficial future. But, more than that, the promise of imaginative criminology is that it is well-designed to be a bridge between critical criminology and a critical politics of criminal justice policy. Imaginative criminology . . . does not pretend to exclude politics from critique."[40] What do you imagine for criminology's future?

PART II "Our Bodies, Ourselves"
TYPES OF CRIMES

When policymakers, the media, and the public talk about the *crime problem*, it is most often without nuance. Crime is overwhelmingly presented as dangerous and scary behavior by Black and Brown men, who must be caged to prevent further harm to innocent victims (i.e., white, straight, abled, cis-gendered females). In the following chapters of part 2, I present different categories of crimes; however, I ask you to think critically about their assumptions of frequency, demographics, and relative harm in the respective categories and whether the theories in the previous section work as frameworks to understand and explain such crimes. You will take your critical eye to crimes against people and property, white-collar crimes, environmental crimes, and public order, drug, and sex crimes. As you read, pay attention to the difference between your expectations and what you are learning, how you developed that perspective, and who benefits from your fear (or lack thereof).

9 Crimes against People

Whereas criminology textbook chapters on "crimes against people" usually define violent crimes and sate students' perennial hunger for stories about rare but terrifying serial killers, this chapter looks at interpersonal violence as a problem with structural roots.

BUT I LOVE MY TRUE CRIME SHOWS!

Most of you reading this book have likely watched a true crime show such as *Investigation Discovery* or listened to a podcast such as *Serial*. Indeed, you would be in good company—the *Serial* podcast was the "fastest podcast ever to reach five million downloads" in 2014 and reached over eighty million downloads by 2016. Popular media (especially "entertainment television") more generally is how most Americans get their impressions and knowledge of the criminal legal system.[1] Oliver Burkeman reviewed this "morbid curiosity" and explained that it is both because we are evolutionarily programmed to focus on threats to our well-being and because we yearn to empathize with people who are suffering as a drive toward meaning and connection with others.[2] Crime entertainment capitalizes on those drives but delivers a picture of the system that is inaccurate and biased and, as a result, dangerous. Justin Pickett and his colleagues found that people with actual experience with the criminal legal system were less likely to rely on the media for information about crime, but that people who *do* rely on the media for crime-related information were particularly ill-informed about the actual system.[3]

The impact of people's (mis)understandings of the reality of our criminal legal system and people who break those laws is not just unfortunate but dangerous for a variety of reasons, including general perceptions that crime and danger are always increasing, even when they are not, and the fact that a lack of awareness of restorative justice practices may account for most of why people oppose them.[4] Given that so many of us get our crime "news" from the media, most of us are afraid of victimization, and this fear of crime has been salient for Americans for many decades; it is particularly high in recent years, even as violent crime is at record lows: as of 2022, 53 percent of Americans worry "a great deal" and 27 percent worry "a fair amount."[5] These worries seem to be based on beliefs that crime has increased where people live—as of 2022, the highest percentage (56 percent) of Americans said that there is more crime in their local area than there was a year ago, the highest since the polling started in 1972. These beliefs are related far more to partisanship than to actual crime rates.[6]

WHAT WE KNOW ABOUT VICTIMS

In chapter 1 you learned about the difference between the National Crime Victimization Survey (NCVS), the Uniform Crime Reports (UCR), and the later National Incident-Based Reporting System (NIBRS). To recap, the UCR and NIBRS rely on police activity to report "crime rates" that are very inaccurate, especially when it comes to intimate partner violence and sexual assault. The NCVS is considered to be a far more accurate picture of crime because it goes straight to the source, asking people if they have been victimized, without requiring that they go to the police. The NCVS shows a rate of 16.5 violent victimizations per 1,000 persons aged twelve or older in 2021, dramatically higher than the rate of 4.0 per 1,000 according to the NIBRS.[7] I preface with these data to remind you to remember that official crime rates, which overwhelmingly come from UCR/NIBRS data, have nothing to do with actual crime (let alone harm) but are merely measures of police activity. While the NCVS is a better measure, it is mostly useful as a way to hint at the magnitude of the "dark figure of crime," which is the harm and lawbreaking that happens but that does not come to the attention of police, which is substantial, especially for crimes against women and other vulnerable populations.

That said, we can see several trends from victimization data from several sources. According to the NCVS, one of the clearest trends is that violent victimization (i.e., rape or sexual assault, robbery, aggravated assault, and simple assault) rates have been declining from 1993 to 2021, from a rate of almost 80 victimizations per 1,000 persons aged twelve or older in 1993 to 16.5 in 2021. This translates to just under 1 percent (0.98 percent or 2.7 million people) aged twelve or older nationwide experiencing at least one violent crime.

Most people who are victims and who victimize are men: the most recent numbers show that of the 4.4 million violent incidents in the United States in 2021, 3.2 million of them involved male offenders. Likewise, when a woman is victimized, it is dramatically more likely to be by a man (1,354,920) rather than a woman (530,370). Victimization rates also show that people most likely to be victimized are Black, young, and poor, with victimization rates going down as people get wealthier, older, and whiter.[8]

PEOPLE MOST AT RISK OF VICTIMIZATION

While many of the people who are afraid of being violently victimized are behind their phone, television, and computer screens, expressing fear of crimes that are statistically almost impossibly unlikely to happen to them, the actual leading cause of death of Black men between fifteen and thirty-four is homicide. However, the impact extends beyond mortality for these young men. Nonfatal injuries due to firearm-related violence among young Black men result in significant physical, psychological, and social difficulties.[9] These challenges were further intensified by obstacles to accessing necessary treatment.[10] This trauma is made even worse by the fact that the young men who end up in emergency rooms for interpersonal violence end up there again and again: emergency room data show that the average rate of repeat violent victimization is on average 35 percent and can be as high as 65 percent.[11] Many of these young men will return to their communities without having received treatment for the trauma they experienced and the resulting posttraumatic stress disorder and acute stress disorder.[12]

While the fearful survey respondents may attribute this to "bad people doing bad things," which in turn justifies the use of mass incarceration for overwhelmingly poor, Black, and Brown people, the research shows that we must focus on the incredible trauma and suffering experienced by these young men suffering from violent injuries. For those who understand that there are both structural (such as mass incarceration and the school-to-prison pipeline) and interpersonal violence (such as firearm violence) roots to the suffering of the victims and perpetrators of this violence, one way to address it is through hospital-based violence intervention programs, which "center and emphasize the perspectives and priorities of young Black male participants" through patient-centered outcomes research. In one study of such a program, young Black men who were the victims of violent crimes reported experiencing a variety of post-traumatic stress symptoms, such as hyper-vigilance, avoidance, sleep disturbance, irritability, isolation, and distrust, all of which impacted their ability to recover.[13]

While women are not as likely as men to be victims of violent crime, it is important to take an intersectional frame when looking at violent victimizations of women. The Urban Indian Health Institute, one of the leading research institutes on Indigenous and Alaska Native people across the United States, works to sound the alarm about high rates of crimes (many unreported) against Indigenous and Alaska Native women. More than one in three Indigenous and Alaska Native women reported that they experienced violence in the past year, including sexual violence and violence by an intimate partner, which is 1.7 times more likely than white women.[14]

WHITE-ON-WHITE CRIME

A popular, though misleading and flawed, argument about crime is that it is a problem almost exclusively of Black people hurting other people, both

Black and white, but with a particular focus on "Black-on-Black" crime to counter the fight against police brutality. One of the most enduring facts about race and crime is that it is almost always intra-racial, which means that they are primarily committed by and against people of the same race. So, just as Black-on-Black crime is most common, so is white-on-white crime, and crime within other racial and ethnic groups.[15]

In addition, by reducing the causes of violent behavior to race, this argument ignores structural factors such as poverty, inadequate education, and racism, which impact Black communities more than others. Ignoring such structural factors is a racist oversimplification that makes policy changes impossible. Finally, by lumping all Black people together, this argument (among other things) obscures the very important factor of place: crime varies quite a lot depending on neighborhood, city, and region, for example, which have profound historical and practical features, such as redlining and disproportionate police practices.

THE ROLE OF PATRIARCHY AND A CRISIS OF MASCULINITY

While violent crimes are so often viewed as interpersonal issues, their existence and persistence are very often rooted in and encouraged by patriarchy and the ways in which toxic masculinities encourage victimization of women and discourage healing in men. Remember that there are many different forms of masculinity, but that hegemonic masculinity remains as the stereotypical notion of masculinity that shapes the socialization and aspirations of young men. Hegemonic masculinity shifts with time and context, but today it includes, "a high degree of ruthless competition, an inability to express emotions other than anger, an unwillingness to admit weakness or dependency, devaluation of women and all feminine attributes in men, homophobia, and so forth."[16] The term *toxic masculinity* embodies the elements of hegemonic masculinity, such as misogyny, homophobia, greed, and violent domination, that are socially destructive, as opposed to the prosocial elements, such as the drive to win at sports, provide for family, or succeed at work. It is this toxic masculinity, valued widely in communities and in the media, that drives much of the violence perpetrated by men against others and themselves and causes such incredible harm in our societies, particularly when coupled with the lethality of firearms. This core element of gender in violence against persons is so prominent that it is widely ignored in discussions of harm.

Before children are even born, American society focuses overwhelmingly on the gender of the fetus, even throwing "gender reveal parties" (or, as Astri Jack calls them, "genital reveal parties") to reveal the sex of their fetus.[17] Gendered socialization then starts before birth and continues throughout people's entire lives so that boys are taught to adhere to rigid gender roles and expectations of being tough, dominant, and controlling and not to act or feel "feminine," such as being vulnerable, empathetic, or nurturing; this is toxic for any human, which is by nature a feeling creature. This is all a part of patriarchy, a system wherein individual men hold power over women, and social structures and institutions (such as legal systems, the media, and religious institutions) are created and maintained to uphold this power imbalance. For example, the media may focus on what a woman was wearing or the fact that she was drunk or a sex worker when reporting a story about her assault, rather than focusing on the person who assaulted her. In addition, patriarchy depends on the dehumanization and objectification of women, whereby they are the objects to men's subject, which in turn leads to a normalization of violence against women as objects of men's pleasure and whims.

PEOPLE WHO ARE "EASY TO KILL"

There is a whole industry centered around serial killers—countless books and movies and whole communities online, fascinated by and terrified of becoming victims of serial killers such as Ted Bundy, who targeted college women in the 1970s. However, research has shown that "invisible victims" who are less likely to be missed, such as homeless people, Black and Brown people, and sex workers, are most often targeted by serial killers. The criminalization of sex work, immigration, and homelessness in the United States means that these groups, and other marginalized groups like them, are loathe to report their own victimization, which makes them easy targets for serial killers looking to go unnoticed.

In fact, Kenna Quinet found that serial killers who kill sex workers "amass a greater average number of victims than do non-prostitute killers, and when analyzed by decade, those who kill primarily prostitutes, kill for slightly longer periods of time."[18] Not only does the criminalization of sex work make them more vulnerable to serial killers, but the victim blaming that comes along with sex work also makes them less likely to report danger. Eric Hickey used his research to shift the blame from the person doing the killing to the victim, suggesting that murders were "victim facilitated" by sex workers.[19] Steven Egger conceptualized the "less dead," whose deaths matter less than others because of their marginalized status as sex workers, drug users, migrant workers, unhoused people, or others.[20] Our data about victims of serial killers are suspected to be undercounted by as much as tenfold because the "missing missing" are targeted—people who are already missing, often in unstable situations, and therefore unknown to be dead.[21] Indeed, Gary Leon Ridgway said explicitly, "I also picked prostitutes as my victims because they were easy to pick up without being noticed. I knew they would not be reported missing. I picked prostitutes because I thought I could kill as many of them as I wanted without getting caught."[22]

Further, most victims of violent crime are men, but among men there is significant resistance to mental health treatment for the significant implications of violent victimization, particularly among poor Black boys and men, who suffer from structural violence from so many sources, such as school failure, arrest, incarceration, and substance use, intertwined with unrecognized and untreated mental health struggles.[23] While young Black men do rely on family members, particularly mothers, to help with depressive and other mental health symptoms, they also express that they are too proud to show their emotions, which is seen as weak, gay, and feminine.[24] Such unwillingness to engage in treatment means not only that men will continue to suffer from anxiety and depression—and the resulting substance abuse, anger, and violence—but that their families, communities, and workplaces also suffer.[25] This resistance is particularly salient in several contexts, including in prison settings, where gender issues are often magnified, including toxic masculinity: "the constellation of socially regressive male traits that serve to foster domination, the devaluation of women, homophobia, and wanton violence," which also leads to resistance to mental health treatment.[26] Even if there were not resistance, structural barriers also make treatment difficult, if not impossible, for men, especially poor, young, Black and Brown men, who are particularly likely to be unemployed (and therefore without health insurance) or in prison (with woefully bad services). Mental health professionals can be complicit in reinforcing masculinity stereotypes, such as over-diagnosing anger issues and under-diagnosing depression among men.[27]

Such toxic masculinity, however, does not only have implications for the men who are dying by the thousands in suicide and homicide rooted in untreated mental health and trauma. This belief in one's domination and the fact that such emotionless expectations are unrealistic (and therefore impossible) often lead to crimes of violence by men against women to assert control and power, including intimate partner violence, sexual assault, and femicide. It is also very important to note that intersectionality has a vital role to play here, for women facing multiple forms of oppression for being non-white, disabled, queer, or immigrants, for example, have their objectification and therefore their victimization compounded.

FEMICIDE

The term *femicide* was first defined by feminist pioneers Jane Caputi and Diana Russell as "the murder of women by men motivated by hatred, contempt, pleasure, or a sense of ownership of women."[28] Femicide is a severe form of gender-based violence that takes a variety of forms, including domestic violence, intimate partner violence, honor killings, and dowry-related killings. It has a variety of motives and indicators, such as gender discrimination, power and control, or forcible attempts to enforce patriarchal values. When women are killed without a sexist motivation, Russell recommended that the term "woman killing" should be used.[29] Where there exists more gender equity, support for victims, education of women and girls, and cultural and societal challenges to gender-based violence and discrimination, there is lower femicide. The term *feminicide* (or *feminicidio*) has emerged more recently to describe the killing of women in particular world regions, including in Latin America, where the term originated. The term encompasses not just the killing of women with misogynist motivation but also the failure of the state to respond to these killings.[30]

Femicide is a global phenomenon, but Juarez, Mexico, is known as the first place that femicides occurred in huge numbers: there have been at least 470 women murdered there since 1993, and over a quarter of those murders included torture, mutilation (often of female body parts), and rape.[31] Many of the victims were teenagers and employed in the U.S. factories just over the border called *maquiladoras*, making poverty wages of four dollars per day. Investigations into these killings are widely considered to be corrupt, illegitimate, and incompetent, which has led to the growth of social movement organizations that have achieved partial goals in pursuit of the eradication of femicide, such as reparations, investigative changes, coalition building, and consciousness raising.[32] The movements and actors who were most successful were those that had culturally relevant framing that mirrored Mexican cultural values.[33] María Encarnación López argues that patriarchy plays a key role in the Juarez femicides: "Femicide in Ciudad Juárez is also enabled by patriarchal modes of production that legitimise despotism and the cruel, racist, and sexist treatment of working-class women. This system confers control over women's sexuality to (male) factory owners, (male) criminals, and (male) authorities. Only a wider renegotiation of the self (amongst subordinated women) and the other (amongst men and male institutions) will allow women to escape the constraints of this system and live free from social prejudice and violence."[34]

DOMESTIC VIOLENCE AND INTIMATE PARTNER VIOLENCE

The terms *domestic violence* and *intimate partner violence* are often used interchangeably, though they refer to different concepts. Domestic violence assumes that the perpetrator(s) and the victim(s) live together, whereas intimate partner violence has a wider net to include current or former spouses or partners in an intimate relationship. Given the huge proportion of violence that is domestic, committed by people known to the victims—and on the other side of the lights, cameras, and locks—one would think that the focus of criminologists and criminal legal system professionals would focus less on crimes like burglary and more on violence between people who know and love one another. But this is not the case.

As you read in the chapter about research methodology, there are vast differences in what we know about victimization depending on the type of crime. In particular, official data (most often used for studies on the validity of theories) such as the arrest data in the FBI's Uniform Crime Reports are notoriously bad at accurately counting victimization in crimes in which women are far more likely to be victims, such as intimate partner violence and sexual assault. The National Crime Victimization Survey is considered to be far more accurate (though still a dramatic undercount) and shows dramatically more gender-based crimes self-reported by victims. According to the NCVS, in 2020 there were 4.6 million violent victimizations, about 40 percent of which were reported to police. Specifically, 41 percent of intimate partner victimizations reported to the NCVS were reported to the police in 2020 (down from 58 percent in 2019).[35] For example, from 2003 to 2012, the Bureau of Justice Statistics found that domestic violence accounted for 21 percent of all violent crime, and, more specifically, within types of domestic violence, intimate partner violence made up the greatest percentage of all violent victimizations (15 percent) than violence committed by immediate family members (4 percent) or other relatives (2 percent). Most domestic violence was committed against females (76 percent) compared to males (24 percent), and over three-quarters occurred at or near the victim's home. Because these data are from the NCVS, at least some of the reluctance to report for both men and women is neutralized: this report is based on data for which only around half was reported to police.

Instead of focusing on what makes people more likely to be victims of domestic and intimate partner violence, it may be more useful to examine risk factors for perpetration of IPV. Despite fear mongering about race and IPV, research shows that poverty and alcohol use are some of the most significant influences on the perpetration of IPV.[36] Beyond that, the CDC itemizes individual (e.g., low self-esteem, low education, heavy alcohol and drug use, belief in strict gender roles, a history of physical or emotional abuse in childhood, and lack of non-violent social problem-solving skills); relationship (e.g., association with antisocial and aggressive peers, a history of experiencing physical discipline as a child, and conflicts such as jealousy, possessiveness, tension, divorce, or separations); community (e.g., communities with high rates of poverty, high unemployment rates, low community involvement among residents, and easy access to drugs and alcohol); and societal factors (e.g., traditional gender norms and gender equality, societal income inequality, and weak health, educational, economic, and social policies or laws) that combine to make IPV perpetration more likely. On the flip side, strong social support networks; neighborhood collective efficacy; the availability of safe, stable housing; and access to economic and financial help can be protective for IPV perpetration.[37]

RAPE IS A MEN'S ISSUE

Your textbook likely has an extensive section on sexual assault and rape, their definitions, prevalence, subjection to myths, and characteristics of survivors and perpetrators. A focus they may not take centers *men:* men get raped too, and their victimization is ignored and ridiculed and underreported because of patriarchy. In fact, about a quarter of men are victims of sexual violence over their lifetimes, but these numbers are likely low because men are especially unlikely to disclose. Male rape myths fall into nine categories and are quite widely believed:

1. Men cannot be raped.
2. "Real" men can defend themselves against rape.
3. Only gay men are victims and/or perpetrators of rape.
4. Men are not affected by rape (or not as much as women).
5. A woman cannot sexually assault a man.
6. Male rape only happens in prisons.
7. Sexual assault by someone of the same sex causes homosexuality.
8. Homosexual and bisexual individuals deserve to be sexually assaulted because they are immoral and deviant.
9. If a victim physically responds to an assault he must have wanted it.[38]

People are particularly likely to deny that Black men are vulnerable to sexual assault, despite high rates of victimization.[39] Also at increased risk of sexual violence are trans and non-binary people, who have been shown to be two to three times more likely to experience sexual violence than their cis-gender counterparts.[40]

Tarana Burke was a sexual assault survivor who worked with other survivors when she founded the #MeToo movement in 2006. In 2017 actor Alyssa Milano and others used #MeToo to call out powerful men like Harvey Weinstein for sexual assault, and Tarana Burke has continued to be a powerful activist for gender equity. When that movement called public attention to sexual assault, they focused on men's responsibility to hold other men accountable: "Because men are (usually) the ones committing sexual assault, they should be held responsible for ending rape by educating themselves about gendered power, changing their behavior, and holding other men accountable."[41]

STATE VIOLENCE

Violence against people is perpetrated not only by individuals but also by the racialized and gendered state violence in our prisons and police force, such as police brutality and racial profiling. Arguably, such violence is more harmful than interpersonal violence because it is structural and has far broader societal impact. Not only does the violence of policing and imprisonment systems have a national impact on millions of people, but that impact is disproportionately against the minds and bodies of marginalized communities, particularly Black and Brown, poor, queer, and disabled people. Research has shown that such uneven focus creates distrust, fear, and trauma within these communities, particularly because state violence operates under the guise of legitimacy and the power of the state. These disproportionate impacts have long-term consequences, as well: the trauma of police brutality and the violence of incarceration can have lifetime impacts on mental health, employability, and much more both for individuals and for generations.

THE CRIMINALIZATION OF PREGNANT WOMEN: THE CASE OF BEI BEI SHUAI

In December 2010 in Indiana, thirty-three-week pregnant Bei Bei Shuai ingested rat poison as a suicide attempt after a breakup with her boyfriend. She survived, but the baby, who was delivered prematurely, died a few days later. Instead of receiving mental health treatment and support, she faced the criminal charges of murder and feticide because, the state argued, she caused the death of her unborn child by attempting suicide. She eventually pleaded guilty to criminal recklessness in March 2013 and was released on time served and placed on probation. Shuai's case is representative of many thousands of cases around the country where pregnant women with mental health challenges are criminalized rather than supported. Organizations such as the National Advocates for Pregnant Women (now Pregnancy Justice) and the American Civil Liberties Union came to Shuai's defense, arguing that punishment is not the appropriate response for pregnant people facing emotional distress and that preventing the criminalization of pregnancy is a part of reproductive justice.

CORPORATE CRIMES AS VIOLENT CRIMES

If you look in the "crimes against persons" chapter in your criminology textbook, you will see an overwhelming focus on the harms of interpersonal violence. While this victimization and the resulting harm and suffering are obviously very important, you will likely not see so-called corporate crimes featured in that same chapter, even though they are physically harmful and deadly to far more people around the world.

CRITICAL THINKING BREAK 18

As you read this chapter, or chapters in your criminology textbook on white-collar and environmental crimes, put on those critical lenses. If those crimes also lead to mass death and injury, how are they not considered and investigated as violent crimes? Should they be?

CONCLUSION

As you read this chapter, I hope you followed the thread of fear with your critical eye, asking yourself who is keeping who afraid of whom and the purpose it serves. Rape and the fear of rape, for example, has been used for thousands of years, including as a tool of war, to subordinate women to men.[42] Nonetheless, still through today, rape prevention literature focuses on women's (body) vulnerability and passivity and men's strength and aggression.[43] It is important to consider how this perspective might shape *your* beliefs about your risk of victimization and your behavior as a result—and who benefits when you make these changes.

10 Crimes against Property

Property crimes, where a victim's property is stolen or destroyed without the use or threat of force against the victim, include such crimes as larceny, theft, arson, burglary, joyriding, and motor vehicle theft.

LARCENY AND THEFT

As you likely learned from your textbook, larceny and theft are when someone takes something from someone else without the use of force or illegal entry. This is the most common property crime, in particular theft from a motor vehicle. Discussions about larceny and theft often focus on the crime of shoplifting, which is commonly known as a "pink collar" crime, because most people believe that it is a crime dominated by women. However, unsurprisingly, the reality is not that simple.

One of the oldest and most persistent arguments in criminology when it comes to women is that, as women have left their more "traditional" roles in the home and entered into the workforce, the lawbreaking in which they engage has also changed and increased because of their increased access.[1] One of the main, more contemporary proponents of this perspective is Mary Dodge, who suggests that the gender gap in crimes such as larceny, fraud, forgery, and embezzlement (LFFE) has diminished with women's increased presence and influence in the workplace.[2]

However, this conclusion is based on data collection that lumps together lawbreaking in a way that obfuscates the fact that the reality is more complicated. While the offenses may be combined as "white collar," on a grander scale, the women committing them are still not doing so from boardrooms but remain within what is considered more traditional roles for women. The overwhelming proportion of the arrests of women that happen for LFFE offenses are of shoplifting, committing welfare and benefit fraud, and passing bad checks, which are consistent with the opportunities available to women, traditional gender-role expectations, and risk preferences found in studies of women who break the law. Almost none of these arrests occurred due to LFFE crimes that happened in the course of anyone's employment, especially for women, and, when people *are* arrested, if it is for small amounts stolen by low- or mid-level employees, not the high-rolling executives stealing millions from company coffers.[3]

So much of these misconceptions and even pure inability to analyze the data in a useful way are due not only to the choices that federal and state officials make when it comes to what data will be collected and how (for example, using arrest data as a proxy for crime or focusing on "index crimes") but also to policing practices, which focus on high presence in poor, usually Black and Brown, neighborhoods and almost never in businesses, where so-called white-collar crimes would likely be detected constantly, were police officers patrolling the hallways of office buildings the way they patrol the hallways of public housing. Rather, such investigations are done by regulatory agencies such as the Securities and Exchange Commission and professional associations such as the Association of Certified Fraud Examiners.[4] Arguments such as those made by Freda Adler suggest that women are finally escaping the bonds of misogyny that have always meant that women are far more impacted by poverty than men, particularly when they are mothers.[5]

PROFESSIONAL OR AMATEUR—AND WHO CARES?

Before continuing, we must cover one of the most common themes in the criminological literature about property crimes: *amateur* and *professional* approaches to taking or destroying property. In your criminology textbook, you likely read about, for example, "professional thieves," who commit crimes with some degree of skill, earn reasonably well from their crimes, and, despite stealing over long periods, spend rather little time incarcerated. They make a regular business of stealing and have technical skills and methods. Persistent thieves continue in common-law property crimes despite an at-best ordinary level of success. They generally do not specialize but alternate between a variety of crimes such as burglary, robbery, car theft, and confidence games. So-called amateurs, on the other hand, do not specialize and do not use their lawbreaking activities as their main source of income. As with most harmful behavior, how we react to these different categories must be different, given their dramatically different motivations.

The vast majority of people who shoplift are amateurs who are more psychologically, situationally, or socially motivated as opposed to using the activity as their primary income.[6] However, many women who shoplift consider themselves to be professionals, making money to often fund drug addictions (I hope this reminds you of pathways theory). Studies of female shoplifters have shown that these women describe their activities using professional language: that it is a job (often stressful!), where they focus on efficiency and competition, create work relationships, make income, and have customers. They subcontract with "hacks" who provide transportation to and from their shoplifting work and create customer bases to ensure the longevity of their profits. These women very explicitly understand their shoplifting as an occupation, and their work does not fit neatly into feminine and masculine categories but rather provides them with income and agency in an otherwise male-dominated world.[7]

STRUCTURED ACTION AND DOING GENDER

The concept of *structured action*, most associated with scholars James Messerschmidt and Jody Miller, is the idea that a social status (such as gender or race or class) impacts and is expressed through people's action and behavior. People express their gender and what it means to "act feminine" or "act masculine" in their activities, with a particular focus on crime. For example, Messerschmidt wrote about the ways in which robbery is just another mechanism by which men express their hegemonic masculinity. When people commit crimes that don't fit what is considered feminine or masculine, Messerschmidt suggests that this transgression of traditional gender roles only maintains and reifies the dichotomy, meaning that if a woman engages in violence, she is simply "acting masculine."[8] Gail Caputo and Anna King argue in their article about shoplifting as work that the reality is closer to Miller's concept of "gender crossing," including an acknowledgement of gender fluidity depending on one's identity and standpoint, and that "rather than explain away this difference using gender roles, we argue that this difference can be interpreted as a fluid, natural expression of both feminine and masculine traits, sometimes leaning toward femininity and sometimes toward maleness" in a way that centralizes women's flexibility and agency.[9]

In a theme that by now should be familiar to you, the concepts of *masculine* and *feminine* in this literature are based largely on centralizing people who are white, cis-gender, straight, and not poor. Instead of suggesting that girls in gangs are acting masculine, we must move toward recognizing that they likely have different views of what it means to be feminine based on, for example, their experiences, cultural expectations, social position, and current (and changeable) situation.

THE ROLE OF CAPITALISM AND PATRIARCHY

As feminist scholars have gained traction in the field of criminology, we have been learning about the ways in which the system of patriarchy is embedded in the criminal legal system. Patriarchy is most commonly defined as a system of male dominance that uses violence to control women. Sherry Ortner shows the ways in which patriarchy can be more clearly understood with an intersectional lens. Using the police as an example, she shows that a patriarchal definition of manhood is not just about having a penis; it *also* requires heterosexuality, able-bodiedness, and racial superiority to embody what it means to be a real man.[10]

Further contextualizing the definition of patriarchy, Carol Christ argues that this simplistic definition obscures the complexity of patriarchy: "In the definition of patriarchy I propose, I bring all of these lines of thought together in a definition that describes patriarchy as an integral system created at the intersection of the control of women, private property, and war—which sanctions and celebrates violence, conquest, rape, looting, exploitation of resources, and the taking of slaves." Christ reviews research on matriarchal societies centered on economic, social, and political egalitarianism, where the mother-child line is unquestioned and where they "honour principles of care, love, and generosity which they associate with motherhood, and believe both women and men can and should practice." Patriarchal societies, on the other hand, customarily require the policing of women's bodies to ensure that children are related to their fathers biologically (not as easy to tell as when a mother gives birth!), resulting in requirements of fidelity, isolation, virginity, and body coverage. Patriarchy, she holds, is also rooted in violence and war, which, in the name of religion, allows for the seizure of land, resources, and people.[11] Indeed, the policing of women's bodies and control of their own reproductive capacity continues to lead to criminalization: Lynn Paltrow and Jeanne Flavin examined hundreds of arrests or their equivalent of pregnant women for miscarriage, stillbirth, and infant death. These arrests are significantly likely to be of Black women, which by this point in the book should not surprise you.[12]

SEGREGATION AND PROPERTY CRIME

While criminological theories have many ways to explain why individual people might engage in property crime, there are undeniable structural factors that impact rates of such activities. Scott Akins found that the level of segregation of Black and Brown people into isolated and disadvantaged areas in U.S. cities was significantly associated with property crime.

This relationship proved to be at least partially related to the fact that neighborhoods with higher police strength (both in terms of numbers and also their suspiciousness) meant a far higher likelihood of arrest.[13] This is important, and a theme you will see over and over again: when there are more police officers, there will be more arrests, simply because there are more observers, but it does not necessarily mean that there is more crime. Akins also found that deprivation was also significantly related to each of the property crimes (burglary in particular). Such relationships between poverty, race, and segregation are long rooted in U.S. slavery, Jim Crow, and racist policies such as redlining. As you read about the different types of property crimes in this chapter, keep those critical glasses on, minding the structural factors that impact individual behaviors but that take time and commitment to fix.

MOTOR VEHICLE THEFT

In 2018 approximately 748,841 vehicles were reported stolen, which is a rate of 228.9 per 100,000 people, with an estimated total value of over $6.3 billion (an average of $8,407 per stolen vehicle). About 75 percent of motor vehicle thefts are reported to the police and about 62 percent of stolen cars are recovered, although not necessarily in their pre-theft condition. Although much of the literature on the relationship between masculinity and crime has focused on crimes of violence, there is also literature that shows that perceptions and performances of masculinity are also related to other crimes, including motor vehicle theft.[14] Motor vehicle theft is a very clearly gendered phenomenon—males are significantly more likely to steal vehicles. Some of the limited research that has been done on this fact has examined the role of "doing masculinity," finding that vehicle theft is significantly considered one of the things that one must do "to be a man" when legal pathways to such "manliness" are unavailable, such as having a job and a car and providing financially for one's family. In that such relationships rarely exist on their own, maleness was also related to problem drinking behaviors and traffic offenses.[15]

Cars in particular are perceived in Western culture as a way to show freedom, success, excitement, power, and change, particularly for marginalized men, who do not have legitimate ways to affirm their identity and status. Men can demonstrate their manhood in many ways when it comes to cars: they can fix them, blast their stereos, race one another or the police, or break traffic laws.[16] Women also steal cars; Clive Kenneth Williams found that young women participated in car theft to prove that they could do something considered so masculine but still be regarded by themselves and others as feminine. They had lower returns from auto theft and limited risk taking and had a subordinate role in thefts.[17]

Motor vehicle theft is also not as simple as one large category: some people, usually young men, steal cars to "joyride," which happens more in good economic times, because owners are less likely to be watching their cars and more likely to be careless with things like leaving their keys in the car. This allows the joyriders to have fun and show off their masculinity to others. Theft of cars for profit, on the other hand, is more often conducted by adult males and increases in bad economic times because people need money to survive.[18]

If we are to work to reduce crimes like motor vehicle theft, then the most effective way to counter car thefts is called *target hardening*, where owners equip their cars with alarms and other anti-theft deterrent devices and are more careful about not leaving keys in their cars. However, if the roots of this crime are, for some, the expression of masculinity in the absence of legitimate opportunities for success, then there must be other ways to escape social marginalization. Williams suggests such things as improved public transportation but focuses mainly on the idea that "providing noncriminal avenues for young men to feel powerful, important and included in society holds potential for preventing not only auto theft but possibly other crimes as well."[19]

ARSON

Arson is defined by the UCR as "any willful or malicious burning or attempt to burn, with or without intent to defraud, a dwelling house, public building, motor vehicle or aircraft, personal property of another, etc."[20] Arson is under-studied in the academic literature, compared to other crimes, even

> **CRITICAL THINKING BREAK 19**
>
> With so much criminological focus on other types of crimes, what does it mean to you that so little research has been done on a crime that may be committed by people burning their own things?

though it is considered very serious (it is categorized as a part 1 crime in the UCR, one of only eight). There is only limited criminological research on people who commit arson, which has focused on presenting the arsonist as a "manic, sexually deviant addict, seemingly intent on firesetting for gratification purposes," with samples mainly drawn from people struggling with their mental health and already in psychiatric institutions.[21] While this titillating picture works well to stoke fear of "crazy" strangers, it does not mesh with research from the fields of economics and insurance, from which emerges a profile of arsonists who own and insure their own property, which they then destroy with fire to receive an insurance payout, often quite high, and significantly higher than the payoff of other property crimes. Some of the small body of criminological research that comes from these economics and insurance literatures has found that arson rates are correlated with economic instability variables such as unemployment, but it has been inconsistent.[22]

THE CRIME DROP AND FEAR OF CRIME

Crime rates around the world have been declining for decades, especially when it comes to property crimes, and no one knows why. Residential burglary, for example, has declined by over 80 percent since the 1980s.[23] There have been many attempts at explaining the international crime drop, from the reduction in lead exposure to the emergence of cybercrime, but there has been a notable lack of consensus in criminology. Nonetheless, U.S. politicians use crime to stoke white racial hatred.[24] Despite this dramatic drop in crime, particularly property crime, fear of crime, especially of crime by Black people, remain high and drive high incarceration rates. Media and political representations of Black people's crime shape viewers' fears: white people tend to overestimate the involvement of Black people in crime, and fear of crime is higher in people with racial biases, though far more people experience fear of crime than actual crime victimization.[25]

One way that this racism and fear, despite the low risk, has shown up in contemporary America is on the internet. The apps Nextdoor and Ring Neighbors (through Amazon), for example, have supercharged neighborhood-watch politics, which used to be maintained through non-digital forms such as mass mailings and phone trees and later emails sent to community listservs about people looking "suspicious" in the neighborhood.[26] The Nextdoor website and mobile app launched in 2011, has over twenty-five million registered users, covers about 90 percent of all U.S. neighborhoods, and has surpassed a valuation of over $2 billion.[27] It, and other platforms like it such as Ring Doorbell, not only allow community members to communicate with one another semi-privately; it also means that they can respond to a moral panic of fear of the increasing diversity and visibility of Black and Brown people in the United States and see themselves as victims.[28]

In fact, Nextdoor had such a problem with racism among its users that it responded with, for example, requiring that any report of a suspicious person had to include at least two other identifiers other than race.[29] A "cesspool of racist gentrification," Nextdoor works as a tool to build a "digitally gated community" in its function of race and class surveillance and exclusion enforced through private and social policing.[30] But it is not just community members who use Nextdoor: police departments partner with Nextdoor to issue warning messages to communities and to communicate with community members, but there are real threats that police may add it to their ever-expanding use of social media surveillance to police citizens without their knowledge or consent.[31] Once people have been digitally labeled as "suspicious," this can be hard to escape, making mere existence difficult for minoritized people.[32]

CONCLUSION

You should recognize by now that one of the main priorities under capitalism is the maintenance of property and social capital to maintain power. The focus of criminology on property crimes by individuals, such as robbery and burglary, obfuscates the overwhelmingly broader harm of not just what the powerful routinely take from the less powerful but also the insistence that the public stay blind to that harm.

11 White-Collar and Environmental Crimes

This chapter covers both white-collar and environmental crimes because of the role of the relative power of the perpetrators and the impacts on large numbers of people who are more likely to be female, poor, and people of color. While most criminology textbooks focus on defining the different types of white-collar crimes, you will instead learn in this chapter about what we *don't* know about white-collar crime and why we don't know it.

WHITE-COLLAR CRIME

Edwin Sutherland first coined the term *white-collar crime* in 1939 as "a crime committed by a person of respectability and high social status in the course of their occupation." At the time any focus on such crimes was quite rare, but Sutherland insisted that the concept of white-collar crime was "the most significant development in criminology, especially since World War Two." He summarized his argument in five points:

1. White-collar criminality is real criminality, being in all cases in violation of the criminal law.

2. White-collar criminality differs from lower-class criminality principally in an implementation of the criminal law which segregates white-collar criminals administratively from other criminals.
3. The theories of the criminologists that crime is due to poverty or to psychopathic and sociopathic conditions statistically associated with poverty are invalid because, first, they are derived from samples which are grossly biased with respect to socioeconomic status; second, they do not apply to the white-collar criminals; and third, they do not even explain the criminality of the lower class, since the factors are not related to a general process characteristic of all criminality.
4. A theory of criminal behavior which will explain both white-collar criminality and lower-class criminality is needed.
5. A hypothesis of this nature is suggested in terms of differential association and social disorganization.[1]

Today theorists fall within three general areas when defining white-collar crime:

1. Those that define white-collar crime by the type of offender (e.g., high socioeconomic status and/or occupation of trust)
2. Those that define it in terms of the type of offense (e.g., economic crime)
3. Those that study it in terms of the organizational culture rather than the offender or offense[2]

When it comes to enforcement, the FBI has defined white-collar crime as "those illegal acts which are characterized by deceit, concealment, or violation of trust and which are not dependent upon the application or threat of physical force or violence. Individuals and organizations commit these acts to obtain money, property, or services; to avoid the payment or loss of money or services; or to secure personal or business advantage."[3] You should notice that this definition does not include any information about the person's occupation or socioeconomic status. This definition is important, however, because it is what the FBI uses to analyze and report data on crime. The FBI's own reporting cautions that there is limited information about white-collar crime because they measure only fraud, forgery and counterfeiting, embezzlement, and a last catch-all category that lumps together *all other offenses*. Because these crimes are not index crimes, police departments report only the age, sex, and race of the person arrested.

These factors might be more interesting if there weren't hardly any white-collar crimes reported by the FBI, though part of that is explained by the fact that the survey itself was being developed while the very concept of white-collar crime was being introduced by Sutherland. The modernized data collection from the National Incident-Based Reporting System is more detailed than its predecessor, but participation by police departments is still quite low. Your textbook may have a lot of data about people who commit white-collar crimes (generally white males in their late twenties to early thirties) or about how many victims there are (millions) or what types of crimes they are arrested for (most commonly fraud and counterfeiting and forgery). However, these statistics remain useful only as a measure of policing activity rather than of lawbreaking behavior. Most of all, we can see that white-collar crimes make up a very small part (13.3 percent) of incidents reported by police departments to the FBI in 2019.[4]

Enron

You may think of Enron when you think of white-collar crime, and you would be right! The case of Enron is a paradigmatic form because it encompasses much of what Sutherland had in mind: "The crimes were committed by privileged, respectable members of society, violating a fundamental trust, through major corporations, for purposes of financial gain (and to avoid financial loss), with devastating economic consequences for many ordinary members of society."[5] It was the largest scale white-collar crime since the savings and loan crisis and insider trading cases of the 1980s. Enron was a prominent U.S. energy company that collapsed in 2001 due to massive accounting fraud and unethical practices. Executives manipulated financial statements to hide debt and inflate profits, leading to its bankruptcy and the loss of billions of dollars for investors and employees.

You Have Probably Been the Victim of Wage Theft

Wage theft is when employers do not pay employees' wages and benefits by, for example, paying below the minimum wage, not paying overtime hours, not paying for social service programs such as unemployment insurance, confiscating tips, forcing people to work off the clock, or prohibiting legally mandated breaks. We do not know the extent of wage theft in the United States, but we do know that it is widespread, especially in low-wage industries such as retail, food services, and construction. Despite public concerns about property crimes such as robbery, theft, and larceny, it is estimated that the amount of stolen wages is more than all three of them put together and costs the United States more than $91 billion tax dollars in the annual gross tax gap.[6]

Women, people of color, people who are already poor, and immigrants working low-wage jobs are most likely to be the victims of wage theft. The Economic Policy Institute found that, while over three billion dollars in stolen wages were recovered by state and federal governments through class and collective action litigation, it represents only a tiny fraction of wages stolen from U.S. workers.[7] While wage theft can be met with criminal penalties for repeat violators, there have been only *ten* criminal convictions between 2005 and 2016. Even civil penalties (the most common recourse) are quite rare: employers have only a 0.5 percent chance that they will be investigated by the U.S. Department of Labor, and the fine is only up to $2,203, which is certainly not a deterrent for large employers.[8]

But back in 1985, Raymond Michalowski contended that the truth is the opposite: "Corporate crime represents the most widespread and costly form of crime in America."[9] Outside of governmental data collection about police enforcement, a small body of research has estimated (conservatively) since then that three hundred thousand people die annually because of white-collar offenses, including "employees injured in the workplace or affected by toxic chemicals due to the company's lack of safety compliance, civilians exposed to toxic waste and deadly pollutants, and consumers victims of faulty products, addictive substances, or subpar medical services."[10] This number dwarfs the number of people (16,425) murdered in 2019.[11] The financial losses are also dire: as of 2021, white-collar crimes had caused financial losses of between $426 billion to $1.7 trillion per year.[12]

The study of white-collar crime began when Sutherland focused his scholarly attention on the crimes of the powerful, which had caused the 1929 stock crash and the Great Depression, but the malfeasance only grew, playing key roles in the past three economic recessions in the United States.[13]

But even so, when you log in to your local social media neighborhood group, you will likely see a lot of people scared of and angry about crime, but it likely isn't white-collar crime! Cedric Michel found that when people compared violent street crime to harmful white-collar crime, people perceived the violent street crime more seriously.[14] This may be because *street crime* is coded language for crime by non-white and poor people or because people are not used to seeing white-collar crime as physically harmful or because media representations of white-collar crime tend to be non-deadly.

White-Collar Crime Is Different from Corporate Crime

In 1964 prominent sociologist Richard Quinney suggested that Sutherland's original definition of white-collar crime needed to be updated to exclude the social status of the offender and focus on violations that occur in the course of occupational activity. He, Marshall Clinard, and John Wildeman later divided white-collar crime into two types: occupational and corporate crime. Specifically, they wrote, "Occupational crime consists of offenses committed by individuals for themselves in the course of their occupations and the offenses of employees against their employers. Corporate crime consists of the offenses committed by corporate officials for their corporation and offenses of the corporation itself." Later in the book, they warn that "criminal law alone does not assure compliance as long as those corporations that are controlled exercise political control and influence over regulatory agencies and courts."[15] In West Virginia in 2022, for example, pharmaceutical manufacturers had to pay $161.5 million in a settlement for overstating the benefits of opioid use while downplaying the risks of addiction.

White-Collar Crimes Remain Men's Crimes, Even as Women Get More Power

In 1975 Freda Adler wrote the now classic book, *Sisters in Crime: The Rise of the New Female Criminal*. While this book was incredibly important because of its focus on women, quite rare in criminology, her contention ended up being completely wrong. Adler suggested that the only reason that women's rates of white-collar crime were so much lower than men's was because of lack of access to those spaces of power. She hypothesized that as women achieved higher positions in the business world, they would take advantage of these new opportunities, both legitimate and illegitimate because, she wrote, women and men are not different except for their opportunities.

Unsurprisingly, if you take a critical criminological perspective, there is not much research about gender and white-collar crime. The research that does exist consistently shows, however, that women's involvement in white-collar crime is low: Kathleen Daly found that women made up less than 5 percent of people convicted of significant organizational or corporate crimes such as antitrust, bribery, and securities fraud and made up only 14 percent of people convicted of *any* fraud or nonviolent economic crime from 1976 to 1978. Even with these low percentages, Daly cautioned that they might be artificially high because of additional surveillance on financial jobs traditionally held by women.[16] Importantly, women's reasons for their actions were family-based, while men's reasons were more about personal finances.

More recently, research has found that fewer than one in ten of the people involved in major corporate frauds of the late twentieth and early twenty-first centuries were women, that men were responsible for all of the solo-executed frauds, and that all conspiracy cases involved groups with either all men or with at least one man involved. In these conspiracies women gained less profit than their male co-conspirators, and most women played minor roles. Finally, they found that women were particularly likely to have become involved in these crimes either because they had a relationship with a male co-conspirator or because their role was useful strategically to the co-conspirators. The authors ended up concluding that more women in positions of corporate power and leadership might be a method to reduce corporate fraud because they might make more ethical decisions, avoid risk-taking excesses, and not create an organizational structure prone to crime.[17]

Corporate Harm Victimization Is Gendered

Helen Baker suggests that social and cultural norms regarding attractiveness and reproductive capacity mean that women are more often subjects of medical examinations and interventions. This makes women more vulnerable to experiencing certain types of pharmaceutical, medical, and surgical harms. Her list of "Gendered Pharma-Harms" is as follows:

- Diethylstilbestrol, sold in the 1930s, was a morning-sickness drug that was known to cause harm to animals but was nonetheless given to women, causing miscarriages, infertility, and birth "deformities."
- Dalkon Sheild, an intra-uterine contraceptive device, was sold in the 1960s, even though it was known that one of its materials could cause an infection in the womb. The device caused miscarriages, infertility, infections, and unwanted pregnancies in thousands of women.
- Thalidomide was prescribed to women in the 1960s for morning sickness even though the manufacturers knew and denied the risks of babies born with "gross deformities."
- Dow Corning's executives knew that the breast implants they were selling were defective and unsafe, but they did it anyway in the 1990s. They paid $3.2 billion to 170,000 women who were made sick as the silicone moved from the implants to their immune systems.
- Poly Implant Prothese breast implants were fraudulently manufactured in 2010, using cheap industrial silicone rather than medical-grade silicone, harming hundreds of thousands of women.[18]

The Absence of Laws

Even though there is no evidence that the number of white-collar crimes is going down, the number of white-collar crime prosecutions and trials has been declining in recent years. Some of this is due to increasing use of "Deferred Prosecution Agreements," in which negotiations between public prosecutors and company attorneys provide leniency for companies that agree to pay fines and implement good governance reforms. While large fines may impact most individuals, even large financial penalties do not impact corporations, which see them as a cost of doing business.[19] When it comes to prevention and arrests, many police departments have established a "white collar crime unit" in recent years. These units, however, spend most of their time and resources on low-level crimes.[20]

Julie O'Sullivan summarizes the very limited literature on race and enforcement of white-collar crime cases: "I am far from the first to note the obvious: there is a jarring disconnect between the race and ethnicity of those who are subjected to the most concerted enforcement efforts and resources and those who benefit from the workings of the white-collar ecosystem."[21] Only about 10 percent of recent federally sentenced cases involved white-collar crimes, and most of the people selected for prosecution and then convicted were not corporate sharks but relatively low-level offenders. Darrell Steffensmeier, Casey Harris, and Noah Painter-Davis found that occupationally related crime is reported rarely but still more than upper-level crime, and most people are charged for minor, "garden variety" crimes rather than anything with widespread impact.[22]

Federal dollars *were* spent, on the other hand, on immigration and drug-trafficking offenses, both categories where Latinx and Black people are over-represented.[23] Indeed, Tracy Sohoni and Melissa Rorie have proposed a "Theory of Racial Privilege and Offending," which considers the racial impact of *whiteness* and examines the impact of concentrated advantage and the resulting entitlement and lack of empathy that impacts involvement in white-collar crime (instead of criminology's obsession with the impact of concentrated *dis*advantage on involvement in *street* crime).[24]

ENVIRONMENTAL CRIMES

Environmental crimes have been a focus of U.S. federal law enforcement only since the late 1960s, with a focus on air, land, and water pollution, and the criminal legal system has used its usual blunt tools to address violations. From the Clean Air Act and the Clean Water Act to the Endangered Species Act, federal responses to environmental crimes are punitive, with adding felony charges to each act being seen as an accomplishment. Angus Nurse found, instead, that because of limited resources, budgets, and staffing, the federal environmental law enforcement is increasingly outsourcing both policy development, practical enforcement, and even direct action, to non-governmental organizations.[25] These interventions can not only be ineffective but also mean that there are a variety of difficult relationships between the state and NGOs, from partners to opponents to somewhere in the middle when it comes to corrupted state processes.[26]

The Environmental Justice Movement

You have likely heard of environmental movements, most of which focus on the impacts of humans and climate change on the earth and the beings that inhabit it. The movements led by communities of color, however, also recognize the disproportionate impact of environmental threats on Black and Brown communities. As Shannon Roesler so clearly expresses it, "By drawing attention to the spaces where people 'live, work, and play,' the [environmental justice] movement exposed how environmental laws and policies fail to protect low-income, minority, and tribal communities from the health effects of air pollution and land contamination, just as they fail to provide basic public goods such as clean drinking water, green space, and safe housing."[27]

Erik Kojola and David Pellow go further by arguing that environmental racism and environmental injustice are forms of institutional and state violence, indelibly linked to environmental and racial privilege.[28] The idea is that the physical, emotional, and spiritual harms of everything from toxic pollution to the placement of pipelines on sacred land to land degradation can lead to trauma, injury, and death in impacted communities and should therefore be considered violent. They link what they refer to as the violence of current environmental injustices to histories of racial capitalism, settler colonialism, and enslavement.

Young Climate Activists Fighting Environmental Injustices

MARI COPENY, AKA LITTLE MISS FLINT

Known as "Little Miss Flint," Mari Copeny became famous when her letter to President Barack Obama about the water crisis in overwhelmingly Black and poor Flint, Michigan, led him to visit the city himself and approve a $100 million relief package for the city. Not only did the city's mis-management mean that there were high levels of lead in the water system, but officials actively ignored and minimized months of complaints from residents about the water's odor, color, and taste. State officials estimate that almost nine thousand children under the age of six in Flint were exposed to high levels of lead. Mari continues to fight for environmental justice, saying in an interview that "Flint is not unique. There are dozens of Flints across the country. Cases of environmental racism are on the rise and disproportionately affect communities of people of color and indigenous communities."[29]

ISRA HIRSI

Climate activist Isra Hirsi is the daughter of Congress representative Ilhan Omar, a refugee from Somalia. As the co-founder of the U.S. Youth Climate Strike, Hirsi is working to spur radical action on climate, with a particular focus on leadership among Muslim and Black youth. "Creating more space for those with marginalized identities in the climate space is necessary for inclusive solutions," she said.[30]

JAMIE MARGOLIN

Jamie Margolin is the co-founder and former executive director of Zero Hour, a climate action organization founded in the wake of Hurricane Maria and the wildfires in Washington State in 2017. Margolin is a first-generation daughter of a Colombian immigrant and identifies as a queer, Jewish, Latina climate activist, focusing her advocacy on the needs of the most vulnerable communities. "I sued the state of Washington because I can't breathe there," she wrote in 2018 at the age of sixteen. She continued, "They ignored me."[31]

XIUHTEZCATL MARTINEZ, AKA X

Xiuhtezcatl Martinez, best known as X, uses hip-hop and R&B music to inspire climate activism. He is the youth director of the Earth Guardians organization, serves as a plaintiff in the Colorado lawsuit seeking to put a stop to fracking, and has sued the U.S. government for failing to act on climate change.[32]

Environmental Racism and Health

One example of this that may be a part of your everyday life is environmental racism and its impact on health. The fact that environmental injustice overwhelmingly impacts Black and Brown people has long been known.[33] In 1987 Rev. Dr. Benjamin Chavis, the former executive director of the National Association for the Advancement of Colored People

(NAACP) and a longtime civil-rights community organizer and activist, coined the term *environmental racism*. He suggested that environmental laws themselves were racist in their implementation and application, with distinct racist and often deadly outcomes. His statement had profound effects on environmental scholarship, law, and policy. For example, the U.S. Environmental Protection Agency (EPA) defines *environmental justice* as requiring that "no group of people should bear a disproportionate share of the negative environmental consequences resulting from industrial, governmental and commercial operations or policies" and calls for "fair treatment and meaningful involvement of all people regardless of race, color, national origin, or income with respect to the development, implementation and enforcement of environmental laws, regulations and policies." The EPA also now explicitly considers environmental justice issues when prioritizing facilities and geographic locations for enforcement.[34]

With inequitable exposure to environmental hazards comes inequitable outcomes, from the most immediate (such as health and educational attainment) to longer term, such as the labor market outcomes of fetuses exposed in utero. This can happen because companies place polluting sites in poor and Black and Brown neighborhoods and because poor people can only afford to live in homes devalued by nearby pollution (and the wealthy are willing and able to pay more to be far away).[35] Others have found that companies who polluted in neighborhoods with more Black and Brown people faced lower penalties, and in those neighborhoods cleanup took more time, and solutions were less strict.[36]

A brownfield is "a property, the expansion, redevelopment, or reuse of which may be complicated by the presence or potential presence of a hazardous substance, pollutant, or contaminant. It is estimated that there are more than 450,000 brownfields in the U.S."[37] Cancer Alley, for example, stretches between New Orleans and Baton Rouge along the Mississippi River, lined with around 150 oil refineries and petrochemical plants. Residents in this area, overwhelmingly Black, are fifty times more likely to develop cancer than the average American. Rev. Dr. William J. Barber said in an interview with *Rolling Stone* about Cancer Alley, "The same land that held people captive through slavery is now holding people captive through this environmental injustice and devastation.... It is killing

> **CRITICAL THINKING BREAK 20**
>
> My community has a brownfield underneath the old middle school building that has been deteriorating for decades. Is there a brownfield in your community? What has come of it?

people by over-polluting them with toxins in their water and in their air. This is slavery of another kind."[38]

In 1985 David Sorokin and Warren Muir, from the environmental organization Inform, wrote an opinion piece for the *New York Times*, "Too Little Toxic-Waste Data," that bemoaned the fact that there existed no data on questions such as "How much of these [toxic] chemicals is being handled at each plant? How much is shipped as a commercial product? How much is released into rivers, lakes, ponds, and sewage treatment plants? How much is emitted into the air? How much becomes solid waste that is burned, buried or stored?" They cited EPA data from the time that showed nearly seven thousand toxic chemical accidents that led to more than 135 people dead and 1,500 injured.[39] Their pleas led to the Toxic Release Inventory (TRI), a publicly available national database of reports from private and government facilities on how much of certain chemicals they emit into air or water or send to landfills annually. There is a concentration of twenty-one TRI facilities—oil refineries, chemical plants, sewage treatment facilities, and hazardous waste sites—in the Harrisburg-Manchester neighborhood of Houston, which has 98 percent Latinx residents. An average of 484,000 pounds of toxic chemicals are released into the Harrisburg-Manchester air annually, while the Rice University neighborhood, ten miles away, is home to no TRI facilities. This means that the Harrisburg-Manchester residents have a 22 percent higher cancer risk than their counterparts in the overall Houston urban area.[40]

Climate Change and Intersectionality

Geraldine Terry wrote that there is "no climate justice without gender justice," because women are over-exposed to climate hazards due to structural barriers and gender discrimination. "Poor women face many gender-specific barriers that limit their ability to cope with and adapt to a changing climate; these must be removed in the interests of both gender equity and adaptation efficiency. At the same time, gender analysis should be integral to the appraisal of public policies designed to reduce carbon emissions."[41] One example of this is that all women, but especially poor women, are more likely to experience over-exposure to extreme temperatures. Women are more likely to be poor and as a result more likely to work in urban areas, live in older housing, and have less access to green areas, which means that they are even disproportionately impacted by the high-heat events that have come with climate change.[42] As another example, Sarah Haley and Bruce Arrigo explored the relationship between climate change and reproductive injustice, showing that bodily autonomy must be central to any movement fighting climate change because of women's disproportionate experiences of health and social inequalities.[43]

Green Criminology

Although three decades old, green criminology is marginalized within criminology, treated as if it were a curiosity rather than a field of research focusing on a tremendously important set of global concerns, from ecological harms such as pollution to the role of environmental laws and environmental justice to so-called green crimes.[44] "At the most abstract level," green criminology is defined as "the study of . . . harms against humanity, . . . the environment (including space) and . . . nonhuman animals committed by both . . . powerful institutions (e.g. governments, transnational corporations, military apparatuses) and . . . ordinary people."[45]

One significant focus of green criminology concerns animals. Some researchers focus on crimes against companion animals, including breeding, abuse, and wildlife trafficking for sale as companion animals; others on wildlife, including poaching and illegal fishing; and others on domesticated animals, including factory farms and the agricultural and industrial use of animals' labor.[46] Piers Beirne has also proposed a term, *theriocide*, specifically to refer to the killing of animals by humans.[47]

Michael Lynch argues that, much like with white-collar crimes, the media and general public are very focused on environmental crimes by individuals rather than those committed by the powerful. While crimes by individuals are a problem, they are far less impactful than corporate crimes against the environment. For example, while one person may unlawfully and harmfully cut down a tree, the widespread deforestation for corporate profit is a much bigger problem. He gives the example of publicized cases of abandoned animals, contrasted with, for example, the 920 million farm animals and 3.1 million minks killed for their pelts annually.[48] Overall, green criminology has grown into a strong field of its own, expanding the purview of criminology to harms that are particularly important at a time of global ecological collapse.[49]

Greenwashing

Have you ever seen a corporation's "Corporate Responsibility Statement," where they outline their work to prevent or remediate the harm their business does to the environment? Originally called *eco-pornography* and then coined as *greenwashing* in 1986, the concept refers to a variety of misleading communications by a company about their environmental practices to make people more comfortable about the organization. This may sound unfamiliar to you, but you likely see it every day in your cupboards, on your phone, or at stores! Specifically, Riccardo Torelli, Federica Balluchi, and Arianna Lazzini suggest four main levels of greenwashing:

- **Corporate-level greenwashing** concerns misleading environmental communication about data and aspects related to the actual firm's image and reputation. This level embodies a static dimension (i.e., the company name and logo, vision, standard adherence, and corporate certification).
- **Strategic-level greenwashing** concerns a misleading environmental communication concerning aspects related to the future firm's strategies (i.e., strategic public communication, corporate medium-long-term goals, strategic plan for improvement or implementation of technology/processes, report communication, and targeted extraordinary operations).
- **Dark level greenwashing** concerns a misleading environmental communication finalized to hide illegal activities (i.e., money laundering, criminal and/or mafia collusion, corruption, and investments with hidden aims).

- **Product level greenwashing** concerns a misleading environmental communication concerning some specific features of a product or a family of products (i.e., label, targeted advertising, packaging, and product certifications).[50]

We know comparatively very little about the extent of green crimes, for there is no centralized data collection like the UCR for mostly street crimes; "yet, with respect to legitimacy, it can be easily shown that there are more green crimes and victimization than street crimes and victimization."[51] Anyone interested in nature and the scope of green crimes would have to gather data from very diverse sources, from wastewater pollution violations and abandoned contaminated brownfields to water extraction crimes. In this way you can see the ways in which political and corporate priorities drive our ability to even know about some crimes (mostly by the less powerful) versus others (mostly by people and organizations with power).

CONCLUSION

Now that you have read through the chapters on crimes against people, crimes against property, and now the crimes of the powerful, I hope that you can see how the critical lens allows us to see harm and power in new ways. The harm is not less—it is often far more—when the powerful victimize people they think no one will care about to advance their own interests, because there is very little recourse.

12 Public Order Crimes

Public order crimes are considered illegal because they go against accepted moral rules, public opinion, and social policy, such as public intoxication, disturbing the peace, and vandalism. However, these "crimes" often have common threads: poverty, race, and trauma. In this chapter you will learn about the criminalization of poverty and the many ways in which the law has moved toward both increasing the population of poor and homeless people *and* criminalizing their very existence, often riddled with trauma. In this chapter we also look at two other "victimless" public order crime categories: drugs and sex work, both quite entangled with homelessness. We'll pay particular attention to the ways in which the U.S. criminal legal system criminalizes the survival strategies of the most marginalized and downtrodden among us.

DISRUPTING THE PUBLIC ORDER

Public order crimes are any acts or behaviors that interfere with society's shared cultural norms, values, and customs. These crimes are viewed as harmful to the public good and disruptive to communities. Most criminology research focuses on, as usual, what is wrong with people that they break these laws. A critical perspective, however, steps back to look at the ways in which the criminalization of these behaviors is a structural issue, which means that one looks at systemic and institutional factors rather than solely individual circumstances and choices. This approach focuses on the larger social, economic, and political structures that contribute to poverty and inequality within a society.

As an example, imagine a veteran who came back from active duty in Afghanistan. When he returned, he was riddled with PTSD and anxiety, which he used drugs and alcohol to tame. He lashed out at people at the smallest inconvenience and got in a variety of altercations, some of which ended up in arrests. He was unable to keep a job because of his behavior and because he would always quit in rages. He had nowhere to live, so he began sleeping on park benches, intoxicated and high to manage the PTSD and the shame and discomfort of sleeping outside, jobless, drunk, and hungry. Most people, and most criminological theories, would look at the ways in which this individual is making bad choices in his individual circumstances. A critical, structural approach looks at how we got here: What systems restricted the opportunities for this man and thousands like him to avoid this in the first place? How can we address the problems that led to his criminalized behaviors? How could, for example, our school, health care, criminal legal, and military systems have done better for this man and the millions of people with similar challenges? What are the unequal and discriminatory practices and systemic barriers that stopped this man and so many like him from achieving economic self-sufficiency?

HOMELESSNESS AND THE CRIMINALIZATION OF POVERTY

In Barbara Ehrenreich's seminal 2009 op-ed, she asks, "Is it now a crime to be poor?" She writes about the many ways in which poor people are criminalized for "the biological necessities of life like sitting, sleeping, lying down or loitering" that are simply not risks to public safety. She traces these laws back to the beginnings of gentrification in the 1980s and 1990s and reports that they in fact *increased* as the economy got worse, meaning more people in poverty.[1] But before gentrification worked as racism and ableism in disguise, there were laws that explicitly allowed police to criminalize people struggling for their very existence. Most well-known were state and local Jim Crow laws (named for a racist blackface performer from the early 1800s), which enforced racial segregation and discrimination in the late nineteenth and early twentieth century and (among other things) meant that public facilities (e.g., bathrooms, restaurants, schools, and transportation) were divided between Black and white people. While these facilities were supposed to be "separate but equal," in reality the segregated facilities were under-funded and inferior to those for white people.

Likewise, several states had "ugly laws" that made it illegal for people with visible disabilities or disfigurements to be in public at all. In her book *The Ugly Laws,* Susan Schweik describes a law from 1867 in San Francisco "to prohibit street begging, and to restrain certain persons from appearing in streets and public places." Section 3 specifically identifies

> any person who is diseased, maimed, mutilated, or in any way deformed to be an unsightly or disgusting object ... [who] shall not therein or thereon expose himself or herself to public view. Any person who shall violate the provisions of this section shall be deemed guilty of a misdemeanour; and on conviction thereof, shall be punished by a fine not exceeding twenty-five dollars, or by imprisonment in the county jail not exceeding twenty-five days, or by both such fine and punishment.[2]

Anti-Okie and vagrancy laws also served similar purposes to keep indigent, disabled, and Black and Brown people out of sight.[3]

Gentrification

Gentrification is the process of a community experiencing an increase in wealthy (usually white) people moving in, causing an increase in property values and the displacement of the original, poorer residents. When low-income districts undergo gentrification, they also see a change in social expectations. Activities that used to be normal are now perceived as suspicious by the new (white and wealthy) residents, which often means an increase in policing, especially in formerly Black and Brown communities.

More specifically, it generally means increases in broken-windows style of policing, which in turn contributes to the cycle of mass incarceration, recurrent poverty, and racial profiling overwhelmingly affecting the Black and Brown members of these communities. Even as crime rates decrease, criminalization increases. In other words, gentrification can be seen as an informal and coercive technique that systematically harms communities of color and low-income communities.[4]

With these laws gone but with homeless populations exploding, U.S. cities began creating policies that allowed them to criminalize homelessness by targeting associated behaviors, such as panhandling and sleeping and sitting in public. While poverty itself is not a crime, systemic failures that continue to exacerbate poverty in communities across the country only add to the idea that it is. Panhandling, loitering, encroaching, and dwelling in vehicles have all been targets of anti-homelessness laws that criminalize some individuals' only way of survival. In their 2019 report "Housing Not Handcuffs 2019: Ending the Criminalization of Homelessness in U.S. Cities," the National Law Center on Homelessness and Poverty examined the city codes of 187 cities across the country to create an overview of laws that punish homelessness. They found that homelessness is rising because of "rising rents, stagnant wages, historically low rental vacancy rates, and the severe decline of federally subsidized housing," leading to a critical shortage of affordable housing units because people cannot afford to get apartments in the first place or get evicted from apartments when they cannot afford the rent. Not surprisingly, this means that homelessness is particularly likely among Black and Brown people, who are disproportionately barred from housing due to racist housing practices and therefore make up over 60 percent of America's homeless population. With the combination of increases in homeless populations and the criminalization of the satisfaction of basic needs in public comes increasing imprisonment of people whose only offense is to be without a safe place to live.[5]

Anti-homelessness laws not only criminalize poverty but also contribute to the continued cycle between imprisonment and homelessness, called the "revolving door" of incarceration: homeless individuals are eleven times more likely to be incarcerated, and being incarcerated makes a person ten times more likely to be homeless. People who have been incarcerated multiple times, people recently released from prison, women, and Black and Brown people are particularly likely to be homeless, not just from unfortunate circumstances but by design, with policies that criminalize people's very existence by making it impossible to panhandle, dumpster dive, store property in public, or camp, sit, lie down, or sleep in public spaces, for example, without being arrested.[6] The root of these laws is in the belief that homelessness is from poor life choices, mental illness, or drug addiction, which must, in turn, be addressed with punitive approaches. The National Law Center on Homelessness and Poverty found that these laws criminalizing poverty are not just harmful but also ineffective because they do not address underlying causes like the lack of affordable housing. Los Angeles, for example, spends $30 million a year in sweeps to clear homeless people, often in violation of the Constitution and anti-discrimination laws.[7]

Housing the Homeless

A variety of homeless advocacy organizations have the same research-based recommendations that would reduce homelessness and increase the dignity of people without homes, while also reducing costs to taxpayers and serving families and communities.[8] The most clear and obvious answer is to house people. One way that communities are doing this is through Housing First, which is a homeless assistance approach that "prioritizes providing permanent housing to people experiencing homelessness, thus ending their homelessness and serving as a platform from which they can pursue personal goals and improve their quality of life. This approach is guided by the belief that people need basic necessities like food and a place to live before attending to anything less critical, such as getting a job, budgeting properly, or attending to substance use issues."[9] By using a Housing First approach, four communities have effectively ended chronic homelessness in the United States: Bergen County in 2017, followed by Rockford, Illinois; Lancaster, Pennsylvania; and the jurisdictions in the Southwest Minnesota Continuum of Care. Even more have effectively ended veteran homelessness, beginning with New Orleans in 2014.[10]

Clearly, there must also be other social services to complement housing, to make sure that people have, for example, the employment, medical care, substance use treatment, mental health care, and social, civic, and family connections they need to thrive.[11] Innovations for preventing homelessness, such as tiny homes, safe parking lots, and community land trusts, as well as stopping police from being the first responders to homelessness, have been proposed as steps toward reducing homelessness.[12] Homelessness prevention efforts will be most effective if they prioritize formerly incarcerated people, who are so much more likely to continue through the revolving doors of homelessness and incarceration, by banning the exclusion of housing applicants due to their criminal record, either before they apply or once they have applied.[13]

Finally, we must realize that the criminalization of homelessness is not just deadly and devastating for people who are already without homes, but that it is also costly and counter-productive for everyone in the community. Cities should end the aggressive enforcement of quality-of-life ordinances. Arresting, fining, and jailing homeless people for acts related to their very survival is not only cruel; it also funnels formerly incarcerated people back through the revolving door of homelessness and punishment, which reduces their chances of successful re-entry at great cost to public safety. Over-policing, including the broken-windows style of enforcement, intensifies and often causes poverty. This means that astronomical costs of the criminal legal system are shifted to the poorest among us.

Examples of Ordinances against the Publicly Poor

Back in 2009, Ehrenreich listed several ways in which poverty itself had been criminalized, including the prohibition of begging or sharing food with the indigent in public places, teenagers charged with trespassing for getting caught in public housing without an ID, fines for turnstile jumping and truancy, and imprisoned people charged for room and board. Once the cycle begins, she argued, it just keeps accelerating and is made even worse by racial profiling. Consider some more recent examples of such ordinances:

- Los Angeles: sleeping in vehicles is prohibited
- Los Angeles: ban on sitting, lying down, and sleeping on sidewalks
- Kansas City: food-sharing regulations
- Las Vegas: illegal to sleep and camp in public places[14]

DRUG "CRIMES"

Over 350,000 people are incarcerated in the United States for drug offenses as of 2023 because police, prosecutors, and judges all punish people harshly for drug offenses, even those as simple as possession.[15] According to the Drug Policy Alliance, someone is arrested for a drug offense once every thirty-one seconds, and 85 percent of those drug arrests are for the relatively low-level crime of possession. Although Black people make up only 13 percent of the population, they are 24 percent of people arrested for drug crimes.[16] Said another way, before the pandemic, police made over one million drug arrests each year. Once people get into prison, there is still access to drugs and alcohol, and it is very often deadly: fatal drug or alcohol overdose increased over 600 percent in state prisons from 2001 to 2018. Treatment or medications for substance use disorder are rarely available in prison.[17]

These statistics, though staggering, represent a slowing down of punitive responses to drugs, which started with the War on Drugs, declared by President Nixon over fifty years ago. The War on Drugs has moved "from political slogan to an actual war" against its own citizens that cost Americans hundreds of billions of dollars in policing that focuses on destroying Black and Brown communities using over-surveillance and incarceration.[18] Your textbook probably covers the reasons behind the War on Drugs and its monumental impacts, particularly on young Black and Brown men, caged at globally unprecedented rates, and the families and communities they leave behind, overwhelmingly Black and Brown mothers. As we shift away from the War on Drugs, however, we must also consider the other ways in which drugs intersect with the criminal legal system. You may be familiar with this type of data from your traditional criminology textbook, because mainstream criminology does a good job of recognizing that crime and substance use and dependence are related. These traditional approaches, however, usually view drug use and addiction simply as moral failures and personal choices without examining the larger structural factors such as poverty, inequality, discrimination, and social marginalization that impact who uses drugs and whether and how they are involved in drug-related lawbreaking activities.

Over these fifty years, Americans have realized that this hyper-punitive response to drugs failed to make anything better and in fact made many things worse. Most Americans now believe that the War on Drugs is a failure and must be ended; support "eliminating criminal penalties for drug possession and reinvesting drug enforcement resources into treatment and addiction services"; and believe that we need a new approach based in public health rather than relying on the police. A full 88 percent of U.S. adults agree marijuana should be legal for medical or recreational use. Even as the War on Drugs slows, drug arrests and their associated extreme racial disparities are still widespread across the United States and have not improved with time. Even in states where marijuana was legalized or decriminalized, and arrests therefore decreased, racial disparities persist.[19]

Racial Disparities Change When We Look at Drug Sales and Use

While Black and Brown people are far over-represented among those we *punish* for drug use, their *usage* rates have historically been lower than those of white people: "for the last twenty years . . . whites have engaged in drug offenses at rates higher than blacks."[20] White people were about 45 percent more likely to sell drugs than Black people in 1980, consistent with findings in 2012, which showed that white adolescents and young adults were 32 percent more likely to sell drugs than their Black counterparts.[21] More recently, use among Black people has moved to being simply comparable to drug usage among white people. The Substance Abuse and Mental Health Services Administration report from 2021 shows that 24.3 percent of Black people, 22.5 percent of white people, and 19.4 percent of Latinx people had used illicit drugs in the past year. These similarities remain when we look specifically at marijuana and opioid (heroin or prescription pain reliever) misuse and substance use disorder among people aged twelve or older. The two racial categories that stand out in each measure of substance use problems are American Indian/Alaskan Native people and multi-racial people, who have higher rates than any other racial group, with as high as 36.1 percent of AI/AN people and 34.6 percent of multiracial people having used illicit drugs in the past year.[22]

Finishing Your Sentence Doesn't Mean Drug Laws Are Finished with You

Once people have been arrested and incarcerated for drug crimes, their "time served" is not only while they are inside. Once people are released, their arrest records follow them in a way that hurts their ability to get and keep jobs and increases their likelihood of longer sentences for future offenses. Being released also does not mean that the appropriate supports will be in place for people in danger of going back to drugs: there is an up-to-fifty times higher risk of overdose in people's first weeks after release from jail or prison compared to their counterparts in the general population.[23]

The War on Drugs Is Shifting, Not Ending

What most people may not realize, however, is that ending the War on Drugs is not just about decriminalizing or legalizing drugs and releasing people convicted of drug offenses. Even if people are not convicted and incarcerated for drug offenses, drugs and alcohol are very often a key element of people's lives when they commit the offense for which they are incarcerated. The Bureau of Justice Statistics performs face-to-face interviews with adults in federal prison and found that, among the almost 1.5 million state and federal prisoners, almost 40 percent reported using drugs and 30 percent reported drinking alcohol at the time of the offense for which they were serving a sentence. These numbers are even higher when they asked whether people had used at least one drug in the month before their arrest (64 percent said yes).[24] However, our punitive responses to drugs are not just in the criminal legal system—nearly a quarter of American workers (thirty-eight million people) are subject to employer-mandated drug testing; drug offenses are one of the leading causes of deportation and of students being referred to the police; and everything from public housing to social services punish people for using drugs.

The Complicated Relationship between Drugs and Crime

So if we move beyond looking at individual choices with drugs and alcohol, what else is there to examine? What we find is a much more complex relationship between drugs and crime, impacted profoundly by the structural and systemic factors that contribute to drug use and drug-related crimes. Specifically, critical criminology examines the role of the pharmaceutical industry, government policies, and law enforcement practices in shaping drug markets and patterns of drug-related crime. It highlights how power imbalances and vested interests influence the definition of illegal drugs, the enforcement of drug laws, and the allocation of resources for drug control.

Data can help us get to these roots. For example, Joseph Friedman and Helena Hansen found that drug overdose deaths among Black and Indigenous Americans surpassed that of white Americans, indicating that "drug overdose mortality is increasingly becoming a racial justice issue in the United States and appears to have been exacerbated by the COVID-19 pandemic." Black and Brown communities, they found, were particularly vulnerable because of "historic inequities, including high rates of incarceration, economic disenfranchisement and loss of community cohesion." There also appears to have been what some have called a "perfect storm," as super-potent synthetic drugs emerged just as the pandemic was increasing people's feelings of isolation and displacement, especially for Black and Brown communities. While the number of overdose deaths rose for all racial groups nationally between 2019 and 2020, the rate increased fastest for African Americans, growing by 49 percent compared with a growth of 26 percent for white people.[25]

Historically, predominantly non-white communities have been socially and economically isolated due to segregation and racism, and this isolation in turn has combined with the unequal distribution of material and symbolic resources by race in a way that funnels wealth and prestige to white communities and poverty and stigma to Black and Brown communities. Private and public infrastructure investments, for example, are comparatively lower in poor Black and Brown communities, whereas investments in institutions such as policing and prisons are quite high. This concentration and continuation of racialized poverty allows police to over-enforce drug policies in the poorer, overwhelmingly Black and Brown communities, which brings with it police brutality and traumatic militarized styles. In a now not-surprising parallel to the criminalization of poverty, the use of targeted and excessive fines and fees overwhelmingly impact these same poor Black and Brown communities, often closing the circle to fund the very police departments waging war on the people paying for their riot gear. The similarly white-dominated media also controls the general perception of these communities as dangerous (the "ghetto"), limiting those communities' access to capital.

Critical criminology also takes a social justice perspective, focused on alternative approaches such as harm reduction, decriminalization, and social policies that address the root causes of drug use and addiction. For example, the interrelatedness of abuse histories and everything from mental health and substance use disorder to criminal behavior has long been shown in research. We know specifically that abuse histories (so, the victimization about which we are so very concerned) are significantly related to mental health outcomes for both men and women.

Safe Consumption Sites

Safe consumption sites are locations where people can use illegal drugs such as heroin, cocaine, or methamphetamine. They are supervised by staff trained to manage accidental overdose, such as with naloxone or oxygen, and the people using them are not at risk of being arrested at the sites. These sites are remarkably effective at harm reduction because the fact that drugs are illegal means that people who use them isolate themselves or engage in risky behavior, which can both be deadly. They also provide referrals to treatment, can help people find housing, and show compassion to people deeply struggling. They reduce overdose deaths, particularly among non-white people and women.[26]

So then what about drug use is "public order" crime? There's not really anything, if policing of crimes has been in isolated communities targeted because of their poverty and non-whiteness, overwhelmed by the consequences of criminalization and ignored in wealthy and white enclaves. The "war" is about Black and Brown and poor people using drugs, not about anyone using drugs. But let's not forget gender! Lisa Maher and Kathleen Daly's revolutionary ethnographic work with women drug users showed that women remained much less powerful in the drug business, taking on selling rather than administration of the business. Sex work therefore became the best way for women to generate income and sustain their drug usage needs.[27]

SEX WORK

Your textbook likely has a section on *prostitution* within the chapter on public order crimes. In this book I instead use the term *sex work*, which rejects the immorality and illegitimacy inferred by such words as *prostitute*. The term was first coined by Carol Leigh, also known as the Scarlet Harlot, who founded the Sex Worker Film and Arts Festival and was the co-founder of BAYSWAN (Bay Area Sex Worker Advocacy Network).[28] The term refers to "a consensual exchange of sexual services for money or other nonmonetary goods such as housing, transportation, food, medicine, or other survival needs," which can cover a wide range of people and needs and which forefronts the *work* inherent in these services and the agency of the people involved in that work. Kimberly Fuentes presents it very clearly: "The broad umbrella of sex work covers full service sex workers, BDSM providers, fetish models, sugar babies, escorts, strippers, porn actors, sex phone operators, and web cam models. Sex work can span a varying level of physical contact with clients, with some workers producing entirely online content and never meeting clients in person. Sex workers may choose to identify as their specific facet of work (i.e., stripper), under the umbrella term of 'sex worker,' or a multitude of other labels such as, 'prostitute,' among other terms."[29]

There is a wide variety of types of sex work, from street work, where clients are solicited in public places, to CB radio work, where workers find truck-driver clients using CB radios, to escorts, where clients contact sex workers by phone or via hotel staff, with widely varying risks depending on, for example, who is in control, whether there is social support for the sex worker, and whether there is penetrative and protected sex.[30] The fact that there is such a wide variety of types of work reflects that there is also a wide variety of characteristics of sex workers, who must in turn be understood within the context of their distinctions and complexities.

The Whorearchy

The Whorearchy is a stratification of types of sex workers, created and maintained by the sex workers themselves, that creates a hierarchy of types of sex work. Fuentes used participatory action research to show that the whorearchy is maintained by whorephobia and criminalization, which turn sex workers against one another. She concludes, "In the fight for justice-seeking, sex workers, practitioners, and researchers alike need to dismantle the power relations that fortify the whorearchy, starting with criminalization. By fully understanding sex workers at all their intersections we can continue the fight for collective liberation."[31]

So then what do we know about this wide range of people who engage in sex work? While it is tempting to put forth an overall portrait or to use arrest data, either would be misleading and would signal universal responses that might be useless or even harmful for diverse populations. A theme you have been learning throughout this book is that the challenges and needs of marginalized members of a community are different from those who are centralized; sex work is no different. The challenges and needs of Black and Brown, poor, and trans or queer sex workers, for example, are different from those who are not poor, who are white, and who are cishet, so, as tempting as it is to come up with one portrait and one approach, it would be counter-productive.[32] For example, we know that female sex workers are disproportionately affected by HIV.[33] We also know that gendered assumptions about sex work even in research mean that we know very little, comparatively, about the significant number of boys and men in sex work and almost nothing about transmen and other gender non-confirming people in sex work, even though almost a third of transgender sex workers identify as non-binary, and almost a fifth are trans men.[34]

Sex Trafficking and Sex Work Are Very Different

Carceral feminism is the belief that the solution to gendered and sexual violence lies in the policing, prosecution, and incarceration of the criminal legal system. The term "carceral feminism" emerges in several different forums, but it was first used by feminist sociologist Elizabeth Bernstein in 2007 within the context of feminist debates about sex work.[35] Specifically, in the 1990s Bernstein writes, an unlikely pairing of Evangelical Christians and anti-trafficking feminists joined together under the common mantle of stopping "modern day slavery," which includes both (involuntary) sex trafficking and (voluntary) sex work and uses aggressive policing to work toward the abolition of both.[36]

The other side of this argument is abolitionist feminism, which holds that the criminal legal system is a large part of and emblematic of the real problems that lead to involuntary sexual labor and the inequities inherent in voluntary sex work. According to abolitionist feminists, if we leave voluntary sex workers alone, we can focus our attention and resources more narrowly on people being trafficked. Whereas sex work is "a consensual exchange of sexual services for money or other nonmonetary goods such as housing, transportation, food, medicine, or other survival needs," sex trafficking is involuntary.[37]

Specifically, in defining sex trafficking, "it is useful to consider the different scenarios that fall under the umbrella term of trafficking. One can think of these as typologies falling along axes of movement (domestic vs. international), type of labor (sexual vs. nonsexual), and age (minor vs. legal adult). Overlaying these axes, then one must also consider the presence or absence of consent. Such a typology is but a first step in thinking about the different scenarios various authors have categorized as trafficking."

1. Underage prostitution (assumed to be involuntary by most legal frameworks)
2. Underage nonsexual labor (assumed to be involuntary by most legal frameworks)
3. Adult sexual labor assumed involuntary without clear evidence of force
4. Adult sexual labor with evidence of force, coercion, or deceit
5. Adult nonsexual labor with evidence of force, coercion, or deceit[38]

Victims of human trafficking often come from very vulnerable populations because they are desperate for resources that the trafficker can easily provide. Climate change, displacement, and poverty are a few examples of factors that exacerbate the vulnerabilities and desperation that enable victims to fall prey to traffickers. Therefore, it is not uncommon for migrants to be targets, especially in places with restrictive migrant policies as well as societal xenophobic sentiments. Women, especially migrant women, are among the most vulnerable because they are the most affected by the factors previously mentioned. Gender discrimination in wages as well as the lack of job opportunities could pressure women to look toward employers or traffickers who put them in situations through coercion or deception, from where they cannot freely escape. Additionally, migrant women with lower levels of education, undocumented immigrant status, and lack of knowledge on U.S. employment protections are also easy targets for recruiters. Additionally, these women usually must work jobs that are unregulated by the government because of their circumstances, which may already be dangerous situations where they can be trafficked by their employer.

The Criminalization—and Decriminalization—of Sex Work

One of the main themes of any discussion of sex work is whether it should be legal. In almost all the United States, sex work, known by the law as prostitution, is criminalized. The criminalization of sex work is often based on the assumption that it will deter people from soliciting sex, though the research has consistently shown that the opposite is true.[39] Criminalization makes sex workers less safe by driving transactions underground, which makes it riskier to negotiate terms with clients, and by specifically criminalizing working in the same space as other sex workers and carrying condoms. These circumstances mean that sex workers, already disproportionately harmed and harassed, are victimized *even more frequently* but also that they are particularly unlikely to report that victimization to the police.[40]

Websites like Backpage and Craigslist that were favored by sex workers to avoid coercion by pimps were targeted by NGOs and bills to protect sex workers for the same reason. These websites gave workers the ability to work for themselves without the fear of coercion (albeit illegally) and sometimes was their only source of income. The closure of these websites due to the Allow States and Victims to Fight Online Sex Trafficking Act (FOSTA) and Stop Enabling Sex Traffickers Act (SESTA) in 2018 led to *less* safety for sex workers, who could no longer advertise their own services; many were forced to go back to using pimps for clients and protection.

LEGAL CHOICES FOR SEX WORK OTHER THAN CRIMINALIZATION

- In the **Swedish model**, an "end demand" approach criminalizes the *buying* of sex work and not sex work itself. The result has been that sex workers have to make riskier choices to protect their clients.
- **Legalization** means that sex work is state controlled (e.g., Nevada), requiring registration and forced health checks. It is often called "back door criminalization."
- **Decriminalization** makes sex work a job like any other. It is overwhelmingly preferred by sex workers because it would reduce police violence against them, would make them less vulnerable to violence from clients, would allow them to protect their own health, would advance equality for the LGBTQIA+ community, and would reduce mass incarceration and racial disparities in the criminal justice system.

Decriminalization of sex work provides sex workers with autonomy and portrays them as workers in need of rights, not victims or criminals. Additionally, outside the general stigma of sex work exists another kind of stigma: the taboo surrounding male sex workers. Often male sex workers are purposely excluded from conversations about sex work because they do not fit the narrative that sex workers are victims in need of rescue from prostitution. (This stems from the radical feminist idea that sex work is embedded in a patriarchal system that is driven by female exploitation.) Male sex workers also must deal with perceived homosexuality. While homosexuality is not inherently negative, it is difficult for homosexuality to be perceived positively in a context of institutionalized discrimination against men who have sex with other men. Ingrained assumptions and ideas of masculinity and femininity can also initiate violence against male sex workers. Ironically, the criminalization of sex workers means that former sex workers have trouble finding employment after exiting sex work. Indeed, during the pandemic many people turned to sex work to make money, and, when the economy reopened, many of those people had trouble as they tried to return to traditional jobs.

PUBLIC ATTITUDES ARE CHANGING, BUT THE LAWS ARE GOING IN THE OPPOSITE DIRECTION

Much as attitudes about the criminalization of drug use have shifted away from "lock 'em up" to support for legalization and decriminalization, attitudes toward sex work have also liberalized. Americans are now more likely to support the legalization or decriminalization of sex work, and states from Maine to California have had bills or legislative task forces on the topic of decriminalization. All the while, and as a backlash to such liberalization, an influential moral crusade has been growing to lobby for enhanced criminalization of sexual services and performances.[41]

Sex Workers Keeping One Another Safe

In Montreal, Canada, a peer-led sex worker organization named Stella, l'amie de Maimie has created a "Bad Client and Aggressor List." This list is made up of reports from sex workers who experienced violence on the job. The list is shared in the monthly bulletin created by and for sex workers in Montreal, and the organization is investigating ways to make it more digital. In this way it serves both as a warning system and to promote solidarity. This list is part of a tradition as old as sex work itself, leading to increased safety and reporting of victimization, which provides an opportunity for sex workers to create alternative forms of reporting violence without having to report it to police, who so often reject sex workers' victimization and do not account for their realities. This practice has many positive impacts, including increasing power and solidarity among sex workers and increasing the public's understanding of sex work and the lived experiences of sex workers.[42]

Working toward Liberation

Most important in the consideration of sex work is that sex workers are humans who deserve life, safety, and joy just as we all do. There are a number of ways in which sex workers are working toward liberation, from the United Kingdom's International Union of Sex Workers to mutual aid, which is "a practice of community helping with roots in anarchist thought and working-class communities, which aims to transgress the hierarchies of established charities and erase distinctions between helpers and helped to prefigure a more equal and stateless society."[43] In this case sex workers can take care of one another when it comes to everything from risks such as poverty, violence, and STDs to access to information, from solidarity to reducing stigma and shame.[44]

CONCLUSION

Our criminal legal system would be far more effective if it focused less on issues that should be managed by other systems, such as public health, or that do not need management at all, such as sex work. If we were to reduce the responsibilities of the criminal legal system, whose mission has risen exponentially in the past hundred years in the United States, what might we be able to accomplish more humanely and more effectively?

PART III "The Master's Tools"
THE CRIMINAL JUSTICE SYSTEM

Now that you have learned about the way we measure and theorize crime and victimization, it is time to look at what we as a society have tried to do to ameliorate these harms. As Black lesbian feminist Audre Lorde taught us, "For the master's tools will never dismantle the master's house. They may allow us temporarily to beat him at his own game, but they will never enable us to bring about genuine change."[1] As you read about our current systems and the options to reform or abolish them, think of Audre Lorde's challenge not to live in fear of the master but to stand up and act boldly in pursuit of that true, liberating change.

In these final two chapters, you should be working under the understanding that, in general, reformers believe that the criminal legal system is broken and that reforms are essential to achieve justice. Abolitionists, on the other hand, generally believe that the system is not broken but is, rather, working exactly as designed: to extend white supremacist patriarchal control with the use of the criminal legal system as an extension of slavery and Jim Crow. These two perspectives are usually presented as an either/or choice. However, most activists recognize that the process of abolition must be a parallel process with reform.

As we work toward dismantling the system rooted in white supremacy and capitalist hetero-patriarchy, there are still human beings in cages. Worth Rises, for example, is an organization that targets the profit centers of the prison industrial complex. Their campaigns have included targeting the pharmaceutical company Absolute Standards for profiteering off the death penalty by supplying the drug pentobarbital for executions. In 2020 the company stopped the manufacturing and sale of pentobarbital and has pledged to no longer supply lethal injection drugs.[2] Another example comes from the collaboration between the national Expanding First Response Commission and the Council of State Governments Justice Center to offer a set of recommendations to reduce reliance on police by growing their crisis response teams.[3] The previous twelve chapters have prepared you to follow criminological understandings of who makes the laws, who breaks the laws, and our ideas of why both of those things happen. You now have the opportunity to explore the ways that our system responds and the ways that people from different perspectives are working to respond.

13 Reforming Police, Courts, and Corrections

When John Laub began his tenure as the director of the National Institute of Justice in 2010, he unveiled a focus on what he called *translational criminology*, which takes academic research and theory and translates it into language that can be understood and applied to criminal justice system practitioners on the job every day. In this chapter you will see that criminology has, in fact, been translational all along, but for a system designed to benefit the powerful at the expense of the very lives of the less powerful. By focusing on men's crimes and on the crimes of poor and Black and Brown people and by institutionalizing gender discrimination in virtually all aspects of the criminal legal system, our system has then focused on punishment, rather than on, for example, the ways in which women in particular avoid criminal behavior; the crimes of powerful, wealthy white people; and the potential for a restorative, communicative system. In this chapter you will learn about the ways in which such a system has gone terribly wrong for almost everyone—victims, "offenders," families, taxpayers, cops, attorneys, judges, and correctional officers—and how people have created reform efforts that they believe will fix these problems.

POLICING

Traditional histories of the first police departments begin with the creation of the London Metropolitan Police in 1829 with its fleet of "Bobbies," patrolling to keep order in their own working-class communities. These Bobbies were specifically civilians in a way that distinguished them from the paramilitary forces of, for example, France's Gendarmerie and Italy's Carabinieri. Departments in the United States soon followed, in New York City (1845), Albany and Chicago (1851), New Orleans and Cincinnati (1853), Philadelphia (1855), Newark and Baltimore (1857). By the 1880s all major U.S. cities had municipal police forces, formed in the face of immigration, urbanization, and increasing crime and disorder (which should remind you of social disorganization theory). These departments were formalized, with taxpayer support, bureaucratic systems, and full-time employees following fixed rules and procedures. They were accountable to a central governmental authority and moved forward, according to these traditional histories, with some reform hiccups, to the community policing focus of the 1990s. Critical perspectives, however, seek to contextualize this story with its erasure of the colonial history of the Bobbies and therefore of the U.S. police that grew from that tradition. These scholars look earlier, to when colonial policing began in India, with brutal tactics meant to maintain order coercively to expand capitalism and maintain British hegemony. The intertwining of empire, slavery, and genocide in the colonial and later independent United States and the connection to Britain meant that they all shaped U.S. policing.[1]

Traditionally, U.S. police historians have focused on northern cities in the mid-nineteenth century as the genesis of policing in the United States. However, there is growing recognition that cities in the U.S. South had

CRITICAL THINKING BREAK 21

You may notice that I do not use the term *law enforcement officer* but instead use words like *police* and *cops*. Now that we are toward the end of the book, why do you think this is?

patrols with the explicit goal of controlling slaves, rooted originally in colonial militias, which later became the police. In Charleston as early as the 1780s, for example, there was a military-style municipal police force focused on controlling slaves, and other cities soon followed.[2] Bryan Wagner's research outlines the rhetoric of proponents of armed police forces, who warned against "superhuman" fugitive slaves and, later, freed Black "savages" invading the cities, if not controlled.[3] Such roots make the current structure of policing (rather than actions of rogue officers), which protects private property and capital with the use of violence and widespread "misconduct" and corruption, far more understandable.

Marching On

Despite the intensification of protests from marginalized groups against police bias and killings since 2020, trends in policing continue toward militarization, which Peter Kraska explains, "is simply the process whereby civilian police increasingly draw from, and pattern themselves around, the tenets of militarism and the military model."[4] With the dust of 9/11 clouding people's minds, Jude McCulloch argues, governments around the world implemented or intensified draconian "safety measures" that never would have been allowed before. The fusion of the police and military action led to these shifts, as U.S. police moved away from significantly more protection of civil liberties afforded civilians and toward acting as a military-like coercive force. As power flows from nation-states to global corporations, she argues, the state is less willing to protect its most vulnerable citizens from capitalism, in a process by which people are moved from being seen as "at risk" and needing support to being seen as "the risk" to be controlled.[5] In the wake of the 1033 program, which allows police departments to obtain surplus equipment from the military, Kraska has shown that the U.S. police and the military are increasingly similar, with over $7 billion of equipment, such as armored vehicles and semi-automatic weapons, having been transferred to police departments since 1996.[6]

With this shift toward the paramilitary has come increasingly lethal weapons with training to "shoot until the target is eliminated," encouraged by the Blue Lives Matter movement, which was an explicit reaction to the 2014 murder of two New York City police officers that the founders blamed on the Black Lives Matter movement.[7] While the political debate focuses on Black Lives Matter versus Blue Lives Matter, the research shows that when police departments are militarized, not only does their use of deadly force increase but confidence in the police decreases, mental health and educational achievement suffer, deaths increase in minoritized communities, and, even with all that, the police's own safety also decreases.[8] But this militarization is not equally distributed: police departments in Black neighborhoods are more likely to acquire and use military equipment, and white U.S. support for police militarization is related to high levels of racial prejudice, which in turn is related to greater amounts of militarized equipment in those areas.[9] Jennifer Cobbina-Dungy and Delores Jones-Brown contend that "warrior style" policing, which is militarized and enforces unquestioned compliance to police authority, is complemented by "proactive" policing strategies that enforce racial dominance.[10] Both of these tiers means that all communities, but Black communities in particular, are over-policed and, as a result, are far less likely to trust the police than other communities.[11]

Say Her Name: Sandra Bland

Sandra Bland was arrested for a traffic violation. Three days later she was dead in a Texas jail, allegedly by suicide. In 2014 the Say Her Name campaign was launched by the African American Policy Forum (with the executive director, Kimberlé Crenshaw, the originator of the concept of intersectionality) and the Columbia Law School Center for Intersectionality and Social Policy Studies to amplify the stories of Black women to refer to the way anti-Black and misogynistic societal attitudes affect Black women specifically. Examples include Black girls often being viewed as more mature and sexually advanced than girls of other races, which causes people to dismiss allegations involving sexual abuse of Black girls, the oversexualization of Black women, and the "angry Black woman" stereotype preventing Black women from being assertive and speaking up for themselves. The accompanying report, "Say Her Name: Resisting Police Brutality against Black Women," shines intersectional light on the distinct experiences and stories of the many Black women profiled, killed, and brutalized by police.[12] As Andrea Ritchie reminds us,

Many people know of Eric Garner, but not Rosann Miller, a seven-month pregnant Black woman put in a chokehold by an NYPD officer just weeks after Eric Garner was killed. Like Garner, who was being harassed by police for allegedly selling loose cigarettes, Miller was being harassed by officers engaged in "broken windows" policing, which posits that targeted enforcement of small offenses is the way to prevent violent crime. In Miller's case, the interaction started when police threatened to ticket her and her husband for grilling outside their own home. Not only does Miller's experience illuminate the broader impacts of the policing practices that killed Eric Garner, it also points us toward the need for focused attention to police use of force against pregnant women.[13]

Cynthia Lum and Daniel Nagin argue that police reform should be driven by two principles: *the primary metric for judging police effectiveness should be crimes prevented rather than arrests made* and, *beyond police effectiveness, citizens' views about the police and their tactics matter*.[14] Your textbook probably covers external commissions such as the Wikersham and Knapp Commissions, cases such as *Mapp v. Ohio* (1961) and *Miranda v. Arizona* (1966), and perhaps the 1994 Crime Bill.

Eight Can't Wait

In 2015, activists launched Campaign Zero, a data-driven movement aimed at ending police brutality. After the murder of George Floyd in Minneapolis in 2020, Campaign Zero launched Eight Can't Wait (#8CantWait), a campaign that advocates for police reforms. Their demands are based on classic research, such as that from James Fyfe, which concludes that more restrictive use of force standards reduces police violence in the form of civilian killings and injuries by police.[15] Eight Can't Wait advocates for the implementation of eight policies in police departments that data have shown reduce police killings: banning chokeholds and strangleholds, requiring de-escalation, requiring warning before shooting, requiring officers to exhaust all other means before shooting, banning shooting at moving vehicles, requiring the use of force continuum, requiring comprehensive reporting, and requiring a duty to intervene. The campaign tracks where these policies are implemented or fail to pass. Likewise, the Black Lives Movement made a list of its seven demands. Demands 3, 5, and 7 focus on the criminal legal system:

> **3. Launch a full investigation into the ties between white supremacy and the Capitol Police, law enforcement, and the military:** The Capitol was able to be breached and overrun by white supremacists attempting to disrupt a political process that is fundamental to our democracy. We know that police departments have been a safe haven for white supremacists to hide malintent behind a badge, because the badge was created for that purpose. We also know off-duty cops and military were among the mob at the Capitol on January 6th. Guilty parties need to be held accountable and fired. We are supporting Rep. Jamaal Bowman's COUP Act to investigate these connections.
>
> **5. Defund the police:** The police that met our BLM protestors this summer with assault rifles, teargas, and military-grade protective gear were the same police that, on Wednesday, met white supremacists with patience and the benefit of the doubt, going so far as to pose for selfies with rioters. The contrast was jarring, but not for Black people. We have always known who the police truly protect and serve. D.C. has the most police per capita in the country; more funding is not the solution.
>
> **7. Pass the BREATHE Act:** The police were born out of slave patrols. We cannot reform an institution built upon white supremacy. We need a new, radical approach to public safety and community investment. President Biden has already drawn on the BREATHE Act in his executive actions calling for racial equity screens in federal programs, investing in environmental justice at historic levels, and engaging with system-impacted communities. The BREATHE Act paints a vision of a world where Black lives matter through investments in housing, education, health, and environmental justice.[16]

One of the mainstream reforms that has passed as high as the U.S. Congress is the Justice in Policing Act of 2020, which, advocates believe, is the first comprehensive attempt to address systemic racism within policing. It passed the House of Representatives but not the Senate, and a reform bill fell apart in 2021. Among other things, the act establishes new reporting requirements for police misconduct, limits qualified immunity as a defense for police in court, lowers the criminal intent standard to convict a law enforcement officer for misconduct, prohibits discriminatory profiling, and limits the amount of force allowed to be used during arrests and investigations.

The Black Lives Matter movement and its related demands resulted in a backlash from police unions, fomented a moral panic about a war on cops, and gave rise to a Blue Lives Matter bill enhancing penalties for violence against police officers, and accompanied a growing white nationalism movement. Both BLM and Eight Can't Wait and its leaders, particularly DeRay Mckesson and Brittany Packnett, have been criticized from the Left for having a "plantation mentality" and for lacking an understanding of the relationship between police and state violence and activism.[17] There are other creative ways to improve policing and its outcomes, especially for minoritized communities. These include Crisis Intervention Teams, which are local community programs made up of law enforcement, mental health professionals, individuals who live with mental illnesses and addiction disorders, and advocates to help people access treatment rather than place them in the criminal justice system. These teams claim to reduce the stigma around mental illnesses and addiction disorders and allow for safer interactions between police officers and individuals with mental illnesses.

Reviews of the research show that, while Crisis Intervention Teams may improve referrals to services, transport, and linkage to care compared to standard policing, they have not been shown to avert arrests, impact the use of force, or resolve crisis calls on scene. Reviews also show that police officers should not be involved in mental health crisis intervention.[18] You will learn more in the last chapter of this book about social work activists, such as Kassandra Frederique, who fight against the use of social workers to accompany police officers to mental health crisis, intimate partner violence, and sexual assault calls. She and other advocates work instead for abolitionist and liberatory social work, which builds practice and guidance for responding to harm outside of state measures, which so often polices and punishes families instead of encouraging their dignity and integrity.[19]

Another alternative is proactive policing, which encompasses community-based methods and strategies to prevent crime before it occurs. This differs from reactive policing, which refers to police response after a crime has occurred. Other ideas, such as reforming qualified immunity, which protects state and local officials (including police officers) from individual liability for their misconduct; creating homeless-outreach

> **CRITICAL THINKING BREAK 22**
>
> What if calling 911 didn't end up in sending only police officers but could, for example, send mental health professionals to crisis situations or traffic experts to accidents? What might be the impact of such changes? What other responsibilities could we take away from armed officers?

teams, reimagining 911, implementing body cams, and problem-oriented policing have been presented by reformers as creative ways to improve policing and policing outcomes, especially for minoritized communities.

The Second Rape

One of the ways in which policing has been damaging when it comes to gender is in responses to sexual violence. Police response to sexual assault is so commonly damaging to victims that it has its own name: the *second rape*. This concept refers to insensitive attitudes and actions of individuals and institutions within the criminal justice system that re-traumatize victims of rape. Police, in particular, may commit the second rape when asking victims questions that imply that the victims themselves contributed to the rape, such as about their use of drugs or their attire. When providers disregard victims' needs and boundaries, the experience can so closely mimic the rape that victims are often left feeling violated yet again. Many police officers themselves are critical of the current methods of responding to sexual violence, seeing the system as archaic and re-traumatizing.[20] There are many ways in which police reformers have suggested improving police responses to sexual violence, such as training police officers in trauma-informed approaches.

Karen Rich's research on trauma-informed responses to rape victims covers the ways in which the demeanors and training at all levels of police response—from patrol officers to detectives to dispatchers—impact victims' comfort level and in turn their motivation to proceed with the case. One of the biggest challenges is a lack of training on victim interviewing, so police officers often use the same techniques they use for people suspected of crimes with victims, including intimidation, confrontation, and lie detection, which inhibit victim comfort and even their recall of events. Trauma-informed approaches to sexual assault include a wide variety of techniques, such as "removing potential triggers in the environment, granting control, choice and agency to clients, demystifying the process, adapting to individual client needs, educating employees on how trauma affects clients, providing 'time out' options for clients, respecting clients' privacy and dignity, and supervising staff to address vicarious trauma."[21] However, no training will be effective if police hierarchies and culture do not change to see victim-centered practices and collaboration as important, effective, and legitimate police practices.

Cops Are Even in Schools

School resource officers (SROs) have become a popular way for schools to outsource difficult situations from teachers and school staff to a police officer specifically focused on safety and crime prevention in schools. While SROs are often seen as acting more as mentors, research shows that they contribute mightily to the school-to-prison pipeline.[22] Denise Gottfredson and colleagues compared schools with and without increased SRO staffing and showed that, over time, increasing SROs increased the number of drug- and weapon-related offenses and exclusionary disciplinary actions that have terrible outcomes for our children. These results in turn increased the criminalization of school discipline, which means that our children get harsh penalties that develop into lawbreaking, poverty, school absence, mental health struggles, and much more. Specifically, when SROs are present, students are more likely to be arrested and referred to the criminal justice system and encounter responses to minor offenses that would otherwise be handled by school administrators.[23]

While some might say that this means that SROs are working, the research shows that these increases persist for at least two years. If SROs were working, there would be an initial spike and then a reduction in such arrests and an increase in safety. This does not happen—recorded offenses get dramatically higher and then stay that way. Districts have started to realize that SROs are not helping our children or our schools but are merely creators and shepherds of the school-to-prison pipeline. One of the problems is that many districts do not have formal agreements about the roles of SROs, which in turn adds to the potential for conflict and confusion. Specifically, there is often a lack of clear boundaries around what types of discipline matters should be handled by police officers or by school personnel. Many states and districts have also instituted reforms to soften their discipline practices, given concerns about increasing use of harsh responses to student behavior that result in exclusion of students from school, reduced exposure to learning, and increased involvement with the criminal justice system both immediately and over time. There are also important questions about the potential for role conflict when police officers engage in dual roles as counselor, teacher, and law enforcer. As you might suspect, these bad impacts are particularly likely for Black and Brown children, whose behaviors are more likely to be criminalized rather than met with help. Research specifically on children with disabilities has found that the combination of the under-resourced special education program and increased security and police personnel in the school resulted in high levels of suspension and expulsion of special needs students.

Instead of spending money on SROs, educational decision-makers wishing to enhance school safety would be wise to consider the many alternatives to programs that require regular police presence in schools. There are many school-based strategies that have been proven to enhance school safety, often with a public health approach rather than a criminalization approach. For example, some of these options increase safety by promoting a more cohesive school environment in which expectations for behavior are clear, and sanctions are consistently applied in response to rule breaking that do not actively harm our children as SROs do.

COURTS

Police officers are only one point of contact between civilians and the criminal legal system. Courts are not as much of a focus of reform efforts, but their racist, misogynist, anti-queer, and ableist impacts have similarly dramatic impacts on marginalized communities. Being released from pre-trial detention, for example, most often requires a money bond, which means that poor people (overwhelmingly Black and Brown people) are more likely to stay in pre-trial detention than their wealthier (and whiter) counterparts. (Bail is the amount of money a judge decides someone must pay to be released. If someone cannot pay it, a small percentage—a bond—can be paid by a bail bond company on the person's behalf, with a promise to pay the rest if the person disappears.) People who stay in pre-trial detention, in turn, are more likely to be denied bond at all, to have a higher bond set, to be convicted, to accept less favorable plea deals, to be sentenced to prison, and to receive longer sentences.[24] Once people are sentenced, the discrimination continues: according to data from the U.S. Sentencing Commission, Black men are significantly more likely to be given harsher prison sentences (20.4 percent longer than white men) than white men who commit the same crimes.[25] Prosecutors are also more likely to charge Black and Brown people with crimes that have longer sentences, and public defenders are plagued with excessively high caseloads, so even the highest quality public defender offices are too overwhelmed to be effective for their indigent clients.[26]

In the United States, bail is often used to ensure that people will return to court by requiring them to deposit money or property to the court in return for releasing them from detention before their trial. If they do not return to court, they forfeit their bail; if they do return to court, their bail is returned to them. Because most people who come into contact with the criminal legal system are poor, they either go into debt to be released, before being convicted of any crime, or they sit in jail, sometimes for very long times: in a study by the Vera Institute of Justice, over half of the people could not afford bail of $2,500 or less until their cases were disposed.[27] Bail bonds businesses, are very profitable in the United States because they use predatory interest rates when people are desperate to be released. Bail funds are organizations that collect donations to post bail money for

CRITICAL THINKING BREAK 23

Listen to your local radio stations. Which stations play bail bond commercials, and which ones don't? Why do you think this happens?

people who are in jail or in pre-trial detention but who cannot afford to post their bail. This allows people to avoid the trauma of detention, gives them the possibility of keeping their jobs and housing, and ensures that they can remain in the community, with their loved ones, while they are still not convicted of anything.

The Sentencing Project, an organization that "advocates for effective and human responses to crime that minimize imprisonment and criminalization of youth and adults by promoting racial, ethnic, economic, and gender justice," offers five recommendations for the court systems to move away from extreme sentencing:

1. Implement community safety solutions—Community-based interventions such as violence interruption programs and changes to the built environment are a promising approach to decreasing violence without incarceration.
2. Transform crisis response—Shifting responses to people in crisis away from police toward trained community-based responders has the potential to reduce police shootings, improve safety, and decrease incarceration.
3. Reduce unnecessary justice involvement—Ending unnecessary police contact and court involvement by decriminalizing and diverting many offenses can improve safety.
4. End the drug war—Shifting away from criminalizing people who use drugs toward public health solutions can improve public health and safety.
5. Strengthen opportunities for youth—Interventions like summer employment opportunities and training youth in effective decision-making skills are a promising means of reducing criminal legal involvement.[28]

They went on in a second report to recommend seven legislative reforms that would cap sentences at twenty years and "right size the sentencing structure":

1. Abolish death and life without parole (LWOP) sentences, limiting maximum sentences to 20 years.
2. Limit murder statutes to intentional killings, excluding offenses such as felony murder, which is when, during the commission of a felony, another person is killed or dies, and reduce homicide penalties.

3. Eliminate mandatory minimum sentences and reform sentencing guidelines to ensure that judges can use their discretion to consider mitigating circumstances.
4. Provide universal access to parole and ensure timely review.
5. Eliminate consecutive sentences and limit sentence enhancements, including repealing "truth-in-sentencing" and "habitual offender" laws.
6. Create an opportunity for judicial "second look" resentencing within a maximum of 10 years of imprisonment, regardless of an individual's offense.
7. Shift all sentences downward, including by de-felonizing many offenses and decriminalizing many misdemeanors.[29]

Alternative Courts

Alternative (also known as experimental) courts are another way that reformers have been working for decades to improve the court system and its outcomes, particularly for people struggling with their mental health and addictive behaviors. The mass de-institutionalization of people with mental illnesses in the 1960s and 1970s, changes in civil commitment statutes that make involuntary placement in psychiatric hospitals more difficult, and policing strategies such as broken windows have meant dramatic increases in the number of people with mental illness in the court system. Alternative courts such as drug courts, mental health courts, and juvenile courts have become entrenched alternative courts that focus on problem solving rather than on punishment. Generally, research has found them to be more effective than their traditional counterparts. For example, mental health court participants have significantly lower recidivism rates than their counterparts in the traditional court system.[30] The first Veterans Treatment Court was established in Buffalo, New York, in January 2008.[31] Veterans Treatment Courts were influenced by these precursor experimental courts to oversee cases involving military veterans and active-duty service members, offering court-supervised treatment rather than incarceration, often in exchange for a reduction or dismissal of charges. One of their key successful components is the use of mentors, also military veterans, who build a relationship based on respect, trust, and understanding and in turn increase their mentees' quality of life and physical and mental health.[32]

CRITICAL THINKING BREAK 24

What theories do you see reflected in alternative courts such as Veterans Treatment Courts, drug courts, and mental health courts?

But the problems with U.S. courts are not just settled in local courts—as with most other things, the structural problems start at the top. A variety of researchers have found that female lawyers are significantly more likely to be interrupted, and for longer times, than their male counterparts and most often by male judges on the U.S. Supreme Court.[33] Lawyers have also been found to be more successful in their arguments before the court if they adhere to gender norms during their oral arguments.[34] Specifically, "women's speech" is more indirect and hyper-polite, whereas men are more assertive and lack hyper-politeness, and Tonja Jacobi and Dylan Schweers found that even the female justices were cut off more often and experienced "mansplaining" far more than their male counterparts.[35]

CORRECTIONS

One of the reasons why the U.S. criminal legal system became the largest in the world is because of the so-called War on Drugs. One of the most important moments, to my mind, of our collective reflection on this "war" is from Dan Baum's interview with John Ehrlichman, former White House counsel and assistant to the president for domestic affairs under President Richard Nixon:

> At the time [1994], I was writing a book about the politics of drug prohibition. I started to ask Ehrlichman a series of earnest, wonky questions that he impatiently waved away. "You want to know what this was really all about?" he asked with the bluntness of a man who, after public disgrace and a stretch in federal prison, had little left to protect. "The Nixon campaign in 1968, and the Nixon White House after that, had two enemies: the antiwar left and black people. You understand what I'm saying? We knew we couldn't

make it illegal to be either against the war or black, but by getting the public to associate the hippies with marijuana and blacks with heroin, and then criminalizing both heavily, we could disrupt those communities. We could arrest their leaders, raid their homes, break up their meetings, and vilify them night after night on the evening news. Did we know we were lying about the drugs? Of course we did." I must have looked shocked. Ehrlichman just shrugged. Then he looked at his watch, handed me a signed copy of his steamy spy novel, *The Company*, and led me to the door.[36]

The War on Drugs Filled Our Prisons

First declared by Richard Nixon, this so-called war was generally made up of three types of laws:

- **Repeat offender statutes:** These laws significantly increase sentences when a person with a previous violent or serious felony is convicted for another felony. The most famous of these is California's Three Strikes and You're Out law, under which Jerry Dewayne Williams was sentenced to twenty-five years to life for stealing a slice of pepperoni pizza from a group of children in 1995. While this normally would have been a misdemeanor, Williams's prior convictions led to the charge being increased to a felony.

- **Truth-in-sentencing statutes:** These laws were created to reduce the disparity between sentences and the amount of time that people actually serve by eliminating the possibility of early release from incarceration on parole or for "good time." These laws are often associated with the Truth-in-Sentencing Incentive Grants Program in the 1994 Crime Act passed by President Bill Clinton and the Violent Crime Control and Law Enforcement Act of 1994, which incentivized expansion of the criminal legal system and focused on punishment rather than rehabilitation. The 1994 Crime Act is considered to be one of the drivers of America's mass incarceration, by rewarding states that built or expanded prisons with federal grants.

- **Mandatory minimum statutes:** These laws ensured that a person convicted of a particular crime must serve a uniform minimum sentence. Mandatory minimum laws are not up for interpretation and do not change based on the circumstances of the crime, such as if the person was coerced into committing the crime, or if the person has no history of criminal legal system involvement.

> **CRITICAL THINKING BREAK 25**
>
> How do repeat offender, truth in sentencing, and mandatory minimum laws remind you of neo-classical theories from earlier in the book? How does this impact your thinking about such theories?

The stated goal of these laws was to use harsh punishment to deter people from committing crimes, but, despite the ratcheting up of penalties for drug crimes, these laws did anything but deter. Between 1974 and 2014, the U.S. state and federal prison population grew from 218,466 people to 1,508,636 (almost 600 percent).[37] The impacts of this tsunami of Black and Brown people into cages have crashed on America's shores for decades: separation from family, interruptions in education and employment, unhealthy and meager food, abuse, assault and rape, disrupted sleep—the list of terrible impacts of prison is quite long and have not resulted in the "intended" deterrence. The impacts extend far beyond prison walls, however, as relatives on the outside, mostly women, take on a support role as a "primary occupation," with myriad responsibilities, such as providing money for commissary, coordination of legal services and criminal legal system compliance, solo parenting, and visiting their loved one, with dramatic impacts on their mental and physical health and financial situation.[38]

The Difference between Prisons and Jails Is Important

Prisons are state or federal facilities caging people who have been convicted, usually of felonies, and are serving sentences longer than a year (and often far longer). Jails are run at the city or county level, and most people have not been convicted but are waiting for trial, many because they can't afford bail. The rest of the people behind jail bars are there after a conviction for a (generally misdemeanor) crime that has a sentence of less than a year. Even though they are all behind bars, people living in jails have very different needs than those in prisons due to the shorter-term nature of jail stays. Jail stays are considered to be far more punitive than prison stays.[39]

One way that state and local governments have worked to save taxpayer money is to contract with private companies to run prisons. These short-term cost savings have turned out to be due to poor staffing, lower staff pay, and fewer trainings for staff, which in turn has led to a higher prevalence of violence and injury to both staff and to people imprisoned there, more overcrowding, and more staff turnover.[40] But the narrative that private prisons are a huge part of the problem with the U.S. prison system is a myth: only 7 percent of all people behind bars are in privately run facilities. As the Prison Policy Institute puts it, "Private prisons are essentially a parasite on the massive publicly owned system—not the root of it."[41]

But these cost savings were also a "business opportunity" in that their profitability to corporations has been so high that their lobbyists, including from GEO Group, Core Civic (formerly Corrections Corporation of America), LaSalle Corrections, and Management and Training Corporation have become powerful voices at all levels of government, with influences that are changing how "justice" is meted out.[42] This includes over $6 million given to politicians who espouse a "tough on crime" rhetoric that leads to higher incarceration rates.[43] The Corrections Corporation of America itself was founded during a forced special session of the state legislature of Tennessee and went on to become the world's largest private prison corporation.[44] And the cycle continues: multiple studies have found that the mere opening or existence of private prisons in a jurisdiction led to longer sentence lengths.[45] Despite the myriad problems with these facilities, according to the Sentencing Project, there were still 90,873 people incarcerated in private prisons in 2022, in twenty-seven states and by the federal government. While this is far higher than it was twenty years before, it is a decrease since the peak in 2012, when it was 137,220 people.[46] Such short-term cost savings, however, only increase costs long term, because the recidivism rates in private facilities are higher than those in public prisons.

The Death Penalty

The very clear relationship between race and the imposition of the death penalty in the United States has existed since its inception. When there were very few colonies and even fewer Black people in the seventeenth century, Black people were more likely to be executed than white people, mainly in New England. This inequity continued through the rise of slavery in the eighteenth century, particularly in the southern states. Not only were Black people more likely to be executed, but it was often for non-homicidal crimes and in more brutal ways, whereas white people were almost always executed for murder.[47] Centuries later, we know that Black and Brown people are far more likely to be prosecuted for capital murder, sentenced to the death penalty, and executed than white people. We also know that this is especially true when the victim was a white person.[48] Beyond being racially biased, the death penalty also does not work to make us safer. Murders are consistently lower in states that have abolished the death penalty, as are the number of police officers killed in the line of duty. As these facts become more widely known, public support for and use of the death penalty are declining: in 2023 only five states executed people, and only seven states imposed new death sentences. For the first time, polls reported that more than half of Americans believe the death penalty is administered unfairly. As of 2023, twenty-nine states have either abolished the death penalty or have used executive action to pause executions.[49]

Reforming Prisons

The overwhelming critical perspective on imprisonment is that the system has such devastating effects not because it is broken but because it is performing exactly as intended as a direct descendant of chattel slavery and Jim Crow laws. In her now classic *The New Jim Crow: Mass Incarceration in the Age of Colorblindness,* Michelle Alexander shows the ways in which mass incarceration has kept the "undercaste" of Black and Brown people under punitive control even after slavery and Jim Crow ended.[50]

Those who wish to reform this system have created several programs that either "divert" people from prison sentences served behind bars or reform the experience of incarceration with programs. Alternatives to incarceration (also known as intermediate sanctions) emerged in the 1980s and 1990s in many forms, from boot camps and ankle monitors to halfway houses and community programs. These programs have been shown to reduce recidivism, increase quality of life, and cost less than incarceration, but they are also significantly less likely to be recommended for Black defendants than white defendants.[51] Programs such as Puppies behind Bars and the Inside/Out college program provide dramatically more humanizing services to people during their incarceration and have also been shown to decrease infractions during incarceration and recidivism upon release.

CONCLUSION

The U.S. criminal legal system is failing almost everyone it touches, from victims to judges to incarcerated people to the community as a whole. In this chapter you have learned about just a few of the problems with the system and some of the responses that researchers and reformers are suggesting and implementing. In our last chapter, we review the work that imagines an entirely new approach to accountability for harm, restoration for victims, and an end to all forms of violence.

14 Abolition

So here we are in our last chapter of this book. Such a critical look at our entrenched criminological theories and criminal justice practices may have made you feel paralyzed. How have we been so wrong, with such disastrous consequences, for so long? Is there anything to be done? But all is not lost! There are many ways in which people are *acting* to change the system in a way that reduces harm. There *are* ways in which a critical, intersectional feminist perspective is the backbone of a living, breathing movement that can upend the criminal "justice" system as we know it. Law professor and activist Dean Spade, who has been working for decades to "build queer and trans liberation based on racial economic justice" and often focuses on prison abolition, reminds us to always seek liberation over reform. Part of his work involved the establishment of the Sylvia Rivera Law Project, which provides transgender and gender non-conforming people with free legal services.[1]

ABOLITION AND REFORM

I went to a conference on prisons in the 1990s hosted by the Barnard Center for Research on Women. One of the speakers referenced the concept of abolition but insisted on calling it simply "the A-word" because she was afraid to even say it for fear of retribution by authorities. Almost thirty years later, in the wake of the Black Lives Matter movement, *abolition* is a word that is now used quite commonly. When I began work on this book, I presented the reform chapter and this abolition chapter as a dichotomy. As we finish this journey together, and on the recommendations of my community of colleagues, I have softened the black and white to a gray. Those of us who work to increase the justice in our world understand that both can be true: the humans in our system need an improved existing system—those arrested and caged, victims and workers, and their families and communities—*and* we can work toward ending a system rooted in slavery, heteropatriarchy, ableism, and domination, imagining and creating a new system of justice, transformed harm, accountability, and restoration.[2]

Relatively simply, abolitionists agree that the criminal legal system is not, in fact, broken but rather working exactly the way it was designed: violently controlling and containing poor, Black, and Brown people to the benefit of private property and capital.[3] While many on both the Left and the Right dismiss abolition as a "fever-dream," the thinkers and advocates of the movement evidence the ways in which social change moves slowly, such as the slavery abolitionist and women's suffrage movements, and show the many pragmatic ways in which the movement has been practically chipping away at the system, from freeing individual prisoners to making it harder for corporations to profit off of phone calls from prison.[4] Finally, abolitionists remind us, when we worry about how we will be safe without police and prisons, that police and prisons do not make us safer. Rather, if they did, the United States would be the safest country in the world, given how many people we arrest, convict, and cage.[5]

Critical Resistance

The formation of Critical Resistance is one of the most important moments in the history of the prison abolition movement. In 1997, activists organized a conference of more than 3,500 people for three days, with almost two hundred panels and workshops with the following goal: "As part of the emerging international movement for penal abolition, we envision a society in which fundamental social problems are no longer 'solved' through the mass warehousing (and periodic torture) of human beings, the overwhelming majority of whom are poor, people of color, and nonviolent. The founders of Critical Resistance included such luminaries as Angela Davis, Ruth Gilmore, Julia Sudbury, and Rose Braz. Critical Resistance's mission is to build a national and international campaign to challenge the prison-industrial complex."[6]

In the ensuing years, Critical Resistance has engaged in a wide variety of activities to that end, such as filing a lawsuit aimed at stopping California from building a new $335 million, 5,160-bed maximum-security prison, with half of the beds devoted to juveniles. Planning began in 1999 for a Northeast Regional Conference that took place in March 2001 in New York City, where organizers worked to develop strategies and share skills so that local activists could be more effective in their fight against the prison industrial complex. Later that year Critical Resistance organized to become "a national organization structured through local chapters that would be connected under a shared mission and organizing principles, but that would operate largely autonomously." Since then the many organizations have had more conferences, anniversary celebrations, and support for local chapters of Critical Resistance.[7]

ABOLITION

The word *abolition* reminds us, as it is meant to, the abolition of slavery. In fact, while the Thirteenth Amendment eradicated the legal category of slavery with its ratification in 1865, it left a loophole: "except as punishment for crime." In reality, the amendment abolished only chattel slavery, where a person is considered the property of another. This exception means that incarcerated people can be used as free, forced labor. Prison abolitionists view their project today as simply an extension of the fight to abolish slavery—to "fulfill the promise of Reconstruction that never took place and provide the set of public goods of citizenship that Reconstruction was to have provided" such as quality health care, housing, and education, which are, after all, what make people safe.[8]

Explained best by Critical Resistance, an organization at both the root and trunk of today's abolitionist movement,

Prison Industrial Complex (PIC) abolition is a political vision with the goal of eliminating imprisonment, policing, and surveillance and creating lasting alternatives to punishment and imprisonment. Abolition isn't just about getting rid of buildings full of cages. It's also about undoing the society we live in because the PIC both feeds on and maintains oppression and inequalities through punishment, violence, and controls millions of people. Because the PIC is not an isolated system, abolition is a broad strategy. An abolitionist vision means that we must build models today that can represent how we want to live in the future. It means developing practical strategies for taking small steps that move us toward making our dreams real and that lead us all to believe that things really could be different. It means living this vision in our daily lives. Abolition is both a practical organizing tool and a long-term goal.[9]

Abolitionist Feminism

As you have seen throughout this book, the tough-on-crime movement is often made up of strange bedfellows: traditionally politically conservative groups joined with white feminists (so called "carceral feminists") looking to use the criminal legal system to convict and sentence people, overwhelmingly Black and Brown men, who have or who are suspected to have harmed women, with a particular focus on "ideal victims"—white, wealthy, abled, and straight. As Victoria Law puts it in her simply named essay "Against Carceral Feminism," "Carceral Feminism describes an approach that sees increased policing, prosecution, and imprisonment as the primary solution to violence against women. This stance does not acknowledge that police are often purveyors of violence and that prisons are always sites of violence. Carceral feminism ignores the ways in which race, class, gender identity, and immigration status leave certain women more vulnerable to violence and that greater criminalization often places these same women at risk of state violence."[10]

With a particularly intense focus on marginalized communities, abolitionist feminism, on the other hand, insists that prison, even when used to punish people who have harmed women, creates far more harm than it solves. Perhaps surprising, this includes the Violence against Women Act of 1994, which focused on addressing crimes against women using policing, surveillance, and incarceration. Abolitionist feminism works to find alternative strategies for both preventing and addressing harm that do not merely expand the harmful impact, particularly in already over-criminalized communities, but instead embody the world we *want* to live in, with strong communities focused on social justice responses to harm. As Reina Sultan so clearly says, "Abolition is feminism.... You can't have an abolitionist movement that isn't feminist."[11]

Follow the Money

One of the ways that abolitionists have worked to dismantle the criminal legal system while envisioning a better future is through money. The United States spends hundreds of billions of dollars on policing, convicting, and imprisoning people. In 2019 state and local governments spent $123 billion on police (4 percent of state and local direct general expenditures), $82 billion on corrections (3 percent), and $50 billion on courts (2 percent). In 2017 (the most recent date for which data are available), the federal government directly spent $30 billion on police, $7 billion on corrections, and $15 billion on courts. These numbers represent dramatic increases in costs, even though crime has gone down: from 1977 to 2019, in 2019 inflation-adjusted dollars, state and local government spending on police increased from $44 billion to $123 billion (179 percent) and corrections expenditures increased from $18 billion to $82 billion (347 percent). Data available for courts show that, from 1992 to 2018, in 2019 inflation-adjusted dollars, state and local government spending on courts increased from $30 billion to $50 billion (66 percent), again even though crime was not also increasing.

CRITICAL THINKING BREAK 26

Abolitionists ask what we could do with the billions of dollars spent on policing, convicting, and imprisoning people if we addressed harm and accountability differently. What would it look like to take funding from the police and prisons (defunding!) and shift public resources toward meeting basic human needs like housing, health care, and childcare? Be creative! What would you pay for with so much money?

Worth Rises is a non-profit organization dedicated to ending the prison industrial complex by starving out the profits for corporations, which are over $80 billion annually from everything from food service to transportation to construction. They have been particularly effective in fighting for phone calls from prisons and jails to be free, with ten bills passed in the past five years in various jurisdictions, starting with Connecticut, the first state to make prison phone calls free in 2022. Prison phone calls provide a huge profit for corporations such as Securus, paid for by the (usually female) family members in the community who know that connection to loved ones is so important to people both while they are inside and in their preparation for release to the community. This is part and parcel of the organization's purpose, which is to use public pressure to force divestment from the prison industrial complex. It becomes so difficult and expensive for governments and investors to secure the funds to build and run prisons that they give up the pursuit.

Another of Worth Rises' campaigns is End the Exception, which refers to the Thirteenth Amendment to the Constitution not completely ending slavery in 1865, for it still allows enslavement as punishment for a crime. Indeed, almost all people behind the walls work, though they are not making the wages made by civilians. There are five states—Alabama, Arkansas, Georgia, Florida, and Texas—that do not pay anything to incarcerated people who work in their facilities. In Texas, state law requires the Department of Criminal Justice to use their labor as much as possible without pay, and they can be punished for refusing to work. For those states that do pay the people caged in their prison facilities, an incarcerated person working a custodial job that pays $0.14 per hour makes as little as $221 for an entire year's worth of work. But if they were required to be paid at least the federal minimum wage, or $7.25 per hour, that custodian would make $11,484 per year, or fifty-two times more. People could instead be participating in other types of programs, such as education or training or re-entry planning, which would prepare them for re-entry without return, but that would not be profitable.

#8ToAbolition

Started by abolitionist activists such as Reina Sultan and Micah Herskind, #8toAbolition (which should remind you of the #8CantWait campaign from the last chapter) was formed in the wake of the Black Lives Matter protests and also in response to calls for reform of a system that Sultan and Herskind believe is fundamentally unfixable. It is not, after all, broken but rather working just as it was designed: to control and punish poor, Black, and Brown people and to maintain capital in the hands of the white supremacist, capitalist state. With abolition instead, #8toAbolition imagines a world where there is "safety for those harmed, changed behaviors for those who caused harm, and a transformation of the conditions that allowed the harm to occur." They are working to accomplish eight goals:

1. **Defund the police,** which includes reducing the power of police unions, slashing police budgets until they are at zero, and ending all police contracts with social services, care services, and government agencies providing care.
2. **Demilitarize communities,** which includes disarming police and private security and ending the use of militaristic policing of Black and Brown communities, such as broken windows and community policing. Whereas reformers believe these are ways to make policing kinder and gentler, abolitionists recognize reforms as ways to make surveillance, coercive control, punishment, and death palatable to the general public.
3. **Remove police from schools,** which means all connection between policing and schools, including removing metal detectors and ending zero-tolerance disciplinary policies, suspensions and expulsions, and truancy laws.
4. **Free people from prisons and jails,** which includes all involuntary confinement, with a particular focus on those who are disabled and those who are incarcerated for their survival strategies.
5. **Repeal laws that criminalize survival,** which focuses on not punishing people working the sex trades, drug trades, street economies, and anything else people need to do to survive homelessness and survive. This would also end all fines and fees, including ticketing, cash bail, court costs, and parole and probation fees.
6. **Invest in community self-governance,** which includes imagining ways in which harms can be addressed by the community, without police, by assessing community needs and investing in community-based resources, from tenant unions to local shop owners.

7. **Provide safe housing for everyone,** which includes repealing laws that bar people from public housing based on income, race, gender, sexuality, immigration status, or history of incarceration. Empty buildings, houses, apartments, and hotels can be repurposed to house people experiencing homelessness.
8. **Invest in care, not cops,** which prioritizes the funding of everything from public transit and teachers to health care infrastructure and community-based food banks, grocery cooperatives, gardens, and farms instead of spending that money on police and prisons.

TRANSFORMATIVE JUSTICE IS THE VISION

Transformative justice is an alternative to the current criminal legal system that instead aims to respond to violence with harm reduction to avoid creating more violence. Restorative justice is an approach that acknowledges harm and seeks to identify the needs and obligations of those impacted by that harm through empowerment and reconciliation. Unlike restorative justice, transformative justice does not overlap with the state at all, from police and prisons to courts and the child "protective" system. Rather, transformative justice is community-based and has a particular focus on building justice for already marginalized and often victimized people such as sex workers, undocumented immigrants, poor children of color, and queer people. Transformative justice addresses current violence but also zooms out to recognize the role of social structures and works to change those systems. As the Bay Area Transformative Justice Collective states, "We envision a world where everyday people can intervene in incidences of child sexual abuse in ways that not only meet immediate needs but also prevent future violence and harm. Our work consists of securing safety and intervening in current violence, while also building long term spaces of accountability and strategies for healing and resilience for all survivors, bystanders, and those who have caused harm."[12] The Incarcerated Workers Organizing Committee, for example, is a prisoner-led organization working to end prison slavery. In 2016 they led the largest prison strike in U.S. history on the anniversary of the Attica uprising.

TRANSFORMING HARM

Mariame Kaba is one of the cornerstones of the abolition movement. One of her many projects is the Transform Harm resource hub, which has materials about transformative justice, restorative justice, community accountability, abolition, carceral feminisms, and healing justice. By transforming harm, we can work to end harm and build relationships. It can be difficult to believe that something can be different from the "criminal justice system" that we have now, particularly when there are people who do, truly, harm others. The scholars who conceptualized imaginative criminology suggest that we break out of our well-worn paths and imagine not just that a better world is possible but what it could possibly look like. You try! Using a fiction format (e.g., film, television, novels, plays, short stories), how could you represent your wildest imaginings in a creative way? In their book *Imaginative Criminology: Of Spaces Past, Present and Future,* for example, Lizzie Seal and Maggie O'Neill examine books like *The Hunger Games,* along with oral histories and films, to see how spaces of "transgression, exclusion, resistance, and possibility" are remembered and represented.[13]

You may be struggling a bit with this idea, wondering, for example, what sexual assault victims would do without the police and prisons, but you must remember that research shows that the police are remarkably inefficient and are often actively harmful in cases of sexual assault, particularly when the victims are from minoritized communities. Prisons, likewise, do not make our country safer—indeed, if they did, the United States would be the safest nation on earth. "The sexual-violence argument, which seeks to uphold the racist criminal justice machine under the guise of pro-woman progressivism, is no different. But victims of sexual violence have always had a place in the transformative justice movement."[14] On the other hand, Black, disabled, and sex-working women and transpeople are especially likely to be assaulted and sexually assaulted by police, and disabled people make up as many as half of people murdered by police, meaning that many of us cannot be safe *with* police and prisons.[15] Abolitionists are implementing many different mutual aid projects to shrink the criminal legal system out of existence, such as Mental Health

First, Collective Action for Safe Spaces, Newark Community Street Team, Moms 4 Housing, and Survived and Punished. Most of these are featured in the #8toAbolition campaign.

MENTAL HEALTH FIRST

In early 2020 the Sacramento chapter of the Anti-Police-Terror Project (APTP) launched a program called Mental Health First, which is now also in Oakland. This program exists partially because one in ten calls to the police are related to mental health, and people with mental illness are particularly likely to be killed by police. Police officers are often in frequent contact with people with mental illnesses, but they are not equipped to manage those calls. Mental Health First, on the other hand, has shifts of three people—a crisis interventionist, a medic, and a safety liaison—who respond to calls, often when the police are already there, which the team sees as a potential threat. These teams can respond to mental health crises including, but not limited to, psychiatric emergencies, substance use support, and domestic violence safety planning with tools such as mobile peer support, de-escalation assistance, and non-punitive and life-affirming interventions. Legislation such as the Community Response Initiative to Strengthen Emergency Systems (CRISES Act) in California have been created to fund community organizations responding to emergency situations—like mental illness, substance use, and homelessness—instead of the police.[16]

COLLECTIVE ACTION FOR SAFE SPACES

CASS is a grassroots organization in Washington, DC, that uses community-based solutions such as public education, cultural organizing, coalition building, and advocacy to build safer communities. The organization is explicitly a Black trans, queer, and non-binary organization focused on using transformative justice and abolitionist frameworks to respond directly to patriarchy and state violence. Their Safe Bar Collective works with staff, using the tools they need to cultivate safe bars and restaurants through training, safety messages on window decals, and advocacy for equitable hiring practices. Their Rethink Masculinity program helps men to identify harmful behaviors rooted in gender norms and to build nurturing relationships of accountability and care.[17]

THE NEWARK COMMUNITY STREET TEAM

The NCST is a community-based violence-reduction strategy based in the South Ward and West Ward of Newark, New Jersey, where outreach workers are hired, trained, and deployed to act as caseworkers for people at risk of violence or victimization, as high-risk interventionists and mediators in ongoing disputes, as Safe Passage actors at participating schools, and as support providers for victims who are overlooked by traditional victims' services. Their work is evidence-based, trauma-informed, and community-focused. While they take referrals from police departments, they explicitly do not cooperate with police.

MOMS 4 HOUSING

Moms 4 Housing is based in Oakland, California, where there are more than four thousand homeless people and thousands of vacant properties. They define themselves as "a collective of unhoused and insecurely housed mothers, organizing to reclaim vacant homes from real estate speculators. We are mothers, we are workers, we are human beings, and we deserve housing. Our children deserve housing. Housing is a human right." In 2019 the collective, led by mom Dominique Walker, occupied a home owned by Wedgewood, a company that profits from flipping "distressed" properties. They advocated to negotiate with Wedgewood to sell them the home at a reasonable price, given the company's role in making a profit off of homelessness.[18]

SURVIVED AND PUNISHED

Marissa Alexander was a Black mother of three living in Florida in 2012. Nine days after giving birth to her daughter prematurely, her estranged husband beat her. She fired a single warning shot upward into a wall to stop the beating, and, even though no one was injured, she was convicted and sentenced to twenty years, in part due to Florida's mandatory minimum sentencing laws. She appealed the verdict in 2013 and accepted a plea in 2014 that resulted in her freedom.[19] In the aftermath of the campaign supporting Marissa Alexander, advocates came together in a collective called Survived and Punished (S&P), which focuses on the intersections of criminalization and surviving domestic and sexual violence.

There are now three collectives, in California, New York, and Chicago, working to raise awareness about criminalized survivors and prison abolition and supporting and freeing criminalized survivors of gender violence.[20]

MUTUAL AID

Beyond programming centered on ending violence, groups focusing on mutual aid are doing the work of abolition by meeting community members' needs and building local models of self-sufficiency. This is related to abolition because social structures will not, and are not designed to, meet community needs. Mutual aid is contrasted with *charity*, which is often the wealthy giving small portions of their fortunes to poor people and non-profits to make themselves look good, with extensive limitations designed to weed out "unworthy" poor people and to give the state, the wealthy, and corporations the power to decide which strategies should be funded. Mutual aid means that communities make decisions from within, for one another and by one another. For example, INCITE! Women of Color against Violence published *The Revolution Will Not Be Funded: Beyond the Non-profit Industrial Complex*, which called out non-profits for maintaining exploitative structures by relying on the state, corporations, and the wealthy to help poor people just enough to keep them powerless while maintaining the power of the capitalist state.[21]

Abolitionist perspectives believe that there is another, more mutually empowering, way:

> Mutual aid projects depart from these norms of charity, social services and non-profitization in several key ways that often include:
>
> - An understanding that it is the system, not the people suffering under it, that creates poverty, crisis, and vulnerability
> - Governance/control by people who are most impacted (can mean having a membership base of those most impacted, or being formed in ways that ensure those providing the aid are from the same group as those giving the aid, or models that allow allies to participate but focus on accountability to those being served)
> - Transparency about how they work, any money they use or manage (many mutual aid projects are not funded and are all volunteer run)

- Open meetings and pathways for new people to join and participate
- Political education within the organization to help those working on the project to expand their awareness of experiences that are not their own, to build solidarity, and to make the project supportive and welcoming to marginalized people
- Humility and willingness to accept feedback about how to make the project more useful to the people it serves
- Long-term commitment to provide the aid the project works on
- Connection to and solidarity with other mutual aid projects and other transformative work
- Commitment to dignity and self-determination of people in need or crisis
- Consensus-based decision making rather than majority rule.[22]

Mutual aid support has been found to be effective in a variety of settings, including with incarcerated mothers seeking social connections and communication skills.[23]

TOWARD LIBERATION AND LOVE

The author bell hooks, one of the giants of feminist thought, Black feminist thought in particular, made the argument that, when love is not present in a society, there cannot be equality. In her book *Feminist Theory: From Margin to Center,* she defines love as "the will to extend one's self for the purpose of nurturing one's own or another's spiritual growth." She continues, "It is essential to our struggle for self-determination that we speak of love. For love is the necessary foundation enabling us to survive the wars, the hardships, the sickness, and the dying with our spirits intact. It is love that allows us to survive whole."[24] Feminism, therefore, is not just a movement to end sexism and gender-based exploitation and oppression but a way to incorporate love into all our interactions, for where there is coercion and domination, there cannot be love. Where we focus on the mutual growth, self-actualization, and emotional well-being of ourselves and all others, we can end oppression with liberation.

The author adrienne maree brown wrote it so beautifully:

Many of us have been looking for that love within an abusive power dynamic with the nation. I speak from the Black experience, from the queer and increasingly disabled experience, from the fat experience. I have felt the punishment this nation metes out in the name of justice and accountability. I have felt the absence of nurture at an individual and collective level. The U.S. has been, and is, the abusive parent, saying that if we change our behavior, it will stop hurting us—making love transactional, offering shoddy inauthentic apologies, confusing the controlling, dominant behavior of wielding power with the extended, nurturing behavior of love. As hooks, Lorde, Hanh, King and so many others teach us, true love is non-negotiably bound up with nurturing, relating, with liberation, with growth toward justice—these are the strands of DNA for a human society that can survive its worst aspects. It's clear enough to echo across love teachers from every background and timeline: Love is a practice that doesn't have room for abuse or injustice.[25]

CONCLUSION

As we end this book together, I will introduce you to one last criminology: compassionate criminology, founded by Josine Junger-Tas. As Michael Tonry describes, compassionate criminology is less a theory than a way of thinking about the world:

> It is predicated on the belief that individual human beings matter, and always matter, and that the only ethical way to think about policies and practices is in terms of their implications for individuals and the lives they have led or potentially can lead. Justice may require that law be even-handedly applied, that like cases be treated alike, but those principles provide little real guidance. Dealing justly with particular cases requires tailoring to this individual, with this background, under these circumstances. Designing policies for handling and preventing delinquency, crime, and other social ills requires that we understand how human beings are shaped and how odds for successful, satisfying lives can be improved.[26]

With what you have learned from this book, I hope that you take this perspective with you on your path.

Notes

INTRODUCTION

1. Black, Cerdeña & Spearman-McCarthy, "Not Your Minority."

PART I

"This Bridge Called My Back": Research Methods and Criminological Theories

1. Sutherland, *Criminology*.
2. Becker & McCorkel, "Gender of Criminal Opportunity," 80.
3. Flavin, "Mainstream Criminologist"; Chesney-Lind & Morash, "Transformative Feminist Criminology"; Cook, "Androcentric Slumber"; Potter, *Intersectionality and Criminology*; Musto, "Transing Critical Criminology," 38.
4. Laub, "Translational Criminology."
5. Henson, Nguyen & Olaghere, "Revising the Critical Gaze."
6. Miles, *Last Supper*.
7. Crenshaw, *Demarginalizing the Intersection*; Rushin, "Bridge Poem."
8. Rushin, "Bridge Poem."

1. Research Methods

1. Digard & Kang-Brown, "New FBI Data."

2. "UCR," 10.
3. Digard & Kang-Brown, "New FBI Data."
4. Digard & Kang-Brown, "New FBI Data."
5. Weiss, "Too Ashamed to Report."
6. Feiring & Taska, "Persistence of Shame."
7. Connell & Messerschmidt, "Hegemonic Masculinity."
8. For reports of rape, see Hohl & Stanko, "Complaints of Rape"; and Shaw et al., "Beyond Surveys and Scales"; for victims' needs, see Hohl & Stanko, "Complaints of Rape"; McGlynn, Downes & Westmarland, "Seeking Justice"; and Smith & Skinner, "Observing Court Responses."
9. Shaw et al., "Beyond Surveys and Scales."
10. Southall, "Negligent and Sexist."
11. Murphy-Oikonen & Egan," Sexual and Gender Minorities," 783.
12. Sheppard & Stowell, "Police Fatal Force."
13. Pezzella, Fetzer & Keller, "Dark Figure."
14. Sullivan & O'Keeffe, "Curtailing Proactive Policing."
15. Eterno, Verma & Silverman, "Police Manipulations."
16. Biderman & Reiss, "Dark Figure," 1.
17. DeKeseredy, "Crime Surveys as Tools"; Currie, "Against Marginality;" Young, "Voodoo Criminology."
18. Weiss, "Neutralizing Sexual Victimization."
19. Vito et al., "Does Daylight Matter?"
20. Jayaratne & Stewart, "Quantitative and Qualitative Methods," quoted in Flavin, "Mainstream Criminologist."
21. Ragin, "Qualitative and Quantitative Research."
22. Aspers & Corte, "Qualitative Research," 155.
23. Aspers & Corte, "Qualitative Research," 156.
24. Flavin, "Mainstream Criminologist"; Wonders, "Postmodern Feminist Criminology," 122, quoted in Flavin "Mainstream Criminologist."
25. Miller & Burack, "General Theory of Crime."
26. Decuir-Gunby, Chapman & Schutz, *Understanding Critical Race*.
27. Briggs, "Caribbean Black Male Youths."
28. Williams, Spencer & Wilson, "Not Your Felon."
29. Laguardia, "She Must Bear."
30. Mondé, "Trying to Get Free."
31. Sudbury, "Celling Black Bodies."
32. Harding, *Feminism and Methodology*.
33. Stanley & Wise, "Method, Methodology and Epistemology."
34. Campbell et al., "Training Interviewers"; Dixson, James & Frieson, "Taking It"; Fine et al. "Participatory Action Research."
35. Fine et al., "Participatory Action Research," 174.
36. Greene, Gabbidon & Wilson, "Included."

37. Young & Easton-Brooks, "Present but Unaccounted For"; Anderson, "Black Male Teachers."
38. Williams, Spencer & Wilson, "Not Your Felon," 1116.
39. Fine et al., "Participatory Action Research."
40. Cho, Crenshaw & McCall, "Field of Intersectionality Studies."
41. Fine et al., "Participatory Action Research," 189.
42. "Regulations."
43. White et al., "IRB Decision-Making."
44. "Vulnerable and Other Populations."

2. Classical and Neo-classical Theories

1. Pratt et al., "Empirical Status."
2. Garland, *Culture of Control*; Clear, *Harm in American Penology*; Whitman, *Harsh Justice*.
3. Fass & Pi, "Getting Tough"; Pratt & Cullen, "Assessing Macro-Level Predictors"; Bennett, DiIulio & Walters, *Body Count*.
4. Pratt et al., "Empirical Status," 382–83.
5. Piquero et al., "Elaborating the Individual Difference," 337.
6. Henson, Nguyen & Olaghere, "Revising the Critical Gaze."
7. Durose & Antenangeli, "Recidivism of Prisoners."
8. Kelling & Wilson, "Broken Windows."
9. Travis, quoted in Berman, "Damage to Undo."
10. Weisburd et al., "Frisk Practices"; Apel, "On the Deterrent Affect."
11. Rosenfeld & Fornango, "Relationship between Crime and Stop."
12. Laurencin & Walker, "Racial Profiling."
13. Morrow, White & Fradella, "After the Stop."
14. Hackney & Glaser, "Reverse Deterrence."
15. Archer & Gartner, "Homicide."
16. Cornish & Clarke, "Understanding Crime Displacement."
17. T. Pratt, "Rational Choice Theory."
18. Neissl et al., "Rational Choice."
19. Neissl et al., "Rational Choice"; Giordano, "Girls, Guys and Gangs"; Morash, "Peer Group Experiences."
20. Loughran et al., "Rational Choice."
21. Tewksbury & Mustaine, "Lifestyle Factors."
22. Potter, "Intersectional Criminology."
23. Blasdell, "Intersection of Race," 263.
24. Turanovic, Pratt & Piquero, "Structural Constraints," 267.
25. For domestic violence, see Johnson & Ferraro, "Research on Domestic Violence"; for intimate partner homicide, see Roberts, "Intimate Partner Homicide"; for rape, see Suarez & Gadalla, "Stop Blaming the Victim"; for sex

trafficking, see Schauer & Wheaton, "Sex Trafficking"; and for stalking, see Spitzberg & Cupach, "Art of Stalking."
  26. Like-Haislip & Miofsky, "Violent Victimization."
  27. Reyns & Scherer, "Stalking Victimization."
  28. Navarro & Jasinski, "Why Girls?"
  29. Wilcox & Gialopsos, "Crime-Event Criminology."

3. Biological and Positivist Theories

  1. Ignatiev, *Irish Became White*; Omi & Winant, *Racial Formation*; Zinn & Damon, *People's History*.
  2. Lombroso, *Criminal Man*; Arford & Madfis, "Whitewashing Criminology," 724–25.
  3. Bieder, "Representations of Indian Bodies."
  4. Harrison, *Belly of the Beast*.
  5. Arford & Madfis, "Whitewashing Criminology."
  6. Rippon, *Gendered Brain*.
  7. Jordan-Young & Karkazis, *Testosterone*.
  8. Martin, "Egg and the Sperm"; Arnold, "Choosy Eggs."
  9. Campo-Engelstein & Johnson, "Fertilization Fairytale."
  10. Sohrabi, "Criminal Gene."
  11. Wertz et al., "Genetics and Crime."
  12. Junger et al., "Parental Criminality."
  13. Van de Weijer, "Intergenerational Continuity of Crime."
  14. Brody, "Harvard Backs Genetic Study"; Garrison, "French Murder Jury."
  15. J. Green, "Media Sensationalisation and Science."
  16. Higney, Hanley & Moro, "Lead-Crime Hypothesis"; Teye et al., "Persistent Racial/Ethnic Disparities."
  17. American Psychiatric Association, *Diagnostic and Statistical Manual*.
  18. Heart, "Historical Trauma Response"
  19. Pettus, "Trauma and Prospects."
  20. American Psychiatric Association, *Diagnostic and Statistical Manual*.
  21. Heide & Solomon, "Childhood Trauma."
  22. Zeidman, *Brain Science*.
  23. Lira & Stern, "Mexican Americans."
  24. Cohn, *Belly of the Beast*.
  25. Chappell, "California's Prison Sterilizations."
  26. Dickerson, Wessler & Jordan, "Unneeded Surgeries."
  27. Chappell, "California's Prison Sterilizations."
  28. Rose, "Biology of Culpability."
  29. Wertz et al., "Genetics and Crime."

4. Psychological Theories

1. Bayne, "Womb Envy."
2. Freud, *Three Essays;* Gilligan & Gerodimos, "Radical Listening."
3. See Bayne, "Womb Envy," for a review.
4. Moreland & Leach, "Black Racial Identity."
5. Gilligan, *In a Different Voice.*
6. Woods, "Gender Differences."
7. Gilligan & Gerodimos, "Radical Listening," 44.
8. Moreland & Leach, "Black Racial Identity," 257.
9. Moreland & Leach, "Black Racial Identity."
10. Gratz & Roemer, "Multidimensional Assessment," 42–43.
11. Garofalo & Velotti, "Negative Emotionality and Aggression."
12. Cohn et al., "Role of Emotion Dysregulation," 60.
13. Brindle, Bowles & Freeman, "Gender, Education and Engagement."
14. Bliton et al., "Emotion Dysregulation."
15. Christian & Teachey, "Yates Believed Children Doomed."
16. Christian & Teachey, "Yates Believed Children Doomed."
17. West & Lichtenstein, "Andrea Yates."
18. Tasca et al., "Women and Hysteria."
19. Hunter, "Hysteria, Psychoanalysis, and Feminism."
20. B. Green, "False Promise," 602.
21. Christin, Rosenblat & Boyd, "Courts and Predictive Algorithms," 1.
22. Eaglin, "Racializing Algorithms."
23. Garland, *Culture of Control.*
24. Mayson, "Bias In, Bias Out," 2225.
25. Semenza & Grosholz, "Mental and Physical Health."
26. Stoliker & Galli, "Examination of Mental Health."
27. Zhong et al., "Risk Factors for Suicide."
28. Ben-Moshe, *Decarcerating Disability.*
29. Jewkes et al., "Designing 'Healthy' Prisons."

5. Social Process and Social Development Theories

1. Akers & Lee, " Longitudinal Test"; Haynie, "Friendship Networks and Delinquency"; Krohn et al., "Social Learning Theory"; Winfree & Bernat, "Social Learning"; Pratt & Cullen, "Empirical Status"; Pratt et al., "Empirical Status"; Stults, Hernandez & Hay, "Low Self-Control"; Burgess & Akers, "Differential Association-Reinforcement Theory."
2. Heimer & De Coster, "Gendering of Violent Delinquency."
3. Fagot, "Influence of Sex"; Fagot, "Beyond the Reinforcement Principle"; Fagot & Hagan, "Observations of Parent Reactions"; Snow, Jacklin & Maccoby, "Sex-of-Child Differences."

4. Schur, *Labeling Women Deviant.*
5. De Coster & Zito, "Social Landscape."
6. Augustyn & McGloin, "Risk of Informal Socializing"; Giordano, Cernkovich & Pugh, "Friendships and Delinquency"; Johnson & Aries, "Talk of Women Friends"; Thorne & Luria, "Sexuality and Gender."
7. Giordano, Cernkovich & Pugh, "Friendships and Delinquency," 1189.
8. De Coster, "Delinquency and Depression."
9. Gilligan, *In a Different Voice.*
10. Connell, *Gender and Power,* 77.
11. Newburn & Stanko, *Just Boys Doing Business.*
12. Messerschmidt, "Hegemonic Masculinity," 86–87.
13. Hughes et al., "Parents' Ethnic-Racial Socialization."
14. Umaña-Taylor & Hill, "Ethnic-Racial Socialization."
15. Naffine, *Female Crime.*
16. Grindal, "Ethnic-Racial Socialization."
17. Vazsonyi, Mikuška, and Kelley, "It's Time."
18. Smart, *Women, Crime and Criminology.*
19. Miller & Burack, "General Theory of Crime," 116.
20. Henson, Nguyen & Olaghere, "Revising the Critical Gaze," 22.
21. Augustyn & McGloin, "Risk of Informal Socializing"; Mears, Ploeger & Warr, "Explaining the Gender Gap"; Piquero et al., "Developmental Trajectories"; Stults, Hernandez & Hay, "Low Self-Control."
22. Belknap, *Invisible Woman;* Kruttschnitt, "Gender and Crime."
23. De Coster, "Delinquency and Depression," 143–44.
24. Toch, *Violent Men;* Shover, *Great Pretenders;* Gove, "Effect of Age."
25. Maruna, *Making Good.*
26. Sommers, Baskin & Fagan, "Getting Out," 144.
27. Giordano, Cernkovich & Rudolph, "Gender, Crime, and Desistance."
28. Michalsen, "Life Course Transition."
29. Laub, "Stockholm Prize."
30. Laub & Sampson, *Shared Beginnings.*
31. Glueck and Glueck, *Five Hundred Delinquent Women.*
32. Laub & Sampson, "Understanding Desistance"; Cook, "Androcentric Slumber."
33. Strazdins & Broom, "Acts of Love."
34. Hall & Harris, "Gendered Weight," 236.
35. Cauffman, Monahan & Thomas, "Pathways to Persistence."
36. Simpson et al., "Age-Graded Pathways."
37. For criminal behavior, see Farrington et al., "Successful Men"; and Glaser, *Effectiveness of a Prison;* for desistance behaviors, see Laub & Sampson, "Turning Points."
38. Heimer, "Gender Gap."

39. Uggen & Kruttschnitt, "Crime in the Breaking."
40. Grace, "Get to Know Me"; Barr, "Working Together."
41. Barr, "Working Together"; Opsal, "Livin' on the Straights"; Low, "Working through Desistance."
42. Holtfreter, Reisig & Morash, "Women Offenders."
43. Pressman, "Gender Poverty Gap"; Proctor & Dalaker, *Poverty;* Dodge & Pogrebin, "Collateral Costs"; Owen & Bloom, "Profiling Women Prisoners"; Richie, "Challenges Incarcerated Women Face."
44. Sampson, Laub & Wimer, "Does Marriage Reduce Crime?"; Farrington & West, "Effects of Marriage"; King, Massoglia & MacMillan "Context of Marriage"; Laub & Sampson, "Turning Points."
45. Lyngstad & Skardhamar, "Changes in Criminal Offending"; Laub, Nagin & Sampson "Trajectories of Change."
46. Farrington & West, "Effects of Marriage"; Horney, Osgood & Marshall, "Criminal Careers."
47. Covington, *Woman's Journey Home,* 74.
48. Giordano, Cernkovich & Rudolph, "Gender, Crime, and Desistance."
49. Leverentz, "Good Man."
50. King, Massoglia & MacMillan, "Context of Marriage."
51. Giordano, Cernkovich & Rudolph, "Gender, Crime and Desistance"; Laub & Sampson, "Turning Points"; Broidy & Cauffman, "Glueck Women"; Michalsen, *Mothering and Desistance;* Michalsen, "Life Course Transition"; Low, "Go and Look."
52. Belknap, *Invisible Woman;* Chesney-Lind & Pasko, *Female Offender;* Fedock & Covington, "Strength-Based Approaches."
53. Daly, "Women's Pathways."

6. Social Structure Theories

1. Shaw & McKay, *Juvenile Delinquency.*
2. Du Bois, *Philadelphia Negro.*
3. Henson, Nguyen & Olaghere, "Revising the Critical Gaze," 21.
4. Gurusami, "Motherwork under the State."
5. Hallett, "For-Profit Imprisonment," 369; Alexander, *New Jim Crow.*
6. Hagan, quoted in Hallett, "For-Profit Imprisonment," 375.
7. Rose & Clear, "Incarceration."
8. Clear, "Impacts of Incarceration."
9. "About."
10. "Colorado Chance to Compete."
11. Swope, Hernández & Cushing, "Relationship of Historical Redlining," 960.
12. Lathan, "50 Years."

13. "Annual Report, 2022."
14. Friedline, Naraharisetti & Weaver, "Digital Redlining."
15. "What Is the PIC?"
16. Klein & Lima, "Prison Industrial Complex."
17. Agnew, "Building on the Foundation," 343–47
18. Peterson & Krivo, *Divergent Social Worlds*.
19. Sue et al., "Racial Microaggressions," 271.
20. De Coster & Thompson, "General Strain Theory."
21. Broidy & Agnew, "Gender and Crime."
22. De Coster & Thompson, "General Strain Theory"; for gender-based discrimination, see Eitle, "Exploring a Source"; for behavioral restrictions, see Bottcher, "Gender as Social Control"; for demands from family members, see Joon Jang, "Gender Differences in Strain"; for greater exposure, see Carbone-López, Kruttschnitt & Macmillan, "Intimate Partner Violence"; Tjaden & Thoennes, "Prevalence and Consequences"; and Tjaden & Thoennes, "Extent, Nature, and Consequences."
23. Chesney-Lind, "Girls' Crime."
24. Giordano, Cernkovich & Pugh, "Friendships and Delinquency"; Conger et al., "Husband and Wife Differences."
25. Nuevelle, "Breaking the Silence."
26. Lerner, "Q&A."
27. Mirowsky & Ross, "Sex Differences in Distress"; Kaufman, "Gendered Responses."
28. For eating disorders, see Sharp et al., "Purging Behavior"; and Sharp, Brewster & RedHawk Love, "Disentangling Strain"; for self-harm, see Piquero et al., "Disordered Eating"; and Piquero and Sealock, "General Strain Theory."
29. Turner, Turner & Hale, "Social Relationships."
30. Joon Jang & Johnson, "Reactions to Strain."
31. Thorne & Luria, "Sexuality and Gender."
32. Broidy & Agnew, "Gender and Crime"; De Coster & Cornell Zito, "General Strain Theory."
33. Collins, "Black Political Economy"; hooks, *Feminist Theory*.
34. Potter, "Black Feminist Criminology."
35. Mondé, "Trying to Get Free."
36. St. Vil et al., "Qualitative Study."
37. Potter, "Black Feminist Criminology"; Mondé, "Trying to Get Free."
38. Middlemiss, "Poverty, Stress, and Support."
39. Miller-Loncar et al., "Characteristics of Social Support."
40. W. Miller, "Lower-Class Culture."
41. Hartley, Maddan & Spohn, "Prosecutorial Discretion"; Steffensmeier, Ulmer & Kramer, "Criminal Sentencing."
42. Galvin & Ulmer, "Expanding our Understanding."

43. Vito, Higgins & Vito, "Police Stop and Frisk."
44. For "real rapes," see Estrich, *Real Rape;* for "genuine victims," see LaFree, *Rape and Criminal Justice;* and Frohmann, "Discrediting Victims' Allegations."
45. O'Neal & Spohn, "Perpetrator Is a Partner."
46. Finkelhor & Yllö, *License to Rape;* Tjaden & Thoennes, *Stalking in America.*
47. O'Neal & Spohn, "Perpetrator Is a Partner."
48. Kaiser, O'Neal & Spohn, "Victim Refuses to Cooperate."
49. Tjaden & Thoennes, "Extent, Nature, and Consequences"; Du Mont, Miller & Myhr, "Police Reporting Practices."
50. Cloward & Ohlin, *Delinquency and Opportunity.*
51. Becker & McCorkel, "Gender of Criminal Opportunity."

7. Theories of Victimology

1. Boysen et al., "Trigger Warnings"; Cares et al., "They Were There."
2. Laguardia, Michalsen & Rider-Milkovich, "Trigger Warnings."
3. Sengstock, "Culpable Victim."
4. Amir, "Victim Precipitated Forcible Rape," 495, 502.
5. Cortina, Rabelo & Holland, "Beyond Blaming the Victim," 84.
6. Meloy & Miller, *Victimization of Women,* 7.
7. Tofte, "I Used to Think."
8. Dhanani, Main & Pueschel, "Yourself to Blame."
9. Stark, "Deviant Places."
10. Ruback & Menard, "Rural-Urban Differences."
11. Rentschler, *Crime Victim Movement,* 131.
12. Fishman, "Crime Waves as Ideology"; Rentschler, *Crime Victim Movement.*
13. Rentschler, *Second Wounds.*
14. Rentschler, *Crime Victim Movement.*
15. Outlaw, "Realizing the Promise."
16. Ruback, Gladfelter & Lantz, "Paying Restitution."
17. Ruback, Cares & Hoskins, "Crime Victims' Perceptions."
18. Haynes, Cares & Ruback, "Harm of Criminal Victimization."
19. Hotaling & Buzawa, *Forgoing Criminal Justice Assistance.*
20. Cheon & Regehr, "Restorative Justice Models"; Van Wormer, "Restorative Justice."
21. Kaba, "TransformHarm.org."
22. Zaykowski, Kleinstuber & McDonough, "Judicial Narratives," 717.
23. Greene, "Polly Klaas' Murder."
24. Berg & Mulford, "Reappraising and Redirecting Research," 17.

25. Gottfredson, *Victims of Crime;* Lauritsen, Laub & Sampson, "Conventional and Delinquent Activities."
26. Berg & Schreck, "Victim-Offender Overlap," 290.
27. Berg & Mulford, "Reappraising and Redirecting Research."
28. Hindelang, "Race and Involvement."
29. Pratt & Turanovic, "Lifestyle and Routine Activity."
30. S. Robinson, *Emotional Abuse and Neglect.*
31. Powers & Oschwald, "Violence and Abuse."
32. "Ins and Outs."
33. Flores et al., "Victimization Rates and Traits."
34. Struckman-Johnson & Struckman-Johnson, "Sexual Coercion Experiences"; Surrell & Johnson, "Examination of Women's Experiences," 562.
35. Meade, Wasileski & Hunter, "Effects of Victimization."
36. Hughto et al., "Victimization."
37. Brömdal et al., "Navigating Intimate Trans Citizenship."
38. Novisky & Peralta, "Gladiator School."
39. Wilson, "Military Sexual Trauma."
40. Monteith et al., "Preventing Suicide."
41. Brownstone et al., "Phenomenology."
42. Bonnes, *Hardship Duty.*
43. "Secretary of the Army."
44. Moyer, "A Poison in the System."
45. Renzetti, "On the Margins."

8. Critical Criminology

1. Henson, Nguyen & Olaghere, "Revising the Critical Gaze," 17.
2. DeKeseredy, "Critical Criminological Understandings."
3. León, "Critical Criminology and Race," 389.
4. Michalowski, "Critique of Domination."
5. León, "Critical Criminology and Race."
6. Lea, "Jock Young," 166.
7. Young, "Failure of Criminology," 25.
8. Arrigo & Bernard, "Postmodern Criminology," 42, 52.
9. Hayward & Young, "Cultural Criminology," 259.
10. Ferrell, "Cultural Criminology," 397.
11. Flavin, "Mainstream Criminologist."
12. Maher & Daly, "Street-Level Drug Economy."
13. Ehrenreich, "What Is Socialist Feminism?"
14. Shohat, *Talking Visions,* 1.
15. Crenshaw, quoted in Steinmetz, "She Coined the Term."
16. "Black Feminist Statement."

17. Springer, "Third Wave Black Feminism?"
18. Liu et al., "Petty and Serious."
19. Warren, Chiricos & Bales, "Imprisonment Penalty."
20. Heidensohn, "On Writing"; Heidensohn, "Deviance of Women."
21. Valcore et al., "Trans-inclusive Criminology."
22. Heidensohn, "Deviance of Women"; Potter, *Intersectionality and Criminology*.
23. Flavin, "Mainstream Criminologist."
24. Potter, "Black Feminist Criminology."
25. Rogers & Rogers, "Advantages and Challenges."
26. Walker et al., "Abolition in Queer Criminology," 1445.
27. Connell, *Masculinities*.
28. Gottzén, Bjørnholt & Boonzaier, "Intimate Partner Violence."
29. Messerschmidt, "Hegemonic Masculinity."
30. Katz, *Seductions of Crime*.
31. Winlow, "Masculinities and Crime."
32. Pepinsky, "Peacemaking Criminology," 321.
33. Currie & MacLean, "Critical Reflections."
34. McEvoy, "Beyond the Metaphor."
35. Cook et al., *Survivor Criminology*, 348.
36. Maruna, *Making Good*.
37. Ross et al., "Convict Criminology," 491.
38. Belknap, "Activist Criminology."
39. Cox & Malkin, "Feminist Convict Criminology."
40. Carlen, quoted in DeKeseredy, "Feminist Perspectives," 84.

PART II

9. Crimes against People

1. Boorsma, "Whole Truth," 213.
2. Burkeman, "This Column Will Change."
3. Pickett et al., "Public (Mis)Understanding."
4. Beckett & Sasson, *Politics of Injustice*; Roberts & Stalans, "Restorative Sentencing."
5. Brenan, "Worry about Crime."
6. Brenan, "Local Crime Has Increased."
7. Morgan & Smith, "National Crime Victimization Survey."
8. Thompson & Tapp, "Criminal Victimization."
9. CDC, "Web-Based Injury Statistics."
10. Richardson et al., "Shook Ones."
11. Cooper et al., "Repeat Victims of Violence."

12. Purtle et al., "Hospital-Based Violence."
13. Richardson et al., "Shook Ones."
14. Rosay, "American Indian."
15. Thompson & Tapp, "Criminal Victimization."
16. Kupers, "Toxic Masculinity," 716.
17. Jack, "Gender Reveal Party."
18. Quinet, "Prostitutes as Victims," 74.
19. Hickey, *Serial Murderers*.
20. Egger, *Killers among Us*.
21. Quinet, "Prostitutes as Victims."
22. State of Washington v. Gary Leon Ridgway, No. 01-1-10270-9 SEA (Superior Court of King County 2003), 7.
23. Lindsey et al., "Help-Seeking Behaviors"; St. Vil et al., "Qualitative Study."
24. Lindsey et al., "Help-Seeking Behaviors."
25. Addis & Cohane, "Social Scientific Paradigms."
26. Kupers, "Toxic Masculinity," 714.
27. Affleck, Carmichael & Whitley, "Men's Mental Health."
28. Caputi & Russell, "Femicide," 34.
29. D. Russell, *Femicide*.
30. Dawson & Carrigan, "Identifying Femicide."
31. Rodriguez, Montana & Pulitzer, *Daughters of Juarez*; "Mexico."
32. Rodriguez, Montana & Pulitzer, *Daughters of Juarez*.
33. Starr, "When Culture Matters."
34. López, "Femicide in Ciudad Juárez."
35. Morgan & Thompson, "Criminal Victimization."
36. Cunradi, Caetano & Schafer, "Socioeconomic Predictors"; Field & Caetano, "Ethnic Differences."
37. Wilkins et al., *Connecting the Dots*.
38. Walfield, "Men Cannot Be Raped"; Turchik & Edwards, "Myths about Male Rape," 211–12.
39. Curry, "Expendables for Whom."
40. Anderson et al., "Differences in Rape Acknowledgment."
41. Metz, Myers & Wallace, "Man's Issue," 52.
42. Mullins, "He Would Kill Me."
43. Campbell, "Keeping the 'Lady' Safe."

10. Crimes against Property

1. Adler, *Sisters in Crime*.
2. Dodge, "Women and White-Collar Crime."
3. Caputo, *Out in the Storm;* Steffensmeier & Allan, "Gender and Crime"; Steffensmeier, Harris & Painter-Davis, "Gender and Arrests."

4. Steffensmeier, Harris & Painter-Davis, "Gender and Arrests."
5. Adler, *Sisters in Crime*.
6. Caputo, *Out in the Storm*.
7. Caputo & King, "Shoplifting."
8. J. Miller, "Strengths and Limits"; Messerschmidt, *Masculinities and Crime*.
9. Caputo & King, "Shoplifting," 162.
10. Ortner, "Patriarchy."
11. Christ, "New Definition of Patriarchy," 216, 217.
12. Paltrow & Flavin, "Forced Interventions."
13. Akins, "Racial Segregation."
14. Cf. Messerschmidt, *Masculinities and Crime*.
15. Williams, "Stealing a Car."
16. O'Connor & Kelly, "Auto Theft."
17. Williams, "Stealing a Car."
18. Paternoster & Bushway, "Theoretical and Empirical Work."
19. Williams, "Stealing a Car," 97.
20. "Offense Definitions."
21. Powell "Burnin' Down the House," 541.
22. Goebel & Harrison, "Money to Burn"; Powell, "Burnin' Down the House."
23. Farrell, "Forty Years."
24. Alexander, *New Jim Crow*.
25. Duxbury, "Fear or Loathing?"; Helfgott et al., "Misdemeanor Arrests."
26. Lowe, Stroud & Nguyen, "Who Looks Suspicious?"
27. Bloch, "Aversive Racism"; Sportsman, "Upholding White Supremacy."
28. Loader, "Consumer Culture."
29. Bloch, "Aversive Racism."
30. Ahmad, "Why I Quit"; Kurwa, "Digitally Gated Community."
31. Patton et al., "Stop and Frisk Online."
32. Gurusami, "Carceral Web We Weave."

11. *White-Collar and Environmental Crimes*

1. Sutherland, "White-Collar Criminality," 9.
2. Barnett, "Measurement," 1.
3. FBI, quoted in Barnett, "Measurement," 1.
4. Barnett, "Measurement."
5. Friedrichs, "Enron et al."
6. Kim & Allmang, "Wage Theft."
7. Mangundayao et al., "More Than $3 Billion."
8. DuBois, "Protecting Workers"; Levin, "Wage Theft Criminalization."

9. Michalowski, *Order, Law, and Crime*, 325.
10. Michel, "Violent Street Crime," 128.
11. "Crime in the U.S."
12. St-Georges et al., "Jobs and Punishment."
13. Steffensmeier, Schwartz & Roche, "Corporate Crime."
14. Michel, "Violent Street Crime."
15. Clinard, Quinney & Wildeman, *Criminal Behavior Systems*, 188, 221.
16. Daly, "Gender and Varieties."
17. Steffensmeier, Schwartz & Roche, "Corporate Crime."
18. H. Baker, "State-Corporate Facilitated Harms."
19. St-Georges et al., "Jobs and Punishment."
20. Steffensmeier, Harris & Painter-Davis, "Gender and Arrests."
21. O'Sullivan, "Corporate Criminal Enforcement Ecosystem," 1065.
22. Steffensmeier, Harris & Painter-Davis, "Gender and Arrests," 213.
23. Rothwell, "Black Social Mobility."
24. Sohoni & Rorie, "White-Collar Crime."
25. Nurse, "Privatising the Green Police."
26. Hasler, Walters & White, "In and Against."
27. Roesler, "Racial Segregation," 10773.
28. Kojola & Pellow, "New Directions."
29. Muhammad, "Meet the Young Activists."
30. Muhammad, "Meet the Young Activists."
31. Muhammad, "Meet the Young Activists."
32. Muhammad, "Meet the Young Activists."
33. Banzhaf, "Regulatory Impact Analysis"; Bowen, "Analytical Review"; Bullard, *Dumping in Dixie*; Cole & Foster, *From the Ground Up*; Mohai, Pellow & Roberts, "Environmental Justice"; Ringquist, "Assessing Evidence."
34. "Air Quality."
35. Banzhaf, Ma & Timmins, "Environmental Justice."
36. Lavelle & Coyle, "Unequal Protection."
37. "Brownfields," 3.
38. Juhasz, "Cancer Alley."
39. Sorokin & Muir, "Little Toxic-Waste Data."
40. Crawford, "Harrisburg Manchester Neighborhood."
41. Terry, "No Climate Justice," 5.
42. Mashhoodi, "Feminization of Surface Temperature."
43. Haley & Arrigo, "Ethical Considerations."
44. Lynch, "Environmental Crime."
45. Beirne & South, "Introduction."
46. Sollund, "Animal Trafficking and Trade."
47. Beirne, "Theriocide."
48. Lynch, "Environmental Crime."

49. Lynch & Long, "Green Criminology."
50. Torelli, Balluchi & Lazzini, "Greenwashing and Environmental Communication," 411.
51. Lynch, "Environmental Crime," 51.

12. Public Order Crimes

1. Ehrenreich, "Crime to Be Poor."
2. Schweik, *Ugly Laws*, 291.
3. Herring, Yarbrough & Alatorre, "Pervasive Penality."
4. Laniyonu, "Coffee Shops."
5. "Housing Not Handcuffs," 11.
6. Couloute, "Nowhere to Go."
7. "Housing Not Handcuffs."
8. Couloute, "Nowhere to Go."
9. "Housing First."
10. "Housing Not Handcuffs."
11. "Success in the Community."
12. "Housing Not Handcuffs."
13. Couloute, "Nowhere to Go."
14. Ehrenreich, "Crime to Be Poor."
15. Sawyer & Wagner, "Mass Incarceration."
16. "Drug War Stats."
17. Carson, "State and Federal Prisons."
18. Alexander, *New Jim Crow*, 74.
19. "Drug Arrests Stayed High"; "Tale of Two Countries."
20. Fellner, "Law Enforcement," 266.
21. Rothwell, "Black Social Mobility."
22. Center for Behavioral Health, *Racial/Ethnic Differences*.
23. Ranapurwala et al., "Opioid Overdose Deaths."
24. Maruschack, Bronson & Alper, "Alcohol and Drug Use."
25. Friedman & Hansen, "Overdose Mortality," 4.
26. Evans, "Massachusetts Has a Drug Problem."
27. Maher & Daly, "Street-Level Drug Economy"; Maher, *Sexed Work*.
28. Leigh, "Inventing Sex Work."
29. Fuentes, "Sex Worker Collectives," 225.
30. See Harcourt & Donovan, "Many Faces," for a typology of direct and indirect sex work.
31. Fuentes, "Sex Worker Collectives," 238.
32. Wahab, "For Their Own Good."
33. Decker et al., "Inconsistent Condom Use."
34. A. Jones, "Trans Men and Enbies."

35. Terwiel, "What Is Carceral Feminism?"
36. Bernstein, "Sexual Politics"; Terwiel, "What Is Carceral Feminism?"
37. Fuentes, "Sex Worker Collectives," 225.
38. Nawyn, Birdal & Glogower, "Extent of Sex Trafficking."
39. Fuentes, "Sex Worker Collectives."
40. Fernandez, "Defending the Less Dead."
41. Weitzer, "Campaign against Sex Work."
42. Strohmayer, Clamen & Liang, "Technologies for Social Justice."
43. Firth, "Mutual Aid," 57.
44. Shimei, "We Are Often Invisible."

PART III

"The Master's Tools": The Criminal Justice System

1. Lorde, "History Is a Weapon," 112.
2. "Demand Absolute Standards Stop."
3. Bayer, McKee & Towles, "Emerging Practices."

13. Reforming Police, Courts, and Corrections

1. Seigel, "Racial Profiling."
2. Rousey, *Policing the Southern City*.
3. Wagner, *Disturbing the Peace*.
4. Kraska, "Militarization and Policing," 503.
5. McCulloch, "Blue Armies."
6. Kraska, "Militarization and Policing."
7. Smith, "Blue Lives Matter."
8. Masera, "Police Safety"; Smith, "Blue Lives Matter."
9. For police in Black neighborhoods, see Mummolo, "Modern Police Tactics"; for white support, see Jimenez, Helm & Arndt, "Racial Prejudice."
10. Cobbina-Dungy & Jones-Brown, "Too Much Policing."
11. Cobbina-Dungy, "I'm Afraid of Cops."
12. Crenshaw et al., "Say Her Name."
13. Ritchie, "#SayHerName," 12.
14. Lum & Nagin, "Reinventing American Policing."
15. Fyfe, "Administrative Interventions."
16. "BLM Demands."
17. Kurti, "Police Power."
18. Marcus & Stergiopoulos, "Re-examining Mental Health."
19. Rasmussen & James, "Trading Cops."
20. Spencer et al., "Re-victimizing Victims."

21. Rich, "Trauma-Informed Police Responses," 466.
22. Heise & Nance, "Defund the (School) Police?"
23. Gottfredson et al., "School Resource Officers."
24. "107th Session."
25. "Demographic Differences in Sentencing."
26. "107th Session."
27. Subramanian et al., *Incarceration's Front Door.*
28. Komar & Porter, "Ending Mass Incarceration."
29. Komar, Nellis & Budd, "Counting Down."
30. Rossman, "Criminal Justice Interventions."
31. R. Russell, "Veterans Treatment Courts."
32. Jalain & Grossi, "Take a Load Off."
33. Patton & Smith, "Gender, Ideology, and Dominance"; Jacobi & Schweers, "Justice, Interrupted."
34. Gleason, "Beyond Mere Presence."
35. Jacobi & Schweers, "Justice, Interrupted."
36. Baum, "Legalize It All."
37. "107th Session."
38. For "primary occupation," see Condry, *Families Shamed;* for responsibilities, see Wildeman, Lee & Comfort, "New Vulnerable Population."
39. May et al., "Going to Jail Sucks."
40. Hallett, "For-Profit Imprisonment."
41. Sawyer & Wagner, "Mass Incarceration."
42. Hallett, "For-Profit Imprisonment."
43. A. Pratt, "Private Prison Companies."
44. Hallett, "For-Profit Imprisonment."
45. Dippel & Poyker, *Private Prisons;* Mukherjee, "Private Prisons."
46. Budd, "Private Prisons."
47. Steiker & Steiker, "American Death Penalty."
48. "Death Penalty."
49. "Capital Punishment."
50. Alexander, *New Jim Crow.*
51. Galvin & Ulnar, "Expanding Our Understanding."

14. Abolition

1. Spade, "Biography."
2. Kaba, "TransformHarm.org."
3. Sultan & Herskind, "What Is Abolition?"
4. Berger, Kaba & Stein, "What Abolitionists Do."
5. Sultan & Herskind, "What Is Abolition?"
6. Braz et al., "Overview."

7. "History."
8. Roth, "Anti-Blackness."
9. "What Is the PIC?"
10. Law, "Against Carceral Feminism."
11. Sultan, quoted in Fisher Quann, "Fresh Framework."
12. "Building Transformative Justice Responses."
13. Seal & O'Neill, *Imaginative Criminology*, v.
14. Fisher Quann, "Fresh Framework."
15. Sultan & Herskind, "What Is Abolition?"
16. Buxbaum, "California Initiative Moves Away."
17. "Our Work."
18. "Home."
19. "Free Marissa Alexander."
20. "About S&P."
21. INCITE!, *Revolution*.
22. "What Is Mutual Aid?"
23. Howard, Clark & Piltch, "Support for Mothers."
24. hooks, *Feminist Theory*.
25. brown, "This Valentine's Day."
26. Tonry, "Learning Cross-Nationally," 85.

Bibliography

"107th Session of the UN Committee on the Elimination of Racial Discrimination." Sentencing Project. July 14, 2022. www.sentencingproject.org/app/uploads/2022/10/07-14-2022_CERD-Shadow-Report-Draft_with-endnotes.pdf.

"About S&P." Survived and Punished. Accessed October 24, 2024. https://survivedandpunished.org/about/.

"About: The Ban the Box Campaign." Ban the Box Campaign. Accessed October 24, 2024. https://bantheboxcampaign.org/about/.

"About Us." Worth Rises. Accessed October 24, 2024. https://worthrises.org/aboutus.

Addis, Michael E., and Geoffrey H. Cohane. "Social Scientific Paradigms of Masculinity and Their Implications for Research and Practice in Men's Mental Health." *Journal of Clinical Psychology* 61, no. 6 (2005): 633–47.

Adler, Freda. *Sisters in Crime: The Rise of the New Female Criminal.* New York: McGraw-Hill, 1975.

Affleck, William, Victoria Carmichael, and Rob Whitley. "Men's Mental Health: Social Determinants and Implications for Services." *Canadian Journal of Psychiatry* 63, no. 9 (2018): 581–89.

Agnew, Robert. "Building on the Foundation of General Strain Theory: Specifying the Types of Strain Most Likely to Lead to Crime and Delinquency." In *Recent Developments in Criminological Theory,* edited by Stuart Henry and Scott A. Lukas, 311–54. London: Routledge, 2017.

Ahmad, Nisa. "Why I Quit the Nextdoor Neighbor App." *Medium,* June 16, 2018. https://medium.com/@MzAhmad/why-i-quit-the-nextdoor-neighbor-app-fcb64bfa1eae.

"Air Quality and Environmental Justice." U.S. Environmental Protection Agency. Accessed January 15, 2025. www.epa.gov/air-quality/air-quality-and-environmental-justice.

Akers, Ronald L., and Gang Lee. "A Longitudinal Test of Social Learning Theory: Adolescent Smoking." *Journal of Drug Issues* 26, no. 2 (1996): 317–43.

Akins, Scott. "Racial Segregation and Property Crime: Examining the Mediating Effect of Police Strength." *Justice Quarterly* 20, no. 4 (2003): 675–95.

Alexander, Michelle. *The New Jim Crow: Mass Incarceration in the Age of Colorblindness.* New York: New Press, 2010.

Allyn, Bobby. "Las Vegas Bans Sleeping, Camping in Public Places." National Public Radio. November 7, 2019. www.npr.org/2019/11/07/777356656/las-vegas-bans-sleeping-camping-in-public-places.

American Psychiatric Association. *Diagnostic and Statistical Manual of Mental Disorders.* 5th ed. Arlington, VA: American Psychiatric Association, 2022.

Amir, Menachem. "Victim Precipitated Forcible Rape." *Journal of Criminal Law, Criminology, and Police Science* 58, no. 4 (1967): 493–502.

Anderson, Christian J. "Black Male Teachers: Diversifying the United States' Teacher Workforce." *Journal for Multicultural Education* 12, no. 2 (2018): 197–202.

Anderson, RaeAnn E., Lesley A. Tarasoff, Nicole VanKim, and Corey Flanders. "Differences in Rape Acknowledgment and Mental Health Outcomes across Transgender, Nonbinary, and Cisgender Bisexual Youth." *Journal of Interpersonal Violence* 36, nos. 13–14 (2021): NP7717–39.

"Annual Report, 2022." African American Redress Network. October 2022. https://redressnetwork.org/wp-content/uploads/2022/10/2022_AARN-ANNUAL-REPORT-.pdf.

Apel, Robert. "On the Deterrent Effect of Stop, Question, and Frisk." *Criminology and Public Policy* 15 (2016): 57.

Archer, Dane, and Rosemary Gartner. "Homicide and the Death Penalty: A Cross-National Test of a Deterrence Hypothesis." In *Crime, Inequality and the State,* edited by Mary Vogel, 469–83. London: Routledge, 2020.

Arford, Tammi, and Eric Madfis. "Whitewashing Criminology: A Critical Tour of Cesare Lombroso's Museum of Criminal Anthropology." *Critical Criminology* 30, no. 3 (2022): 723–40.

Arnold, Carrie. "Choosy Eggs May Pick Sperm for Their Genes, Defying Mendel's Law." *Quanta Magazine,* November 15, 2017. www.quantamagazine.org/choosy-eggs-may-pick-sperm-for-their-genes-defying-mendels-law-20171115.

Arrigo, Bruce A., and Thomas J. Bernard. "Postmodern Criminology in Relation to Radical and Conflict Criminology." *Critical Criminology* 8, no. 2 (1997): 39–60.

Aspers, Patrik, and Ugo Corte. "What Is Qualitative in Qualitative Research." *Qualitative Sociology* 42 (2019): 139–60.

Augustyn, Megan Bears, and Jean Marie McGloin. "The Risk of Informal Socializing with Peers: Considering Gender Differences across Predatory Delinquency and Substance Use." *Justice Quarterly* 30, no. 1 (2013): 117–43.

Baker, Helen. "'State-Corporate Facilitated Harms of the Pharmaceutical Industry: A Gendered Perspective.'" *Justice, Power and Resistance: The Journal of the European Group for the Study of Deviance and Social Control* 3, no. 1 (2019): 89–114.

Baker, Katie. "Here's the Powerful Letter the Stanford Victim Read to Her Attacker." BuzzFeedNews. June 3, 2016. www.buzzfeednews.com/article/katiejmbaker/heres-the-powerful-letter-the-stanford-victim-read-to-her-ra.

Banzhaf, H. Spencer. "Regulatory Impact Analysis of Environmental Justice Effects." *Journal of Land Use and Environmental Law* 27 (2011): 1–30.

Banzhaf, Spencer, Lala Ma, and Christopher Timmins. "Environmental Justice: The Economics of Race, Place, and Pollution." *Journal of Economic Perspectives* 33, no. 1 (2019): 185–208.

Barnett, Cynthia. "The Measurement of White-Collar Crime Using Uniform Crime Reporting (UCR) Data." U.S. Department of Justice. 2000. www.ojp.gov/ncjrs/virtual-library/abstracts/measurement-white-collar-crime-using-uniform-crime-reporting-ucr.

Barr, Una. "Working Together? Gendered Barriers to Employment and Desistance from Harm amongst Criminalised English Women." *Feminist Criminology* 18, no. 2 (2023): 156–77.

Baum, Dan. "Legalize it All: How to Win the War on Drugs." *Harpers*, April, 2016. https://harpers.org/archive/2016/04/legalize-it-all/.

Bayer, Mari, Melissa McKee, and Ashtan Towles. "Emerging Practices to Elevate and Replicate Community Responder Programs Nationwide: Expanding First Response National Commission Report." CSG Justice Center. May 2024. https://csgjusticecenter.org/publications/emerging-practices-to-elevate-and-replicate-community-responder-programs-nationwide/.

Bayne, Emma. "Womb Envy: The Cause of Misogyny and Even Male Achievement?" *Women's Studies International Forum* 34, no. 2 (2011): 151–60.

Beccaria, Cesare. *On Crimes and Punishments*. 1764. Reprint, London: Transaction, 2016.

Becker, Sarah, and Jill A. McCorkel. "The Gender of Criminal Opportunity: The Impact of Male Co-offenders on Women's Crime." *Feminist Criminology* 6, no. 2 (2011): 79–110.

Beckett, Katherine, and Theodore Sasson. *The Politics of Injustice: Crime and Punishment in America.* Thousand Oaks, CA: Sage, 2003.

Beirne, Piers. "Theriocide: Naming Animal Killing." *International Journal for Crime, Justice and Social Democracy* 3, no. 2 (2014): 49–66.

Beirne, Piers, and Nigel South. "Introduction: Approaching Green Criminology." In *Issues in Green Criminology: Confronting Harms against Environments, Humanity and Other Animals,* edited by Piers Beirne and Nigel South, 13–22. Portland, OR: Willan, 2007

Belknap, Joanne. "Activist Criminology: Criminologists' Responsibility to Advocate for Social and Legal Justice." *Criminology* 53, no. 1 (2015): 1–22.

Belknap, Joanne. *The Invisible Woman: Gender, Crime, and Justice.* 3rd ed. Belmont, CA: Thompson Wadsworth, 2007.

Ben-Moshe, Liat. *Decarcerating Disability: Deinstitutionalization and Prison Abolition.* Minneapolis: University of Minnesota Press, 2020.

Bennett, William J., John J. DiIulio, and John P. Walters. *Body Count: Moral Poverty and How to Win America's War against Crime and Drugs.* New York: Simon and Schuster, 1996.

Berg, Mark T., and Carrie F. Mulford. "Reappraising and Redirecting Research on the Victim-Offender Overlap." *Trauma, Violence, and Abuse* 21, no. 1 (2020): 16–30.

Berg, Mark T., and Christopher J. Schreck. "The Meaning of the Victim-Offender Overlap for Criminological Theory and Crime Prevention Policy." *Annual Review of Criminology* 5 (2022): 277–97.

Berger, Dan, Mariame Kaba, and David Stein. "What Abolitionists Do." Jacobin. August 2017. https://jacobin.com/2017/08/prison-abolition-reform-mass-incarceration.

Berman, Greg. "'We Have a Lot of Damage to Undo': A Conversation with Jeremy Travis." Guggenheim Foundation. September 21, 2021. www.hfg.org/conversations/we-have-a-lot-of-damage-to-undo/.

Bernstein, Elizabeth. "The Sexual Politics of the 'New Abolitionism.'" *Differences* 18, no. 3 (2007): 128–51.

Biderman, Albert D., and Albert J. Reiss Jr. "On Exploring the 'dark figure' of crime." *Annals of the American Academy of Political and Social Science* 374, no. 1 (1967): 1–15.

Bieder, Robert E. "The Representations of Indian Bodies in Nineteenth-Century American Anthropology." *American Indian Quarterly* 20, no. 2 (1996): 165–79.

Black, Carmen, Jessica P. Cerdeña, and E. Vanessa Spearman-McCarthy. "I Am Not Your Minority." *Lancet Regional Health-Americas* 19 (2023): 100464.

"A Black Feminist Statement." Combahee River Collective. *Women's Studies Quarterly* 42, nos. 3–4 (2014): 271–80.

Blasdell, Raleigh. "The Intersection of Race, Gender, and Class in Routine Activities: A Proposed Criminological Model of Victimization and Offending." *Race, Gender, and Class* 22, nos. 3–4 (2015): 260–73.

Bliton, Chloe F., Caitlin Wolford-Clevenger, Heather Zapor, JoAnna Elmquist, Meagan J. Brem, Ryan C. Shorey, and Gregory L. Stuart. "Emotion Dysregulation, Gender, and Intimate Partner Violence Perpetration: An Exploratory Study in College Students." *Journal of Family Violence* 31 (2016): 371–77.

"BLM Demands." Black Lives Matter. Accessed October 2, 2023. https://blacklivesmatter.com/blm-demands/.

Bloch, Stefano. "Aversive Racism and Community-Instigated Policing: The Spatial Politics of Nextdoor." *Environment and Planning C: Politics and Space* 40, no. 1 (2022): 260–78.

Bonnes, Stephanie. *Hardship Duty: Women's Experiences with Sexual Harassment, Sexual Assault, and Discrimination in the US Military*. Oxford: Oxford University Press, 2023.

Boorsma, Megan. "The Whole Truth: The Implications of America's True Crime Obsession." *Elon Law Review* 9 (2017): 209–24.

Bottcher, Jean. "Gender as Social Control: A Qualitative Study of Incarcerated Youths and Their Siblings in Greater Sacramento." *Justice Quarterly* 12, no. 1 (1995): 33–57.

Bowen, William. "An Analytical Review of Environmental Justice Research: What Do We Really Know?" *Environmental Management* 29 (2002): 3–15.

Boysen, Guy A., Loreto R. Prieto, Jeffrey D. Holmes, R. Eric Landrum, Richard L. Miller, Annette Kujawski Taylor, J. Noland White, and Dakota J. Kaiser. "Trigger Warnings in Psychology Classes: What Do Students Think?" *Scholarship of Teaching and Learning in Psychology* 4, no. 2 (2018): 69–80.

Braz, Rose, Bo Brown, Leslie DiBenedetto, and Ruthie Gilmore. "Overview: Critical Resistance to the Prison-Industrial Complex." *Social Justice* 27, no. 3 (2000): 1–5.

Brenan, Megan. "Record-High 56% in U.S. Perceive Local Crime Has Increased." Gallup. October 28, 2022. https://news.gallup.com/poll/404048/record-high-perceive-local-crime-increased.aspx.

Brenan, Megan. "Worry about Crime in U.S. at Highest Level since 2016." Gallup. April 7, 2022. https://news.gallup.com/poll/391610/worry-crime-highest-level-2016.aspx.

Briggs, Anthony Q. "Second Generation Caribbean Black Male Youths Discuss Obstacles to Educational and Employment Opportunities: A Critical Race Counter-Narrative Analysis." *Journal of Youth Studies* 21, no. 4 (2018): 533–49.

Brindle, Kimberley A., Terence V. Bowles, and Elizabeth Freeman. "Gender, Education and Engagement in Antisocial and Risk-Taking Behaviours and Emotional Dysregulation." *Issues in Educational Research* 29, no. 3 (2019): 633–48.

Briond, Joshua. (2017). "Navigating Justice for Sexual Abuse Survivors, When You're a Prison Abolitionist and a Survivor." Afropunk. December 17, 2019. https://afropunk.com/2017/12/navigating-need-justice-sexual-abuse-survivors-youre-abolitionist-survivor/.

Brody, Jane E. "Harvard Backs Genetic Study." *New York Times*, December 14, 1974.

Broidy, Lisa, and Robert Agnew. "Gender and Crime: A General Strain Theory Perspective." *Journal of Research in Crime and Delinquency* 34, no. 3 (1997): 275–306.

Broidy, Lisa, and Elizabeth Cauffman. "The Glueck Women: Using the Past to Assess and Extend Contemporary Understandings of Women's Desistance from Crime." *Journal of Developmental and Life-Course Criminology* 3 (2017): 102–25.

Brömdal, Annette, Sherree Halliwell, Tait Sanders, Kirsty A. Clark, Jessica Gildersleeve, Amy B. Mullens, Tania M. Phillips, et al. "Navigating Intimate Trans Citizenship While Incarcerated in Australia and the United States." *Feminism and Psychology* 33, no. 1 (2023): 42–64.

brown, adrienne maree. "This Valentine's Day, Celebrate Love as Growth and Liberation." Truthout. February 14, 2021. https://truthout.org/articles/this-valentines-day-celebrate-love-as-growth-and-liberation/.

"Brownfields Program Overview." Environmental Protection Agency. Accessed October 24, 2024. https://19january2021snapshot.epa.gov/sites/static/files/2019-11/documents/brownfields-program-overview-ne.pdf.

"Brownfields: Properties with New Purpose." Environmental Protection Agency. June 2019. www.epa.gov/sites/default/files/2019-06/documents/bf_booklet.pdf.

Brownmiller, Susan. *Against Our Will: Men, Women, and Rape.* New York: Ballantine Books, 1993.

Brownstone, Lisa M., Brooke Dorsey Holliman, Holly R. Gerber, and Lindsey L. Monteith. "The Phenomenology of Military Sexual Trauma among Women Veterans." *Psychology of Women Quarterly* 42, no. 4 (2018): 399–413.

Budd, Kristen M. "Private Prisons in the United States." Sentencing Project. February 21, 2024. www.sentencingproject.org/reports/private-prisons-in-the-united-states/.

"Building Transformative Justice Responses to Child Sexual Abuse." Bay Area Transformative Justice Collective. Accessed January 9, 2025. https://batjc.wordpress.com/.

Bullard, Robert D. *Dumping in Dixie: Race, Class, and Environmental Quality.* Boulder, CO: Westview, 2000.

Burgess, Robert L., and Ronald L. Akers. "A Differential Association-Reinforcement Theory of Criminal Behavior." *Social Problems* 14 (1966): 128–47.

Burkeman, Oliver. "This Column Will Change Your Life: Empathy." *Guardian,* September 19, 2014. www.theguardian.com/lifeandstyle/2014/sep/19/column-change-life-empathy-oliver-burkeman.

Buxbaum, Jessica. "California Initiative Moves Away from Relying on Police to Address Mental Health Crises." Shadowproof. July 23, 2020. https://shadowproof.com/2020/07/23/california-initiative-moves-away-from-relying-on-police-to-address-mental-health-crises/.

Campbell, Alex. "Keeping the 'Lady' Safe: The Regulation of Femininity through Crime Prevention Literature." *Critical Criminology* 13, no. 2 (2005): 119–40.

Campbell, Rebecca, Adrienne E. Adams, Sharon M. Wasco, Courtney E. Ahrens, and Tracy Sefl. "Training Interviewers for Research on Sexual Violence: A Qualitative Study of Rape Survivors' Recommendations for Interview Practice." *Violence against Women* 15, no. 5 (2009): 595–617.

Campo-Engelstein, Lisa, and Nadia L. Johnson. "Revisiting 'The Fertilization Fairytale': An Analysis of Gendered Language Used to Describe Fertilization in Science Textbooks from Middle School to Medical School." *Cultural Studies of Science Education* 9 (2014): 201–20.

"Capital Punishment and Police Safety." Death Penalty Information Center. Accessed October 24, 2024. https://deathpenaltyinfo.org/policy-issues/deterrence/capital-punishment-and-police-safety.

Caputi, Jane, and Diana E. H. Russell. (1990) "Femicide: Speaking the Unspeakable." *Ms.: The World of Women* 1, no. 2 (1990): 34–37.

Caputo, Gail A. *Out in the Storm: Drug-Addicted Women Living as Shoplifters and Sex Workers.* Boston: Northeastern University Press, 2008.

Caputo, Gail A., and Anna King. "Shoplifting by Male and Female Drug Users: Gender, Agency, and Work." *Criminal Justice Review* 40, no. 1 (2015): 47–66.

Caputo, Gail A., and Anna King. "Shoplifting: Work, Agency, and Gender." *Feminist Criminology* 6, no. 3 (2011): 159–77.

Carbone-López, Kristin, Candace Kruttschnitt, and Ross Macmillan. "Patterns of Intimate Partner Violence and Their Associations with Physical Health, Psychological Distress, and Substance Use." *Public Health Reports* 121, no. 4 (2006): 382–92.

Cares, Alison C., Cortney A. Franklin, Bonnie S. Fisher, and Lisa Growette Bostaph. "'They Were There for People who Needed Them': Student Attitudes toward the Use of Trigger Warnings in Victimology Classrooms." *Journal of Criminal Justice Education* 30, no. 1 (2019): 22–45.

Carmichael, Stephanie, Lynn Langton, Gretchen Pendell, John D. Reitzel, and Alex R. Piquero. "Do the Experiential and Deterrent Effect Operate Differently across Gender?" *Journal of Criminal Justice* 33, no. 3 (2005): 267–76.

Carson, E. Ann. "Mortality in State and Federal Prisons, 2001–2018: Statistical Tables." U.S. Department of Justice. April 2021. https://bjs.ojp.gov/content/pub/pdf/msfp0118st.pdf.

Cauffman, Elizabeth, Kathryn C. Monahan, and April Gile Thomas. "Pathways to Persistence: Female Offending from 14 to 25." *Journal of Developmental and Life-Course Criminology* 1 (2015): 236–68.

CDC (Centers for Disease Control and Prevention). "Web-Based Injury Statistics Query and Reporting System, Fatal Injury Data." Hyattsville, MD: National Center on Injury Prevention, 2020.

Center for Behavioral Health Statistics and Quality. *Racial/Ethnic Differences in Substance Use, Substance Use Disorders, and Substance Use Treatment Utilization among People Aged 12 or Older (2015–2019)*. Publication PEP21-07-01-001. Rockville, MD: Substance Abuse and Mental Health Services Administration, 2021.

Chappell, Bill. "California's Prison Sterilizations Reportedly Echo Eugenics Era." National Public Radio. July 9, 2013. www.npr.org/sections/thetwo-way/2013/07/09/200444613/californias-prison-sterilizations-reportedly-echoes-eugenics-era.

Cheon, Aileen, and Cheryl Regehr. "Restorative Justice Models in Cases of Intimate Partner Violence: Reviewing the Evidence." *Victims and Offenders* 1, no. 4 (2006): 369–94.

Chesney-Lind, Meda. "Girls' Crime and Woman's Place: Toward a Feminist Model of Female Delinquency." *Crime and Delinquency* 35, no. 1 (1989): 5–29.

Chesney-Lind, Meda, and Merry Morash, eds. *Feminist Theories of Crime*. Oxon, England: Routledge, 2016.

Chesney-Lind, Meda, and Merry Morash. "Transformative Feminist Criminology: A Critical Re-thinking of a Discipline." *Critical Criminology* 21 (2013): 287–304.

Chesney-Lind, Meda, and Lisa Pasko. *The Female Offender: Girls, Women, and Crime*. Los Angeles: Sage, 2012.

Cho, Sumi, Kimberlé Williams Crenshaw, and Leslie McCall. "Toward a Field of Intersectionality Studies: Theory, Applications, and Praxis." *Signs: Journal of Women in Culture and Society* 38, no. 4 (2013): 78–810.

Chou, Elizabeth. "What's Next: LA Ban on Sitting, Lying Down and Sleeping on Sidewalks Will Launch Sept. 3." *Daily News*, July 30, 2021. www.dailynews.com/2021/07/30/whats-next-la-ban-on-sitting-lying-down-and-sleeping-on-sidewalks-will-launch-sept-3/.

Christ, Carol P. "A New Definition of Patriarchy: Control of Women's Sexuality, Private Property, and War." *Feminist Theology* 24, no. 3 (2016): 214–25.

Christian, Carol, and Lisa Teachey. "Yates Believed Children Doomed." *Houston Chronicle*, March 6, 2002. https://web.archive.org/web/20070902232526/http://www.chron.com/disp/story.mpl/special/drownings/1268306.html.

Christin, Angèle, Alex Rosenblat, and Danah Boyd. "Courts and Predictive Algorithms." *Data and Civil Rights* (2015): 1–11.

Clear, Todd R. *Harm in American Penology: Offenders, Victims, and Their Communities*. New York: State University of New York Press, 1994.

Clear, Todd R. "The Impacts of Incarceration on Public Safety." *Social Research: An International Quarterly* 74, no. 2 (2007): 613–30.

Clinard, Marshall, Richard Quinney, and John Wildeman. *Criminal Behavior Systems: A Typology*. 2nd ed. New York: Holt, Rinehart, and Winston, 1973.

Cloward, Richard A., and Lloyd E. Ohlin. *Delinquency and Opportunity: A Study of Delinquent Gangs*. London: Routledge, 2013.

Cobbina-Dungy, Jennifer. "'I'm Afraid of Cops': Black Protesters' and Residents' Perceptions of Policing in the United States." *Journal of Ethnicity in Criminal Justice* 19, nos. 3–4 (2021): 244–66.

Cobbina-Dungy, Jennifer E., and Delores Jones-Brown. "Too Much Policing: Why Calls Are Made to Defund the Police." *Punishment and Society* 25, no. 1 (2023): 3–20.

Cohen, Stanley. *Folk Devils and Moral Panics*. London: Routledge, 2011.

Cohn, Amy M., Matthew Jakupcak, L. Alana Seibert, Thomas B. Hildebrandt, and Amos Zeichner. "The Role of Emotion Dysregulation in the Association between Men's Restrictive Emotionality and Use of Physical Aggression." *Psychology of Men and Masculinity* 11, no. 1 (2010): 53–64.

Cohn, Erika. *Belly of the Beast*. Accessed November 15, 2024. www.bellyofthebeastfilm.com/.

Cole, Luke W., and Sheila R. Foster. *From the Ground Up: Environmental Racism and the Rise of the Environmental Justice Movement*. Vol. 34. New York: New York University Press, 2001.

"Colorado Chance to Compete Rules." Colorado Department of Labor and Employment. August 2019. www.sos.state.co.us/CCR/Upload/AGORequest-Emergency/AdoptedRules02019-00439.doc.

Collins, Patricia Hill. "Gender, Black Feminism, and Black Political Economy." *Annals of the American Academy of Political and Social Science* 568, no. 1 (2000): 41–53.

Condry, Rachel. *Families Shamed: The Consequences of Crime for Relatives of Serious Offenders*. London: Routledge, 2013.

Conger, Rand D., Frederick O. Lorenz, Glen H. Elder Jr., Ronald L. Simons, and Xiaojia Ge. "Husband and Wife Differences in Response to Undesirable

Life Events." *Journal of Health and Social Behavior* 34. no. 1 (1993): 71–88.

Connell, Raewyn. *Gender and Power: Society, the Person and Sexual Politics*. Stanford, CA: Stanford University Press, 1987.

Connell, Raewyn. *Masculinities*. Berkeley: University of California Press, 1995.

Connell, Raewyn, and James W. Messerschmidt. "Hegemonic Masculinity: Rethinking the Concept." *Gender and Society* 19, no. 6 (2005): 829–59.

Cook, Kimberly J. "Has Criminology Awakened from Its 'Androcentric Slumber?'" *Feminist Criminology* 11, no. 4 (2016): 334–53.

Cook, Kimberly J., Jason M. Williams, Reneè D. Lamphere, Stacy L. Mallicoat, and Alissa R. Ackerman. *Survivor Criminology: A Radical Act of Hope*. Lanham, MD: Rowman and Littlefield, 2022.

Cooper, Carnell, Dawn Eslinger, Denis Nash, Jalal Al Zawahri, and Paul Stolley. "Repeat Victims of Violence: Report of a Large Concurrent Case-Control Study." *Archives of Surgery* 135, no. 7 (2000): 837–43.

Copeny, Mari. "About Mari." Mari Copeny. Accessed October 24, 2024. www.maricopeny.com/about.

Cornish, Derek B., and Ronald V. Clarke. "Understanding Crime Displacement: An Application of Rational Choice Theory." In *Crime Opportunity Theories: Routine Activity, Rational Choice and Their Variants*, edited by Mangai Natarajan, 197–211. London: Routledge, 2017.

Cortina, Lilia M., Verónica Caridad Rabelo, and Kathryn J. Holland. "Beyond Blaming the Victim: Toward a More Progressive Understanding of Workplace Mistreatment." *Industrial and Organizational Psychology* 11, no. 1 (2018): 81–100.

Couloute, Lucius. "Nowhere to Go: Homelessness among Formerly Incarcerated People." Prison Policy Institute. 2018. www.prisonpolicy.org/reports/housing.html.

Covington, Stephanie S. "Women in Prison: Approaches in the Treatment of Our Most Invisible Population." In *Breaking the Rules*, edited by Marcia Hill and Judith Harden, 141–55. London: Routledge, 2018.

Covington, Stephanie S. *A Woman's Journey Home: Challenges for Female Offenders*. Washington, DC: U.S. Department of Health and Human Services, 2002.

Cox, Alison, and Michelle L. Malkin. "Feminist Convict Criminology for the Future." *Critical Criminology* 31, no. 3 (2023): 685–705.

Crawford, Julianne. "Environmental Racism in Houston's Harrisburg Manchester Neighborhood." Stanford University. March 15, 2018. http://bay.stanford.edu/blog/2018/3/15/environmental-racism-in-houstons-harrisburgmanchester-neighborhood.

Crenshaw, Kimberlé. *Demarginalizing the Intersection of Race and Sex: A Black Feminist Critique of Antidiscrimination Doctrine*. Chicago: University of Chicago Legal Forum, 1989.

Crenshaw, Kimberlé W., Andrea J. Ritchie, Rachel Anspach, Rachel Gilmer, and Luke Harris. "Say Her Name: Resisting Police Brutality against Black Women." Columbia University. 2015. https://scholarship.law.columbia.edu/faculty_scholarship/3226/.

"Crime in the U.S., 2019." Federal Bureau of Investigation. Accessed October 24, 2024. https://ucr.fbi.gov/crime-in-the-u.s/2019/crime-in-the-u.s.-2019/home.

Cunradi, Carol B., Raul Caetano, and John Schafer. "Socioeconomic Predictors of Intimate Partner Violence among White, Black, and Hispanic Couples in the United States." *Journal of Family Violence* 17 (2002): 377–89.

Currie, Dawn H., and Brian D. MacLean. "Critical Reflections on the Peace Process in Northern Ireland: Implications for 'Peacethinking Criminology.'" *Humanity and Society* 19, no. 3 (1995): 99–108.

Currie, Elliott. "Against Marginality: Arguments for a Public Criminology." *Theoretical Criminology* 11, no. 2 (2007): 175–90.

Curry, Tommy J. "Expendables for Whom: Terry Crews and the Erasure of Black Male Victims of Sexual Assault and Rape." *Women's Studies in Communication* 42, no. 3 (2019): 287–307.

Daly, Kathleen. "Gender and Varieties of White-Collar Crime." *Criminology* 27, no. 4 (1989): 769–94.

Daly, Kathleen. "Women's Pathways to Felony Court: Feminist Theories of Lawbreaking and Problems of Representation." *Southern California Review of Law and Women's Studies* 2 (1992): 11–52.

Davis, Angela Y., Gina Dent, Erica R. Meiners, and Beth E. Richie. *Abolition. Feminism. Now.* Vol. 2. Chicago: Haymarket Books, 2022.

Dawson, Myrna, and Michelle Carrigan. "Identifying Femicide Locally and Globally: Understanding the Utility and Accessibility of Sex/Gender-Related Motives and Indicators." *Current Sociology* 69, no. 5 (2021): 682–704.

"The Death Penalty." Equal Justice Initiative. Accessed October 24, 2024. https://eji.org/issues/death-penalty/.

Decker, Michele R., Ju Nyeong Park, Sean T. Allen, Bradley Silberzahn, Katherine Footer, Steven Huettner, Noya Galai, and Susan G. Sherman. "Inconsistent Condom Use among Female Sex Workers: Partner-Specific Influences of Substance Use, Violence, and Condom Coercion." *AIDS and Behavior* 24 (2020): 762–74.

De Coster, Stacy. "Delinquency and Depression: A Gendered Role-Taking and Social Learning Perspective." In *Social Learning Theory and the Explanation of Crime*, edited by Ronald L. Akers and Gary F. Jensen, 129–50. London: Routledge, 2017.

De Coster, Stacy, and Maxine S. Thompson. "Race and General Strain Theory: Microaggressions as Mundane Extreme Environmental Stresses." *Justice Quarterly* 34, no. 5 (2017): 903–30.

De Coster, Stacy, and Rena C. Zito. "The Social Landscape of Intractable Offending among African-American Males in Marginalized Contexts." In *Preventing Crime and Violence*, edited by Bret Teasdale and Mindy S. Bradley, 113–22. New York: Springer International, 2017.

De Coster, Stacy, and Rena Cornell Zito. "Gender and General Strain Theory: The Gendering of Emotional Experiences and Expressions." *Journal of Contemporary Criminal Justice* 26, no. 2 (2010): 224–45.

Decuir-Gunby, Jessica T., Thandeka K. Chapman, and Paul A. Schutz, eds. *Understanding Critical Race: Research Methods and Methodologies: Lessons from the Field*. London: Routledge, 2018.

DeKeseredy, Walter S. "Critical Criminological Understandings of Adult Pornography and Woman Abuse: New Progressive Directions in Research and Theory." *International Journal for Crime, Justice and Social Democracy* 4, no. 4 (2015): 4–21.

DeKeseredy, Walter S. "Feminist Perspectives on Woman Abuse in Rural and Remote Places: Pushing the Criminological Envelope." In *Rural Transformations and Rural Crime*, edited by Matt Bowden and Alistair Harkness, 66–86. Bristol: Bristol University Press, 2022.

DeKeseredy, Walter S. "Using Crime Surveys as Tools of Critical Insight and Progressive Change." In *Liquid Criminology*, edited by Michael Hviid Jacobsen and Sandra Walklate, 31–48. London: Routledge, 2016.

"Demand Absolute Standards Stop Profiting from Executions." Worth Rises. Accessed October 24, 2024. https://worthrises.org/lethalinjections.

"Demographic Differences in Sentencing: An Update to the 2012 Booker Report." Sentencing Commission. November 2017. www.ussc.gov/sites/default/files/pdf/research-and-publications/research-publications/2017/20171114_Demographics.pdf.

Dhanani, Lindsay Y., Amanda M. Main, and Andrew Pueschel. "Do You Only Have Yourself to Blame? A Meta-analytic Test of the Victim Precipitation Model." *Journal of Organizational Behavior* 41, no. 8 (2020): 706–21.

Dickerson, Caitlin, Seth Freed Wessler, and Miriam Jordan. "Immigrants Say They Were Pressured into Unneeded Surgeries." *New York Times*, September 29, 2020. www.nytimes.com/2020/09/29/us/ice-hysterectomies-surgeries-georgia.html.

Digard, Léon, and Jacob Kang-Brown. "Yes, the New FBI Data Is Poor Quality but We've Always Needed Better." Vera Institute of Justice. October 12, 2022. www.vera.org/news/yes-the-new-fbi-data-is-poor-quality-but-weve-always-needed-better.

Dippel, Christian, and Michael Poyker. *Do Private Prisons Affect Criminal Sentencing?* Cambridge, MA: National Bureau of Economic Research, 2019.

Dixson, Adrienne D., ArCasia James, and Brittany L. Frieson. "Taking It to the Streets: Critical Race Theory, Participatory Research and Social Justice." In Decuir-Gunby, Chapman, and Schutz, *Understanding Critical Race*, 64–75.

Dodge, Mary. "Women and White-Collar Crime." In *Oxford Research Encyclopedia of Criminology and Criminal Justice*, edited by Henry Pontell. Oxford: Oxford University Press, 2019.

Dodge, Mary, and Mark R. Pogrebin. "Collateral Costs of Imprisonment for Women: Complications of Reintegration." *Prison Journal* 81, no. 1 (2001): 42–54.

"Drug Arrests Stayed High Even as Imprisonment Fell from 2009 to 2019." Pew Charitable Trusts. Accessed January 11, 2025. www.pewtrusts.org/-/media/assets/2022/02/drug-arrests-stayed-high-even-as-imprisonment-fell-from-2009-to-2019.pdf.

"Drug War Stats." Drug Policy Alliance. Accessed October 24, 2024. https://drugpolicy.org/drug-war-stats/.

DuBois, Grace. "Protecting Workers by Prosecuting Wage Theft as a Crime." Center for Progressive Reform. July 19, 2022. https://progressivereform.org/cpr-blog/protecting-workers-prosecuting-wage-theft-crime/.

Du Bois, William Edward Burghardt. *The Philadelphia Negro: A Social Study*. Philadelphia: Atlanta University, 1899.

Du Mont, Janice, Karen-Lee Miller, and Terri L. Myhr. "The Role of 'Real Rape' and 'Real Victim' Stereotypes in the Police Reporting Practices of Sexually Assaulted Women." *Violence against Women* 9, no. 4 (2003): 466–86.

Durose, Matthew R., and Leonardo Antenangeli. "Recidivism of Prisoners Released in 34 States in 2012: A 5-Year Follow-Up Period (2012–2017)." Washington, DC: Bureau of Justice Statistics, 2021.

Duxbury, Scott W. "Fear or Loathing in the United States? Public Opinion and the Rise of Racial Disparity in Mass Incarceration, 1978–2015." *Social Forces* 100, no. 2 (2021): 427–53.

Eaglin, Jessica M. "Racializing Algorithms." *California Law Review* 111 (2023): 753–800.

Egger, Steven A. *The Killers among Us: An Examination of Serial Murder and Its Investigation*. Upper Saddle River, NJ: Prentice Hall, 2002.

Ehrenreich, Barbara. "Is It Now a Crime to Be Poor?" *New York Times*, August 8, 2009.

Ehrenreich, Barbara. "What Is Socialist Feminism?" *Win Magazine*, June 3, 1976.

Eitle, David J. "Exploring a Source of Deviance-Producing Strain for Females: Perceived Discrimination and General Strain Theory." *Journal of Criminal Justice* 30, no. 5 (2002): 429–42.

Elbasheir, Aziz, Seyma Katrinli, Breanne E. Kearney, Ruth A. Lanius, Nathaniel G. Harnett, Sierra E. Carter, Timothy D. Ely, et al. "Racial Discrimination, Neural Connectivity, and Epigenetic Aging among Black Women." *JAMA Network Open* 7, no. 6 (2024): e2416588–e2416588.

Eligon, John. "You Want to Feed the Hungry? Lovely. Let's See Your Permit." *New York Times*, November 21, 2018.

"Eight Can't Wait." Campaign Zero. Accessed October 24, 2024. https://8cantwait.org/.

Estrich, Susan. *Real Rape*. Cambridge, MA: Harvard University Press, 1987.

Eterno, John A., Arvind Verma, and Eli B. Silverman. "Police Manipulations of Crime Reporting: Insiders' Revelations." *Justice Quarterly* 33, no. 5 (2016): 811–35.

Evans, Sarah. "Massachusetts Has a Drug Problem. Somerville's Bold Plan Should Be a Part of the Solution." WBUR. July 10, 2023. www.wbur.org/cognoscenti/2023/07/10/massachusetts-drug-problem-safe-reduction-site-opioids-sarah-evans.

Fagot, Beverly I. "Beyond the Reinforcement Principle: Another Step toward Understanding Sex Role Development." *Developmental Psychology* 21, no. 6 (1985): 1097–104.

Fagot, Beverly I. "The Influence of Sex of Child on Parental Reactions to Toddler Children." *Child Development* (1978): 459–65.

Fagot, Beverly I., and Richard Hagan. "Observations of Parent Reactions to Sex-Stereotyped Behaviors: Age and Sex Effects." *Child Development* 62, no. 3 (1991): 617–28.

Farrell, Graham. "Forty Years of Declining Burglary in the United States: Explanation and Evidence Relating to the Security Hypothesis." *Security Journal* 35, no. 2 (2022): 444–62.

Farrington, David P., Bernard Gallagher, Lynda Morley, Raymond J. St. Ledger, and Donald J. West. "Are There Any Successful Men from Criminogenic Backgrounds?" *Psychiatry* 51, no. 2 (1988): 116–30.

Farrington, David P., and Donald J. West. "Effects of Marriage, Separation, and Children on Offending by Adult Males." *Current Perspectives on Aging and the Life Cycle* 4 (1995): 249–81.

Fass, Simon M., and Chung-Ron Pi. "Getting Tough on Juvenile Crime: An Analysis of Costs and Benefits." *Journal of Research in Crime and Delinquency* 39, no. 4 (2002): 363–99.

Fedock, Gina, and Stephanie S. Covington. (2022) "Strengths-Based Approaches to the Treatment of Incarcerated Women and Girls." In *Facilitating Desistance from Aggression and Crime: Theory, Research and*

Strengths-Based Practices, edited by Calvin M. Langton and James R. Worling, 378–96. Hoboken, NJ: Wiley-Blackwell.

Feiring, Candice, and Lynn S. Taska. "The Persistence of Shame Following Sexual Abuse: A Longitudinal Look at Risk and Recovery." *Child Maltreatment* 10, no. 4 (2005): 337–49.

Fellner, Jamie. "Race, Drugs, and Law Enforcement in the United States." *Stanford Law and Policy Review* 20 (2009): 257–92.

Fernandez, Lauren E. "Defending the Less Dead: Using the Decriminalization of Sex Work to Combat the High Incidence of Serial Homicide of Street-Based Sex Workers." *William and Mary Journal of Race, Gender, and Social Justice* 29 (2022): 205–28.

Ferrell, Jeff. "Cultural Criminology." *Annual Review of Sociology* 25, no. 1 (1999): 395–418.

Field, Craig A., and Raul Caetano. "Ethnic Differences in Intimate Partner Violence in the US General Population: The Role of Alcohol Use and Socioeconomic Status." *Trauma, Violence, and Abuse* 5, no. 4 (2004): 303–17.

Fine, Michelle, Maria Elena Torre, Kathy Boudin, Iris Bowen, Judith Clark, Donna Hylton, Migdalia Martinez, et al. "Participatory Action Research: Within and beyond Bars." In *Qualitative Research in Psychology: Expanding Perspectives in Methodology and Design*, edited by Paul Camic, Jean E. Rhodes, and Lucy Yardley, 173–98. Washington, DC: American Psychological Association, 2003.

Finkelhor, David, and Kersti Yllö. *License to Rape: Sexual Abuse of Wives*. New York: Simon and Schuster, 1987.

Firth, Rhiannon. "Mutual Aid, Anarchist Preparedness and COVID-19." In *Coronavirus, Class and Mutual Aid in the United Kingdom*, edited by John Preston and Rhiannon Firth, 57–111. London: Palgrave Macmillan, 2020.

Fisher Quann, Rayne. "A Fresh Framework: The Feminism of the Abolition Movement." Anarchist Agency. July 6, 2020. https://anarchistagency.com/rayne-fisher-quann-a-fresh-framework-the-feminism-of-the-abolition-movement/.

Fishman, Mark. "Crime Waves as Ideology." *Social Problems* 25, no. 5 (1978): 531–43.

Flavin, Jeanne. "Feminism for the Mainstream Criminologist: An Invitation." *Journal of Criminal Justice* 29, no. 4 (2001): 271–85.

Flores, Andrew R., Lynn Langton, Ilan H. Meyer, and Adam P. Romero. "Victimization Rates and Traits of Sexual and Gender Minorities in the United States: Results from the National Crime Victimization Survey, 2017." *Science Advances* 6, no. 40 (2020): eaba6910.

"Free Marissa Alexander." Free Marissa Now. Accessed October 24, 2024. www.freemarissanow.org/.

Freud, Sigmund. *Three Essays on the Theory of Sexuality.* 1905. Reprint, New York: Verso, 2017.
Friedline, Terri, Sruthi Naraharisetti, and Addie Weaver. "Digital Redlining: Poor Rural Communities' Access to Fintech and Implications for Financial Inclusion." *Journal of Poverty* 24, nos. 5–6 (2020): 517–41.
Friedman, Joseph, and Helena Hansen. "Black and Native Overdose Mortality Overtook That of White Individuals during the COVID-19 Pandemic." *MedRxiv* (2021): 1–8.
Friedrichs, David. "Enron et al.: Paradigmatic White Collar Crime Cases for the New Century." In *Transnational Financial Crime,* edited by Nikos Passas, 59–78. London: Routledge, 2017.
Frohmann, Lisa. "Discrediting Victims' Allegations of Sexual Assault: Prosecutorial Accounts of Case Rejections." *Social Problems* 38, no. 2 (1991): 213–26.
Fuentes, Kimberly. "Sex Worker Collectives within the Whorearchy: Intersectional Inquiry with Sex Workers in Los Angeles, CA." *Affilia* 38, no. 2 (2023): 224–43.
Fyfe, James J. "Administrative Interventions on Police Shooting Discretion: An Empirical Examination." *Journal of Criminal Justice* 7, no. 4 (1979): 309–23.
Gabbidon, Shaun L. *W. E. B. Du Bois on Crime and Justice: Laying the Foundations of Sociological Criminology.* London: Routledge, 2016.
Galvin, Miranda A., and Jeffery T. Ulmer. "Expanding Our Understanding of Focal Concerns: Alternative Sentences, Race, and 'Salvageability.'" *Justice Quarterly* 39, no. 6 (2022): 1332–53.
Garland, David. *The Culture of Control: Crime and Social Order in Contemporary Society.* Chicago: University of Chicago Press, 2012.
Garofalo, Carlo, and Patrizia Velotti. "Negative Emotionality and Aggression in Violent Offenders: The Moderating Role of Emotion Dysregulation." *Journal of Criminal Justice* 51 (2017): 9–16.
Garrison, Lloyd. "French Murder Jury Rejects Chromosome Defect as Defense." *New York Times,* October 15, 1968. www.nytimes.com/1968/10/15/archives/french-murder-jury-rejects-chromosome-defect-as-defense.html.
Gilligan, Carol. *In a Different Voice: Psychological Theory and Women's Development.* Cambridge, MA: Harvard University Press, 1993.
Gilligan, Carol, and Roman Gerodimos. "Shame, Gender and Radical Listening: Carol Gilligan in Conversation with Roman Gerodimos." In *Interdisciplinary Applications of Shame/Violence Theory: Breaking the Cycle,* edited by Roman Gerodimos, 39–58. Cham: Springer International, 2022.
Giordano, Peggy C. "Girls, Guys and Gangs: The Changing Social Context of Female Delinquency." *Journal of Criminal Law and Criminology* 69 (1978): 126–32.

Giordano, Peggy C., Stephen A. Cernkovich, and Meredith D. Pugh. "Friendships and Delinquency." *American Journal of Sociology* 91, no. 5 (1986): 1170–202.

Giordano, Peggy C., Stephen A. Cernkovich, and Jennifer L. Rudolph. "Gender, Crime, and Desistance: Toward a Theory of Cognitive Transformation." *American Journal of Sociology* 107, no. 4 (2002): 990–1064.

Glaser, Daniel. *The Effectiveness of a Prison and Parole System*, Indianapolis: Bobb-Merrill, 1969.

Gleason, Shane A. "Beyond Mere Presence: Gender Norms in Oral Arguments at the US Supreme Court." *Political Research Quarterly* 73, no. 3 (2020): 596–608.

Glueck, Sheldon, and Eleanor Glueck. *Delinquents and Nondelinquents in Perspective*. Cambridge, MA: Harvard University Press, 1968.

Glueck, Sheldon, and Eleanor Touroff Glueck. *Five Hundred Delinquent Women*. New York: Knopf, 1934.

Glueck, Sheldon, and Eleanor Touroff Glueck. *One Thousand Juvenile Delinquents*. Cambridge, MA: Harvard University Press, 1934.

Goebel, Paul, and David Harrison. "Money to Burn: Economic Incentives and the Incidence of Arson." *Journal of Housing Research* 21, no. 1 (2012): 49–65.

Gottfredson, Denise C., Scott Crosse, Zhiqun Tang, Erin L. Bauer, Michele A. Harmon, Carol A. Hagen, and Angela D. Greene. "Effects of School Resource Officers on School Crime and Responses to School Crime." *Criminology and Public Policy* 19, no. 3 (2020): 905–40.

Gottfredson, Michael R. *Victims of Crime: The Dimensions of Risk*. Vol. 81. London: H. M. Stationery Office, 1984.

Gottfredson, Michael R., and Travis Hirschi. *A General Theory of Crime*. Stanford, CA: Stanford University Press, 1990.

Gottzén, Lucas, Margunn Bjørnholt, and Floretta Boonzaier. "What Has Masculinity to Do with Intimate Partner Violence?" In *Men, Masculinities and Intimate Partner Violence*, edited by Lucas Gottzén, Margunn Bjørnholt, and Floretta Boonzaier 1–15. London: Routledge, 2020.

Gove, Walter R. 1985. "The Effect of Age and Gender on Deviant Behavior: A Biopsychosocial Perspective." In *Gender and the Life Course*, edited by Alice S. Rossi, 115–44. New York: Aldine.

Grace, Anita. "'Get to Know Me, Not the Inmate': Women's Management of the Stigma of Criminal Records." *British Journal of Criminology* 62, no. 1 (2022): 73–89.

Graham, John, and Benjamin Bowling. *Young People and Crime*. London: Home Office, 1995.

Gratz, Kim L., and Lizabeth Roemer. "Multidimensional Assessment of Emotion Regulation and Dysregulation: Development, Factor Structure, and Initial Validation of the Difficulties in Emotion Regulation Scale." *Journal of Psychopathology and Behavioral Assessment* 26 (2004): 41–54.

Green, Ben. "The False Promise of Risk Assessments: Epistemic Reform and the Limits of Fairness." Paper presented at the Conference on Fairness, Accountability, and Transparency, Barcelona, January 27–30, 2020.

Green, Jeremy. "Media Sensationalisation and Science: The Case of the Criminal Chromosome." In *Expository Science: Forms and Functions of Popularisation*, edited by Terry Shinn and Richard P. Whitley, 139–61. Dordrecht: Springer Netherlands, 1985.

Greene, Helen Taylor, Shaun L. Gabbidon, and Sean K. Wilson. "Included? The Status of African American Scholars in the Discipline of Criminology and Criminal Justice since 2004." *Journal of Criminal Justice Education* 29, no. 1 (2018): 96–115.

Greene, Robert. "Polly Klaas' Murder Accelerated the Tough-on-Crime Movement. Her Sisters Want to Stop It." *Los Angeles Times*, October 17, 2021. www.latimes.com/opinion/story/2021-10-17/polly-klaas-jess-annie-nichol-criminal-justice-reforms.

Grindal, Matthew. "Ethnic-Racial Socialization, Social Bonds, and College Student Substance Use." *Deviant Behavior* 38, no. 10 (2017): 1102–19.

Gurusami, Susila. "The Carceral Web We Weave: Carceral Citizens' Experiences of Digital Punishment and Solidarity." *Punishment and Society* 21, no. 4 (2019): 435–53.

Gurusami, Susila. "Motherwork under the State: The Maternal Labor of Formerly Incarcerated Black Women." *Social Problems* 66, no. 1 (2019): 128–43.

Gurusami, Susila. "Working for Redemption: Formerly Incarcerated Black Women and Punishment in the Labor Market." *Gender and Society* 31, no. 4 (2017): 433–56.

Hackney, Amy A., and Jack Glaser. "Reverse Deterrence in Racial Profiling: Increased Transgressions by Nonprofiled Whites." *Law and Human Behavior* 37, no. 5 (2013): 348.

Haley, Sarah, and Bruce Arrigo. "Ethical Considerations at the Intersection of Climate Change and Reproductive Justice: Directions from Green Criminology." *Critical Criminology* 30, no. 4 (2022): 1001–18.

Hall, Lauren, and Lyndsey Harris. "The Gendered Weight of Desistance and Understanding the 'Love of a Good Woman': Desistance Emotional Work (DEW)." *Probation Journal* 70, no. 3 (2023): 224–41.

Hallett, Michael A. "Race, Crime, and For-Profit Imprisonment: Social Disorganization as Market Opportunity." *Punishment and Society* 4, no. 3 (2002): 369–93.

Harcourt, Christine, and Basil Donovan. "The Many Faces of Sex Work." *Sexually Transmitted Infections* 81, no. 3 (2005): 201–6.

Harding, Sandra G., ed. *Feminism and Methodology: Social Science Issues*. Indianapolis: Indiana University Press, 1987.

Harrison, Da'Shaun. *Belly of the Beast: The Politics of Anti-fatness as anti-Blackness*. Berkeley, CA: North Atlantic Books, 2021.

Hartley, Richard D., Sean Maddan, and Cassia C. Spohn. "Prosecutorial Discretion: An Examination of Substantial Assistance Departures in Federal Crack-Cocaine and Powder-Cocaine Cases." *Justice Quarterly* 24, no. 3 (2007): 382–407.

Hasler, Olivia, Reece Walters, and Rob White. "In and against the State: The Dynamics of Environmental Activism." *Critical Criminology* 28 (2020): 517–31.

Haynes, Stacy Hoskins, Alison C. Cares, and R. Barry Ruback. "Reducing the Harm of Criminal Victimization: The Role of Restitution." *Violence and Victims* 30, no. 3 (2015): 450–69.

Haynie, Dana L. "Friendship Networks and Delinquency: The Relative Nature of Peer Delinquency." *Journal of Quantitative Criminology* 18 (2002): 99–134.

Hayward, Keith J., and Jock Young. "Cultural Criminology: Some Notes on the Script." *Theoretical Criminology* 8, no. 3 (2004): 259–73.

Heart, Maria Yellow Horse Brave. "The Historical Trauma Response among Natives and Its Relationship with Substance Abuse: A Lakota Illustration." *Journal of Psychoactive Drugs* 35, no. 1 (2003): 7–13.

Heide, Kathleen M., and Eldra P. Solomon. "Biology, Childhood Trauma, and Murder: Rethinking Justice." *International Journal of Law and Psychiatry* 29, no. 3 (2006): 220–33.

Heidensohn, Frances. "The Deviance of Women: A Critique and an Enquiry." *British Journal of Sociology* 19, no. 2 (1968): 160–75.

Heidensohn, Frances. "On Writing 'The Deviance of Women': Observations and Analysis." Supplement, *British Journal of Sociology* 61, no. S1 (2010): 127–32.

Heimer, Karen. "Changes in the Gender Gap in Crime and Women's Economic Marginalization." *Criminal Justice* 1 (2000): 427–83.

Heimer, Karen, and Stacy De Coster. "The Gendering of Violent Delinquency." *Criminology* 37, no. 2 (1999): 277–318.

Heise, Michael, and Jason P. Nance. "'Defund the (School) Police?' Bringing Data to Key School-to-Prison Pipeline Claims." *Journal of Criminal Law and Criminology* 111, no. 3 (2021): 717–72.

Helfgott, Jacqueline B., William S. Parkin, Christopher Fisher, and Adrian Diaz. "Misdemeanor Arrests and Community Perceptions of Fear of Crime in Seattle." *Journal of Criminal Justice* 69 (2020): 101695.

Helmer, Markus, Manuel Schottdorf, Andreas Neef, and Demian Battaglia. "Gender Bias in Scholarly Peer Review." *Elife* 6 (2017): 1–18.

Henson, Abigail, Thuy-Trinh Nguyen, and Ajima Olaghere. "Revising the Critical Gaze: An Inversion of Criminological Theories to Center Race, Racism, and Resistance." *Critical Criminology* 31, no. 1 (2023): 17–33.

Herring, Chris, Dilara Yarbrough, and Lisa Marie Alatorre. "Pervasive Penality: How the Criminalization of Poverty Perpetuates Homelessness." *Social Problems* 67, no. 1 (2020): 131–49.

Hickey, Eric W. *Serial Murderers and Their Victims*. Boston: Cengage Learning, 2015.

Higney, Anthony, Nick Hanley, and Mirko Moro. "The Lead-Crime Hypothesis: A Meta-analysis." *Regional Science and Urban Economics* 97 (2022): 1–18.

Hindelang, Michael J. "Race and Involvement in Common Law Personal Crimes." *American Sociological Review* 34, no. 1 (1978): 93–109.

Hirschi, Travis. *Causes of Delinquency*. London: Routledge, 2017.

"Historical Development of Environmental Criminal Law." Environment and Natural Resources Division. Accessed October 24, 2024. www.justice.gov/enrd/about-division/historical-development-environmental-criminal-law.

"History." Critical Resistance. Accessed October 24, 2024. https://criticalresistance.org/mission-vision/history/.

"The History of Critical Resistance." *Social Justice* 27, no. 3 (2000): 6–10. www.jstor.org/stable/29767223.

Hohl, Katrin, and Elisabeth A. Stanko. "Complaints of Rape and the Criminal Justice System: Fresh Evidence on the Attrition Problem in England and Wales." *European Journal of Criminology* 12, no. 3 (2015): 324–41.

Holtfreter, Kristy, Michael D. Reisig, and Merry Morash. "Poverty, State Capital, and Recidivism among Women Offenders." *Criminology and Public Policy* 3, no. 2 (2004): 185–208.

"Home." Moms 4 Housing. Accessed January 10, 2025. https://moms4housing.org/.

hooks, bell. *Feminist Theory: From Margin to Center*. London: Pluto, 2000.

Horney, Julie, D. Wayne Osgood, and Ineke Haen Marshall. "Criminal Careers in the Short-Term: Intra-individual Variability in Crime and Its Relation to Local Life Circumstances." *American Sociological Review* 60, no. 5 (1995): 655–73.

Hotaling, Gerald T., and Eva Schlesinger Buzawa. *Forging Criminal Justice Assistance: The Non-reporting of New Incidents of Abuse in a Court Sample of Domestic Violence Victims*. Self published, 2003.

"Housing First." National Alliance to End Homelessness. March 20, 2022. https://endhomelessness.org/resource/housing-first/.

"Housing Not Handcuffs, 2019: Ending the Criminalization of Homelessness in U.S. Cities." National Law Center on Homelessness and Poverty. December 2019. https://homelesslaw.org/wp-content/uploads/2019/12/HOUSING-NOT-HANDCUFFS-2019-FINAL.pdf.

Howard, Heather, Katie Clark, and Mary Piltch. "Support for Mothers Who Are Incarcerated: Impact of Mutual Aid Support Groups." *Urban Social Work* 4, no. 1 (2020): 77–93.

Hughes, Diane, James Rodriguez, Emilie P. Smith, Deborah J. Johnson, Howard C. Stevenson, and Paul Spicer. "Parents' Ethnic-Racial Socialization Practices: A Review of Research and Directions for Future Study." *Developmental Psychology* 42, no. 5 (2006): 747–70.

Hughto, Jaclyn M. W., Kirsty A. Clark, Kirstie Daken, Annette Brömdal, Amy B. Mullens, Tait Sanders, Tania Phillips, et al. "Victimization within and beyond the Prison Walls: A Latent Profile Analysis of Transgender and Gender Diverse Adults." *Journal of Interpersonal Violence* 37, nos. 23–24 (2022): NP23075–106.

Hunter, Dianne. "Hysteria, Psychoanalysis, and Feminism: The Case of Anna O." *Feminist Studies* 9, no. 3 (1983): 465–88.

Ignatiev, Noel. *How the Irish Became White*. London: Routledge, 2012.

"Incidents, Offenses, Victims, and Known Offenders by Offense Category, 2019." Federal Bureau of Investigation. Accessed October 24, 2024. https://ucr.fbi.gov/nibrs/2019/tables/pdfs/incidents_offenses_victims_and_known_offenders_by_offense_category_2019.pdf.

INCITE! Women of Color against Violence. *The Revolution Will Not Be Funded: Beyond the Non-profit Industrial Complex*. Durham, NC: Duke University Press, 2020.

"The Ins and Outs of Assistive Technology Safety." End Abuse of People with Disabilities. Presentation. May 5, 2022. www.endabusepwd.org/wp-content/uploads/2022/05/May-2022-EAPWD-Webinar.pdf.

Jack, Astri. "The Gender Reveal Party: A New Means of Performing Parenthood and Reifying Gender under Capitalism." *International Journal of Child, Youth and Family Studies* 11, no. 2 (2020): 82–93.

Jacobi, Tonja, and Dylan Schweers. "Justice, Interrupted: The Effect of Gender, Ideology, and Seniority at Supreme Court Oral Arguments." *Virginia Law Review* 103 (2017): 1379–486.

Jalain, Caroline I., and Elizabeth L. Grossi. "'Take a Load Off Fanny': Peer Mentors in Veterans Treatment Courts." *Criminal Justice Policy Review* 31, no. 8 (2020): 1165–92.

Jayaratne, Toby Epstein, and Abigail J. Stewart. "Quantitative and Qualitative Methods in the Social Sciences: Feminist Issues and Practical Strategies." *Debates and Issues in Feminist Research and Pedagogy* (1995): 217–34.

Jewkes, Yvonne, Melanie Jordan, Serena Wright, and Gillian Bendelow. "Designing 'Healthy' Prisons for Women: Incorporating Trauma-Informed Care and Practice (TICP) into Prison Planning and Design." *International Journal of Environmental Research and Public Health* 16, no. 20 (2019): 1–15.

Jimenez, Tyler, Peter J. Helm, and Jamie Arndt. "Racial Prejudice Predicts Police Militarization." *Psychological Science* 33, no. 12 (2022): 2009–26.

Johnson, Fern L., and Elizabeth J. Aries. "The Talk of Women Friends." *Women's Studies International Forum* 6, no. 4 (1983): 353–61.

Johnson, Michael P., and Kathleen J. Ferraro. "Research on Domestic Violence in the 1990s: Making Distinctions." *Journal of Marriage and Family* 62, no. 4 (2000): 948–63.

Jones, Angela. "'Where the Trans Men and Enbies At?' Cissexism, Sexual Threat, and the Study of Sex Work." *Sociology Compass* 14, no. 2 (2020): 1–15.

Jones, Nikki. "W. E. B. Du Bois." *Encyclopedia of Race and Crime*, edited by Helen Taylor Greene and Shaun L. Gabbidon, 242–46. Thousand Oaks, CA: Sage, 2009.

Joon Jang, Sung. "Gender Differences in Strain, Negative Emotions, and Coping Behaviors: A General Strain Theory Approach." *Justice Quarterly* 24, no. 3 (2007): 523–53.

Joon Jang, Sung, and Byron R. Johnson. "Gender, Religiosity, and Reactions to Strain among African Americans." *Sociological Quarterly* 46, no. 2 (2005): 323–57.

Jordan-Young, Rebecca M., and Katrina Karkazis. *Testosterone: An Unauthorized Biography*. Cambridge, MA: Harvard University Press, 2019.

Juhasz, Antonia. "Louisiana's 'Cancer Alley' Is Getting Even More Toxic—But Residents Are Fighting Back." *Rolling Stone*, October 30, 2019. www.rollingstone.com/politics/politics-features/louisiana-cancer-alley-getting-more-toxic-905534/.

Junger, Marianne, Jack Greene, Ruth Schipper, Floreyne Hesper, and Veronique Estourgie. "Parental Criminality, Family Violence and Intergenerational Transmission of Crime within a Birth Cohort." *European Journal on Criminal Policy and Research* 19 (2013): 117–33.

Kaba, Mariame. "TransformHarm.org: A Resource Hub for Ending Violence." Transform Harm. Accessed January 10, 2025. https://transformharm.org/.

Kaba, Mariame, and Andrea J. Ritchie. *No More Police: A Case for Abolition*. New York: New Press, 2022.

Kaiser, Kimberly A., Eryn N. O'Neal, and Cassia Spohn. "'Victim Refuses to Cooperate': A Focal Concerns Analysis of Victim Cooperation in Sexual Assault Cases." *Victims and Offenders* 12, no. 2 (2017): 297–322.

Katz, Jack. *Seductions of Crime: Moral and Sensual Attractions in Doing Evil*. New York: Basic Books, 1988.

Kaufman, Joanne M. "Gendered Responses to Serious Strain: The Argument for a General Strain Theory of Deviance." *Justice Quarterly* 26, no. 3 (2009): 410–44.

Kelling, George L., and James Q. Wilson. "Broken Windows: The Police and Neighborhood Safety." *Atlantic*, March 1982. www.theatlantic.com/magazine/archive/1982/03/broken-windows/304465/.

Kim, Joy Jeounghee, and Skye Allmang. "Wage Theft in the United States: Towards New Research Agendas." *Economic and Labour Relations Review* 32, no. 4 (2021): 534–51.

King, Ryan D., Michael Massoglia, and Ross MacMillan. "The Context of Marriage and Crime: Gender, the Propensity to Marry, and Offending in Early Adulthood." *Criminology* 45, no. 1 (2007): 33–65.

Kingsnorth, Rodney F., and Randall C. Macintosh. "Domestic Violence: Predictors of Victim Support for Official Action." *Justice Quarterly* 21, no. 2 (2004): 301–28.

Klein, Daniel Eisenkraft, and Joana Madureira Lima. "The Prison Industrial Complex as a Commercial Determinant of Health." *American Journal of Public Health* 111, no. 10 (2021): 1750–52.

Klemko, Robert, and John Sullivan, "Unaccountable: The Push to Remake Policing Takes Decades, Only to Begin Again." *Washington Post*, June 16, 2021. www.washingtonpost.com/investigations/interactive/2021/police-reform-failure/.

Kojola, Erik, and David N. Pellow. "New Directions in Environmental Justice Studies: Examining the State and Violence." *Environmental Politics* 30, nos. 1–2 (2021): 100–18.

Komar, Liz, Ashley Nellis, and Kristin M. Budd. "Counting Down: Paths to a 20-Year Maximum Prison Sentence." Sentencing Project. February 15, 2023. www.sentencingproject.org/reports/counting-down-paths-to-a-20-year-maximum-prison-sentence/.

Komar, Liz, and Nicole D. Porter. "Ending Mass Incarceration: Safety beyond Sentencing." Sentencing Project. July 2023. www.sentencingproject.org/app/uploads/2023/07/Safety-Beyond-Sentencing.pdf.

Kraska, Peter B. "Militarization and Policing—Its Relevance to 21st Century Police." *Policing: A Journal of Policy and Practice* 1, no. 4 (2007): 501–13.

Krohn, Marvin D., William F. Skinner, James L. Massey, and Ronald L. Akers. "Social Learning Theory and Adolescent Cigarette Smoking: A Longitudinal Study." *Social Problems* 32, no. 5 (1985): 455–73.

Kruttschnitt, Candace. "Gender and Crime." *Annual Review of Sociology* 39, no. 1 (2013): 291–308.

Kupers, Terry A. "Toxic Masculinity as a Barrier to Mental Health Treatment in Prison." *Journal of Clinical Psychology* 61, no. 6 (2005): 713–24.

Kurti, Zhandarka. "Police Power in the Aftermath of Black Lives Matter." *Social Justice* 47, nos. 3–4 (2020): 137–50.

Kurwa, Rahim. "Building the Digitally Gated Community: The Case of Nextdoor." *Surveillance and Society* 17, nos. 1–2 (2019): 111–17.

LaFree, Gary D. *Rape and Criminal Justice: The Social Construction of Sexual Assault*. Belmont, CA: Wadsworth, 1989.

Laguardia, Francesca. "Pain That Only She Must Bear: On the Invisibility of Women in Judicial Abortion Rhetoric." *Journal of Law and the Biosciences* 9, no. 1 (2022): 1–36.

Laguardia, Francesca, Venezia Michalsen, and Holly Rider-Milkovich. "Trigger Warnings." *Journal of Legal Education* 66, no. 4 (2017): 882–903.
Laniyonu, Ayobami. "Coffee Shops and Street Stops: Policing Practices in Gentrifying Neighborhoods." *Urban Affairs Review* 54, no. 5 (2018): 898–930.
Lathan, Nadia. "50 Years after Being Outlawed, Redlining Still Drives Neighborhood Health Inequities." Berkeley School of Public Health. September 20, 2023. https://publichealth.berkeley.edu/news-media/research-highlights/50-years-after-being-outlawed-redlining-still-drives-neighborhood-health-inequities .
Laub, John. "Stockholm Prize: Conversation with John Laub and Rob Sampson." National Institute of Justice. February 11, 2011. https://nij.ojp.gov/speech/stockholm-prize-conversation-john-laub-and-rob-sampson.
Laub, John H. "Translational Criminology." National Institute of Justice. March 1, 2011. https://nij.ojp.gov/speech/translational-criminology.
Laub, John H., Daniel S. Nagin, and Robert J. Sampson. "Trajectories of Change in Criminal Offending: Good Marriages and the Desistance Process." In *The Termination of Criminal Careers*, edited by Stephen Farrall, 433–46. London: Routledge, 2017.
Laub, John H., and Robert J. Sampson. *Shared Beginnings, Divergent Lives: Delinquent Boys to Age 70*. Cambridge, MA: Harvard University Press, 2006.
Laub, John H., and Robert J. Sampson. "Turning Points in the Life Course: Why Change Matters to the Study of Crime." *Criminology* 31, no. 3 (1993): 301–25.
Laub, John H., and Robert J. Sampson. "Understanding Desistance from Crime." *Crime and Justice* 28 (2001): 1–69.
Laurencin, Cato T., and Joanne M. Walker. "Racial Profiling Is a Public Health and Health Disparities Issue." *Journal of Racial and Ethnic Health Disparities* 7 (2020): 393–97.
Lauritsen, Janet L., John H. Laub, and Robert J. Sampson. "Conventional and Delinquent Activities: Implications for the Prevention of Violent Victimization among Adolescents." *Violence and Victims* 7, no. 2 (1992): 91–108.
Lavelle, Marianne, and Marcia Coyle. "Unequal Protection: The Racial Divide in Environmental Law." *National Law Journal* 15, no. 3 (1992): S1–12.
Law, Victoria. "Against Carceral Feminism." Jacobin. October 17, 2014. https://jacobin.com/2014/10/against-carceral-feminism/.
Lazarus, Richard J. "Environmental Racism—That's What It Is." *University of Illinois Law Review* 2000, no. 1 (2000): 255–74.
Lea, John. "Jock Young and the Development of Left Realist Criminology." *Critical Criminology* 23 (2015): 165–77.
Leigh, Carol. "Inventing Sex Work." In *Whores and Other Feminists*, edited by Jill Nagle, 223–32. London: Routledge, 1997.

León, Kenneth Sebastian. "Critical Criminology and Race: Re-examining the Whiteness of US Criminological Thought." *Howard Journal of Crime and Justice* 60, no. 3 (2021): 388–408.

Lerner, Kira. "Q&A: A Search for Healing in the 'Trauma-to-Prison Pipeline.'" Arnold Ventures. October 14, 2021. www.arnoldventures.org/stories/a-search-for-healing-in-the-trauma-to-prison-pipeline.

Leverentz, Andrea M. "The Love of a Good Man? Romantic Relationships as a Source of Support or Hindrance for Female Ex-offenders." *Journal of Research in Crime and Delinquency* 43, no. 4 (2006): 459–88.

Levin, Benjamin. "Wage Theft Criminalization." *UC Davis Law Review* 54 (2020): 1429–506.

Like-Haislip, Toya Z., and Karin Tusinski Miofsky. "Race, Ethnicity, Gender, and Violent Victimization." *Race and Justice* 1, no. 3 (2011): 254–76.

Lindsey, Michael A., Wynne S. Korr, Marina Broitman, Lee Bone, Alan Green, and Philip J. Leaf. "Help-Seeking Behaviors and Depression among African American Adolescent Boys." *Social Work* 51, no. 1 (2006): 49–58.

Lira, Natalie, and Alexandra Minna Stern. "Mexican Americans and Eugenic Sterilization: Resisting Reproductive Injustice in California, 1920–1950." *Aztlán: A Journal of Chicano Studies* 39, no. 2 (2014): 9–34.

Liu, Lin, Ronet Bachman, Jing Qiu, and Dayu Sun. "Do Both Petty and Serious Female Offenders Have Shorter Incarcerations Than Their Male Counterparts? Testing the Universality of Chivalrous Treatment." *Women and Criminal Justice* 33, no. 4 (2023): 310–24.

Loader, Ian. "Consumer Culture and the Commodification of Policing and Security." *Sociology* 33, no. 2 (1999): 373–92.

Lombroso, Cesare. *Criminal Man*. New York: Putnam, 1911.

López, María Encarnación. "Femicide in Ciudad Juárez Is Enabled by the Regulation of Gender, Justice, and Production in Mexico." *LSE Latin America and Caribbean Blog*. February 15, 2018. https://eprints.lse.ac.uk/88766/1/latamcaribbean-2018-02-15-femicide-in-ciudad-juarez-is-enabled-by-the.pdf.

López Haney, Ian. *White by Law*. New York: New York University Press, 1996.

Lorde, Audre. "History Is a Weapon: The Master's Tools Will Never Dismantle the Master's House." In *Sister Outsider: Essays and Speeches*, 110–14. New York: Crossing, 1984.

Loughran, Thomas A., Ray Paternoster, Aaron Chalfin, and Theodore Wilson. "Can Rational Choice Be Considered a General Theory of Crime? Evidence from Individual-Level Panel Data." *Criminology* 54, no. 1 (2016): 86–112.

Low, Grace. "'Go and Look in the Mirror and Make a Change, Mum': Motherhood and Identity Change in Women's Desistance in New Zealand." *Women and Criminal Justice* 33, no. 5 (2023): 325–48.

Low, Grace. "Working through Desistance: Employment in Women's Identity and Relational Desistance." *British Journal of Criminology* 64, no. 4 (2024): 846–62.

Lowe, Maria R., Angela Stroud, and Alice Nguyen. "Who Looks Suspicious? Racialized Surveillance in a Predominantly White Neighborhood." *Social Currents* 4, no. 1 (2017): 34–50.

Lum, Cynthia, and Daniel S. Nagin. "Reinventing American Policing." *Crime and Justice* 46, no. 1 (2017): 339–93.

Lynch, Michael J. "Green Criminology and Environmental Crime: Criminology That Matters in the Age of Global Ecological Collapse." *Journal of White Collar and Corporate Crime* 1, no. 1 (2020): 50–61.

Lynch, Michael J., and Michael A. Long. "Green Criminology: Capitalism, Green Crime and Justice, and Environmental Destruction." *Annual Review of Criminology* 5 (2022): 255–76.

Lyngstad, Torkild Hovde, and Torbjørn Skardhamar. "Changes in Criminal Offending around the Time of Marriage." *Journal of Research in Crime and Delinquency* 50, no. 4 (2013): 608–15.

Maher, Lisa. *Sexed Work: Gender, Race, and Resistance in a Brooklyn Drug Market.* Oxford: Clarendon, 1997.

Maher, Lisa, and Kathleen Daly. "Women in the Street-Level Drug Economy: Continuity or Change?" *Criminology* 34, no. 4 (1996): 465–92.

Mangundayao, Ihna, Celine McNicholas, Margaret Poydock, and Ali Sait. "More Than $3 Billion in Stolen Wages Recovered for Workers between 2017 and 2020." Economic Policy Institute. December 22, 2021. www.epi.org/publication/wage-theft-2021/.

Marcus, Natania, and Vicky Stergiopoulos. "Re-examining Mental Health Crisis Intervention: A Rapid Review Comparing Outcomes across Police, Co-responder and Non-police Models." *Health and Social Care in the Community* 30, no. 5 (2022): 1665–79.

Margolin, Jamie. "I Sued the State of Washington Because I Can't Breathe There. They Ignored Me." *Guardian,* October 6, 2018. www.theguardian.com/commentisfree/2018/oct/06/i-sued-the-state-of-washington-because-i-cant-breathe-there-they-ignored-me.

Martin, Emily. "The Egg and the Sperm: How Science Has Constructed a Romance Based on Stereotypical Male-Female Roles." *Signs: Journal of Women in Culture and Society,* 16, no. 3 (1991): 485–501.

Martinez, Xiuhtezcatl. "Xiuhtezcatl Martinez Explains Why He's Fighting Climate Change." *Teen Vogue,* April 30, 2018. www.teenvogue.com/story/xiuhtezcatl-martinez-explains-why-hes-fighting-climate-change.

Maruna, Shadd. Foreword to *Convict Criminology for the Future,* edited by J. I. Ross and F. A. Vianello, Ross, Jeffrey Ian, and Francesca Alice Vianello, eds. xviii–xix. New York: Routledge, 2020.

Maruna, Shadd. *Making Good*. Vol. 86. Washington, DC: American Psychological Association, 2001.

Maruschack, Laura, Jennifer Bronson, and Mariel Alper. "Alcohol and Drug Use and Treatment Reported by Prisoners." Bureau of Justice Statistics. July 2021. https://bjs.ojp.gov/sites/g/files/xyckuh236/files/media/document/adutrpspi16st.pdf.

Masera, Federico. "Police Safety, Killings by the Police, and the Militarization of US Law Enforcement." *Journal of Urban Economics* 124 (2021): 1–22.

Mashhoodi, Bardia. "Feminization of Surface Temperature: Environmental Justice and Gender Inequality among Socioeconomic Groups." *Urban Climate* 40 (2021): 1–12.

Matsueda, Ross L. "Rational Choice Research in Criminology: A Multi-level Framework." In *Handbook of Rational Choice Social Research*, edited by Rafael Wittek, Tom A. B. Snijders, and Victor Nee, 283–321. Stanford, CA: Stanford University Press., 2013.

May, David C., Brandon K. Applegate, Rick Ruddell, and Peter B. Wood. "Going to Jail Sucks (and It Really Doesn't Matter Who You Ask)." *American Journal of Criminal Justice* 39 (2014): 250–66.

Mayson, Sandra G. "Bias In, Bias Out." *Yale Law Journal* 128, no. 8 (2019): 2218–300.

McCulloch, Jude. "Blue Armies, Khaki Police and the Cavalry on the New American Frontier: Critical Criminology for the 21st Century." *Critical Criminology* 12 (2003): 309–26.

McEvoy, Kieran. "Beyond the Metaphor: Political Violence, Human Rights and New 'Peacemaking Criminology.'" *Theoretical Criminology* 7, no. 3 (2003): 319–46.

McGlynn, Clare, Julia Downes, and Nicole Westmarland. "Seeking Justice for Survivors of Sexual Violence: Recognition, Voice and Consequences." In *Restorative Responses to Sexual Violence*, edited by Estelle Zinsstag and Marie Keenan, 179–91. London: Routledge, 2017.

McKay, Hollie. "New Documentary Highlights the Forced Sterilization of Women in California Prison." Fox News. June 15, 2020. www.foxnews.com/entertainment/new-documentary-illuminates-the-forced-sterilization-of-women-in-california-prison.

Meade, Benjamin, Gabriela Wasileski, and Alisha Hunter. "The Effects of Victimization Prior to Prison on Victimization, Misconduct, and Sanction Severity during Incarceration." *Crime and Delinquency* 67, no. 12 (2021): 1856–78.

Mears, Daniel P., Matthew Ploeger, and Mark Warr. "Explaining the Gender Gap in Delinquency: Peer Influence and Moral Evaluations of Behavior." *Journal of Research in Crime and Delinquency* 35, no. 3 (1998): 251–66.

Meloy, Michelle L., and Susan L. Miller. *The Victimization of Women: Law, Policies, and Politics.* Oxford: Oxford University Press, 2010.

Messerschmidt, James W. "From Patriarchy to Gender: Feminist Theory, Criminology and the Challenge of Diversity." In *International Feminist Perspectives in Criminology: Engendering a Discipline,* edited by Nicole Hahn Rafter and Frances Heidensohn, 167–88. Buckingham: Open University, 1995.

Messerschmidt, James W. *Masculinities and Crime: Critique and Reconceptualization of Theory.* Lanham, MD: Rowman and Littlefield, 1993.

Messerschmidt, James W. "The Salience of 'Hegemonic Masculinity.'" *Men and Masculinities* 22, no. 1 (2019): 85–91.

Metz, Julia, Kristen Myers, and Patricia Wallace. "'Rape Is a Man's Issue': Gender and Power in the Era of Affirmative Sexual Consent." *Journal of Gender Studies* 30, no. 1 (2021): 52–65.

"Mexico: Intolerable Killings; 10 Years of Abductions and Murder of Women in Ciudad Juárez and Chihuahua." Amnesty International. August 10, 2023. www.amnesty.org/en/wp-content/uploads/2021/06/amr410262003en.pdf.

Michalowski, Raymond J. "Critical Criminology and the Critique of Domination: The Story of an Intellectual Movement." *Critical Criminology* 7 (1996): 9–16.

Michalowski, Raymond J. *Order, Law, and Crime: An Introduction to Criminology.* New York: Random House, 1985.

Michalsen, Venezia. *Mothering and Desistance in Re-entry.* London: Routledge, 2018.

Michalsen, Venezia. "Mothering as a Life Course Transition: Do Women Go Straight for Their Children?" *Journal of Offender Rehabilitation* 50, no. 6 (2011): 349–66.

Michel, Cedric. "Violent Street Crime versus Harmful White-Collar Crime: A Comparison of Perceived Seriousness and Punitiveness." *Critical Criminology* 24 (2016): 127–43.

Middlemiss, Wendy. "Poverty, Stress, and Support: Patterns of Parenting Behaviour among Lower-Income Black and Lower-Income White Mothers." *Infant and Child Development: An International Journal of Research and Practice* 12, no. 3 (2003): 293–300.

Miles, Rosalind. *Who Cooked the Last Supper? The Women's History of the World.* New York: Crown, 2007.

Miller, Jody. "The Strengths and Limits of 'Doing Gender' for Understanding Street Crime." *Theoretical Criminology* 6, no. 4 (2002): 433–60.

Miller, Jody. "Up It Up: Gender and the Accomplishment of Street Robbery." *Criminology* 36, no. 1 (1998): 37–66.

Miller, Susan L., and Cynthia Burack. "A Critique of Gottfredson and Hirschi's General Theory of Crime: Selective (In)Attention to Gender and Power Positions." *Women and Criminal Justice* 4, no. 2 (1993): 115–34.

Miller, Walter B. "Lower-Class Culture as a Generating Milieu of Gang Delinquency." *Journal of Social Issues* 14, no. 3 (1958): 5–19.

Miller-Loncar, Cynthia L., Loeta Jeanette Erwin, Susan H. Landry, Karen E. Smith, and Paul R. Swank. "Characteristics of Social Support Networks of Low Socioeconomic Status African American, Anglo American, and Mexican American Mothers of Full-Term and Preterm Infants." *Journal of Community Psychology* 26, no. 2 (1998): 131–43.

Mirowsky, John, and Catherine E. Ross. "Sex Differences in Distress: Real or Artifact?" *American Sociological Review* 60 (1995): 449–68.

Mohai, Paul, David Pellow, and J. Timmons Roberts. "Environmental Justice." *Annual Review of Environment and Resources* 34 (2009): 405–30.

Mondé, Geniece Crawford. "'Trying to Get Free': A Theoretical Centering of Black Women's Post-carceral Narratives of Systemic Unfreedom." *Journal of Qualitative Criminal Justice and Criminology* 11, no. 3 (2021): 352–82.

Monteith, Lindsey L., Ryan Holliday, Melissa E. Dichter, and Claire A. Hoffmire. "Preventing Suicide among Women Veterans: Gender-Sensitive, Trauma-Informed Conceptualization." *Current Treatment Options in Psychiatry* 9, no. 3 (2022): 186–201.

Moraga, Cherríe, and Gloria Anzaldúa, eds. *This Bridge Called My Back: Writings by Radical Women of Color*. 1981. Reprint, New York: State University of New York Press, 2022.

Morash, Merry. "Gender, Peer Group Experiences, and Seriousness of Delinquency." *Journal of Research in Crime and Delinquency* 23, no. 1 (1986): 43–67.

Moreland, Cheryl, and Mark M. Leach. "The Relationship between Black Racial Identity and Moral Development." *Journal of Black Psychology* 27, no. 3 (2001): 255–71.

Morgan, Rachel E., and Erica L. Smith. "The National Crime Victimization Survey and National Incident-Based Reporting System: A Complementary Picture of Crime in 2021." Bureau of Justice Statistics. October 2022. https://bjs.ojp.gov/sites/g/files/xyckuh236/files/media/document/ncvsnibrscpc21.pdf.

Morgan, Rachel E., and Alexandra Thompson. "Criminal Victimization, 2020." Bureau of Justice Statistics. October 2021. https://bjs.ojp.gov/library/publications/criminal-victimization-2020.

Morrison, Toni. *Playing in the Dark: Whiteness and the Literary Imagination*. New York: Vintage, 1992.

Morrow, Weston J., Michael D. White, and Henry F. Fradella. "After the Stop: Exploring the Racial/Ethnic Disparities in Police Use of Force during Terry Stops." *Police Quarterly* 20, no. 4 (2017): 367–96.

Moyer, Melinda Wenner. "'A Poison in the System': The Epidemic of Military Sexual Assault." *New York Times*, October 11, 2021. www.nytimes.com/2021/08/03/magazine/military-sexual-assault.html.

Muhammad, Nylah Iqbal. "Meet the Young Activists of Color Who Are Leading the Charge against Climate Disaster." Vox. October 11, 2019. www.vox.com/identities/2019/10/11/20904791/young-climate-activists-of-color.

Mukherjee, Anita. "Do Private Prisons Distort Justice? Evidence on Time Served and Recidivism." *Social Sciences Research Network* 15 (2015): 1–77.

Mullins, Christopher W. "'He Would Kill Me with His Penis': Genocidal Rape in Rwanda as a State Crime." *Critical Criminology* 17 (2009): 15–33.

Mummolo, Jonathan. "Modern Police Tactics, Police-Citizen Interactions, and the Prospects for Reform." *Journal of Politics* 80, no. 1 (2018): 1–15.

Murphy-Oikonen, Jodie, and Rachel Egan. "Sexual and Gender Minorities: Reporting Sexual Assault to the Police." *Journal of Homosexuality* 69, no. 5 (2022): 773–95.

Musto, Jennifer. "Transing Critical Criminology: A Critical Unsettling and Transformative Anti-carceral Feminist Reframing." *Critical Criminology* 27 (2019): 37–54.

Naffine, Ngaire. *Female Crime: The Construction of Women in Criminology.* London: Routledge, 2015.

Navarro, Jordana N., and Jana L. Jasinski. "Why Girls? Using Routine Activities Theory to Predict Cyberbullying Experiences between Girls and Boys." *Women and Criminal Justice* 23, no. 4 (2013): 286–303.

Nawyn, Stephanie J., Nur Banu Kavakli Birdal, and Naomi Glogower. "Estimating the Extent of Sex Trafficking: Problems in Definition and Methodology." *International Journal of Sociology* 43, no. 3 (2013): 55–71.

Neissl, Katharina, Ekaterina V. Botchkovar, Olena Antonaccio, and Lorine A. Hughes. "Rational Choice and the Gender Gap in Crime: Establishing the Generality of Rational Choice Theory in Russia and Ukraine." *Justice Quarterly* 36, no. 6 (2019): 1096–121.

Newburn, Tim, and Elizabeth A. Stanko. *Just Boys Doing Business? Men, Masculinities and Crime.* London: Routledge, 2013.

Novisky, Meghan A., and Robert L. Peralta. "Gladiator School: Returning Citizens' Experiences with Secondary Violence Exposure in Prison." *Victims and Offenders* 15, no. 5 (2020): 594–618.

Nuevelle, Taylar. "Breaking the Silence about Women in Prison." Vera Institute of Justice. August 22, 2016. www.vera.org/blog/gender-and-justice-in-america/breaking-the-silence-about-women-in-prison.

Nurse, Angus. "Privatising the Green Police: The Role of NGOs in Wildlife Law Enforcement." *Crime, Law and Social Change* 59 (2013): 305–18.
O'Connor, Christopher, and Katharine Kelly. "Auto Theft and Youth Culture: A Nexus of Masculinities, Femininities and Car Culture." *Journal of Youth Studies* 9, no. 3 (2006): 247–67.
"Offense Definitions." Federal Bureau of Investigation. Accessed October 24, 2024. https://ucr.fbi.gov/crime-in-the-u.s/2019/crime-in-the-u.s.-2019/topic-pages/offense-definitions.
O'Hare, Peggy. "Nurse: Yates Overwrought as Mother." *Houston Chronicle*, July 8, 2006. www.chron.com/news/houston-texas/article/nurse-yates-overwrought-as-mother-1666444.php.
Omi, Michael, and Howard Winant. *Racial Formation in the United States*. London: Routledge, 2014.
"On 50th Anniversary of 'War on Drugs,' Poll Shows Majority of Voters Support Ending Criminal Penalties for Drug Possession, Think Drug War Is a Failure." American Civil Liberties Union. June 9, 2021. www.aclu.org/press-releases/50th-anniversary-war-drugs-poll-shows-majority-voters-support-ending-criminal.
O'Neal, Eryn Nicole, and Cassia Spohn. "When the Perpetrator Is a Partner: Arrest and Charging Decisions in Intimate Partner Sexual Assault Cases—A Focal Concerns Analysis." *Violence against Women* 23, no. 6 (2017): 707–29.
Opsal, Tara. "'Livin' on the Straights': Identity, Desistance, and Work among Women Post-incarceration." *Sociological Inquiry* 82, no. 3 (2012): 378–403.
Ortner, Sherry B. "Patriarchy." *Feminist Anthropology* 3, no. 2 (2022): 307–14.
O'Sullivan, Julie R. "Is the Corporate Criminal Enforcement Ecosystem Defensible?" *Journal of Corporation Law* 47 (2021): 1047–71.
"Our Work." Collective Action for Safe Spaces. Accessed October 24, 2024. www.collectiveactiondc.org/our-work/.
Outlaw, Maureen C. "Realizing the Promise of Restitution." *Criminology and Public Policy* 13 (2014): 401–4.
Owen, Barbara, and Barbara Bloom. "Profiling Women Prisoners: Findings from National Surveys and a California Sample." *Prison Journal* 75, no. 2 (1995): 165–85.
Paltrow, Lynn M., and Jeanne Flavin. "Arrests of and Forced Interventions on Pregnant Women in the United States, 1973–2005: Implications for Women's Legal Status and Public Health." *Journal of Health Politics, Policy and Law* 38, no. 2 (2013): 299–343.
Park, Peter, and Paulo Freire. *Voices of Change: Participatory Research in the United States and Canada*. Toronto: Ontario Institute for Studies in Education, 1993.

"Past Cases and Projects." Public Interest Law Center. Accessed October 24, 2024. https://pubintlaw.org/practice-area/environmental-justice/archive/past-cases-projects/.

Paternoster, Raymond, and Shawn D. Bushway. "Theoretical and Empirical Work on the Relationship between Unemployment and Crime." *Journal of Quantitative Criminology* 17 (2001): 391–407.

Patton, Dana, and Joseph L. Smith. "Gender, Ideology, and Dominance in Supreme Court Oral Arguments." *Journal of Women, Politics and Policy* 41, no. 4 (2020): 393–415.

Patton, Desmond Upton, Douglas-Wade Brunton, Andrea Dixon, Reuben Jonathan Miller, Patrick Leonard, and Rose Hackman. "Stop and Frisk Online: Theorizing Everyday Racism in Digital Policing in the Use of Social Media for Identification of Criminal Conduct and Associations." *Social Media + Society* 3, no. 3 (2017): 1–10.

Pepinsky, Hal. "Peacemaking Criminology." *Critical Criminology* 21, no. 3 (2013): 319–39.

Peterson, Ruth D., and Lauren J. Krivo. *Divergent Social Worlds: Neighborhood Crime and the Racial-Spatial Divide*. New York: Sage Foundation, 2010.

Pettus, Carrie A. "Trauma and Prospects for Reentry." *Annual Review of Criminology* 6 (2023): 423–46.

Pezzella, Frank S., Matthew D. Fetzer, and Tyler Keller. "The Dark Figure of Hate Crime Underreporting." *American Behavioral Scientist* (2019): 1–24.

"Phrenology and 'Scientific Racism' in the 19th Century." Real Archaeology. Accessed October 24, 2024. https://pages.vassar.edu/realarchaeology/2017/03/05/phrenology-and-scientific-racism-in-the-19th-century/.

Pickett, Justin T., Christina Mancini, Daniel P. Mears, and Marc Gertz. "Public (Mis)Understanding of Crime Policy: The Effects of Criminal Justice Experience and Media Reliance." *Criminal Justice Policy Review* 26, no. 5 (2015): 500–522.

Piliavin, Irving, Rosemary Gartner, Craig Thornton, and Ross L. Matsueda. "Crime, Deterrence, and Rational Choice." *American Sociological Review* 51, no. 1 (1986): 101–19.

Piquero, Alex R., Jeffrey Fagan, Edward P. Mulvey, Laurence Steinberg, and Candice Odgers. "Developmental Trajectories of Legal Socialization among Serious Adolescent Offenders." *Journal of Criminal Law and Criminology* 96, no. 1 (2005): 267–98.

Piquero, Nicole Leeper, Kristan Fox, Alex R. Piquero, George Capowich, and Paul Mazerolle. "Gender, General Strain Theory, Negative Emotions, and Disordered Eating." *Journal of Youth and Adolescence* 39 (2010): 380–92.

Piquero, Nicole Leeper, and Miriam D. Sealock. "Gender and General Strain Theory: A Preliminary Test of Broidy and Agnew's Gender/GST Hypotheses." *Justice Quarterly* 21, no. 1 (2004): 125–58.

Piquero, Alex R., Raymond Paternoster, Greg Pogarsky, and Thomas Loughran. "Elaborating the Individual Difference Component in Deterrence Theory." *Annual Review of Law and Social Science* 7 (2011): 335–60.

Posey, Brianne M., Melissa A. Kowalski, and Mary K. Stohr. "Thirty Years of Scholarship in the Women and Criminal Justice Journal: Gender, Feminism, and Intersectionality." *Women and Criminal Justice* 30, no. 1 (2020): 5–29.

Potter, Hillary. "An Argument for Black Feminist Criminology: Understanding African American Women's Experiences with Intimate Partner Abuse Using an Integrated Approach." *Feminist Criminology* 1, no. 2 (2006): 106–24.

Potter, Hillary. "Intersectional Criminology: Interrogating Identity and Power in Criminological Research and Theory." *Critical Criminology* 21 (2013): 305–18.

Potter, Hillary. *Intersectionality and Criminology: Disrupting and Revolutionizing Studies of Crime*. London: Routledge, 2015.

Powell, Zachary A. "Burnin' Down the House: The 2007 Recession and the Effect on Arson." *Deviant Behavior* 39, no. 5 (2018): 541–53.

Powers, Laurie E., and Mary Oschwald. "Violence and Abuse against People with Disabilities: Experiences, Barriers and Prevention Strategies." Oregon Health and Science University. www.phinational.org/wp-content/uploads/legacy/clearinghouse/AbuseandViolenceBrief%203-7-04.pdf.

Pratt, Amy. "Private Prison Companies and Sentencing." Ohio State Legal Studies Research Paper 677. Drug Enforcement and Policy Center. January 26, 2022. http://dx.doi.org/10.2139/ssrn.4018475.

Pratt, Travis C. "Rational Choice Theory, Crime Control Policy, and Criminological Relevance." *Criminology and Public Policy* 7 (2008): 43–52.

Pratt, Travis C., and Francis T. Cullen. "Assessing Macro-Level Predictors and Theories of Crime: A Meta-analysis." *Crime and Justice* 32 (2005): 373–450.

Pratt, Travis C., and Francis T. Cullen. "The Empirical Status of Gottfredson and Hirschi's General Theory of Crime: A Meta-analysis." *Criminology* 38, no. 3 (2000): 931–64.

Pratt, Travis C., Francis T. Cullen, Kristie R. Blevins, Leah E. Daigle, and Tamara D. Madensen. "The Empirical Status of Deterrence Theory: A Meta-analysis." *Taking Stock: The Status of Criminological Theory* 15 (2006): 367–96.

Pratt, Travis C., Francis T. Cullen, Christine S. Sellers, L. Thomas Winfree Jr., Tamara D. Madensen, Leah E. Daigle, Noelle E. Fearn, and Jacinta M. Gau. "The Empirical Status of Social Learning Theory: A Meta-analysis." *Justice Quarterly* 27, no. 6 (2010): 765–802.

Pratt, Travis C., and Jillian J. Turanovic. "Lifestyle and Routine Activity Theories Revisited: The Importance of 'Risk' to the Study of Victimization." *Victims and Offenders* 11, no. 3 (2016): 335–54.

Pressman, Steven. "Explaining the Gender Poverty Gap in Developed and Transitional Economies." *Journal of Economic Issues* 36, no. 1 (2002): 17–40.

Proctor, Bernadette D., and Joseph Dalaker. *Poverty in the United States: 2001 Current Population Reports*. Washington, DC: United States Census, 2002.

Purtle, Jonathan, Rochelle Dicker, Carnell Cooper, Theodore Corbin, Michael B. Greene, Anne Marks, Diana Creaser, Deric Topp, and Dawn Moreland. "Hospital-Based Violence Intervention Programs Save Lives and Money." *Journal of Trauma and Acute Care Surgery* 75, no. 2 (2013): 331–33.

Quinet, Kenna. "The Missing Missing: Toward a Quantification of Serial Murder Victimization in the United States." *Homicide Studies* 11, no. 4 (2007): 319–39.

Quinet, Kenna. "Prostitutes as Victims of Serial Homicide: Trends and Case Characteristics, 1970–2009." *Homicide Studies* 15, no. 1 (2011): 74–100.

"Racial Disparities in Sentencing in the United States." Sentencing Project. July 14, 2022. www.sentencingproject.org/app/uploads/2022/10/07-14-2022_CERD-Shadow-Report-Draft_with-endnotes.pdf.

Ragin, Charles. "Combining Qualitative and Quantitative Research." Paper presented at the Workshop on Scientific Foundations of Qualitative Research, National Science Foundation, Arlington, VA, 2004.

Ragin, Charles C., Joane Nagel, and Patricia White. *Workshop on Scientific Foundations of Qualitative Research*. Alexandra, VA: National Science Foundation, 2004.

Ranapurwala, Shabbar I., Mary C. Figgatt, Molly Remch, Carrie Brown, Lauren Brinkley-Rubinstein, David L. Rosen, Mary E. Cox, and Scott K. Proescholdbell. "Opioid Overdose Deaths among Formerly Incarcerated Persons and the General Population: North Carolina, 2000–2018." *American Journal of Public Health* 112, no. 2 (2022): 300–303.

Rasmussen, Cameron, and Kirk "Jae" James. "Trading Cops for Social Workers Isn't the Solution to Police Violence." Truthout. July 17, 2020. https://truthout.org/articles/trading-cops-for-social-workers-isnt-the-solution-to-police-violence/.

Raven, Leila, Mon Mohapatra, and Rachel Kuo. "8 to Abolition Is Advocating to Abolish Police to Keep Us All Safe." *Teen Vogue*, June 25, 2020. www.teenvogue.com/story/8-to-abolition-abolish-police-keep-us-safe-op-ed.

"Regulations: 45 CFR 46." U.S. Department of Health and Human Services. Accessed January 10, 2025. www.hhs.gov/ohrp/regulations-and-policy/regulations/45-cfr-46/index.html.

Rentschler, Carrie. *The Crime Victim Movement and United States Public Culture*. Champaign: University of Illinois at Urbana-Champaign, 2002.

Rentschler, Carrie A. *Second Wounds: Victims' Rights and the Media in the US*. Durham, NC: Duke University Press, 2011.

Renzetti, Claire M. "On the Margins of the Malestream (or, They Still Don't Get It, Do They?): Feminist Analyses in Criminal Justice Education." *Journal of Criminal Justice Education* 4, no. 2 (1993): 219–34.

Reyes, Emily Alpert. "L.A. City Council Votes to Reimpose Limits on Living in Vehicles." *Los Angeles Times*, July 30, 2019. www.latimes.com/california/story/2019-07-30/homeless-cars-la-law.

Reyns, Bradford W., and Heidi Scherer. "Stalking Victimization among College Students: The Role of Disability within a Lifestyle-Routine Activity Framework." *Crime and Delinquency* 64, no. 5 (2018): 650–73.

Rich, Karen. "Trauma-Informed Police Responses to Rape Victims." *Journal of Aggression, Maltreatment and Trauma* 28, no. 4 (2019): 463–80.

Richardson, Joseph B., Jr., William Wical, Nipun Kottage, and Che Bullock. "Shook Ones: Understanding the Intersection of Nonfatal Violent Firearm Injury, Incarceration, and Traumatic Stress among Young Black Men." *American Journal of Men's Health* 14, no. 6 (2020): 1–15.

Richie, Beth E. "Challenges Incarcerated Women Face as They Return to Their Communities: Findings from Life History Interviews." *Crime and Delinquency* 47, no. 3 (2001): 368–89.

Richie, Beth. *Compelled to Crime: The Gender Entrapment of Battered, Black Women*. London: Routledge, 2018.

Ringquist, Evan J. "Assessing Evidence of Environmental Inequities: A Meta-analysis." *Journal of Policy Analysis and Management: The Journal of the Association for Public Policy Analysis and Management* 24, no. 2 (2005): 223–47.

Rippon, Gina. *The Gendered Brain: The New Neuroscience That Shatters the Myth of the Female Brain*. New York: Random House, 2019.

"Risk and Protective Factors." Centers for Disease Control and Prevention. Accessed October 24, 2024. www.cdc.gov/aces/risk-factors/index.html.

Ritchie, Andrea J. "#SayHerName: Racial Profiling and Police Violence against Black Women." *Harbinger* 41 (2016): 11–24.

Roberts, Darryl W. "Intimate Partner Homicide: Relationships to Alcohol and Firearms." *Journal of Contemporary Criminal Justice* 25, no. 1 (2009): 67–88.

Roberts, Julian V., and Loretta J. Stalans. "Restorative Sentencing: Exploring the Views of the Public." *Social Justice Research* 17 (2004): 315–34.

Robinson, Jackie. "People with Disabilities Affected by Violence: Court Advocacy and Intervention Tips." Virginia Victim Assistance Network. 2012. www.vanetwork.org/Resources/Robinson%20-%20People%20with%20Disabilities%20Affected%20By%20Violence%20PowerPoint.Final.%2011.29.12.pdf.

Robinson, Sally. *Preventing the Emotional Abuse and Neglect of People with Intellectual Disability: Stopping Insult and Injury*. London: Kingsley, 2013.

Rodriguez, T., M. Montana, and L. Pulitzer. *The Daughters of Juarez: The True Story of Serial Murder South of the Border.* New York: Atria Books, 2007.

Roesler, Shannon. "Racial Segregation and Environmental Injustice." *Environmental Law Reporter* 51 (2021): 10773–84.

Rogers, Sarah A., and Baker A. Rogers. "Advantages and Challenges of Queer Scholars Doing Qualitative Queer Criminology and Criminal Justice Research." *Crime and Delinquency* 69, no. 2 (2023): 464–82.

Rosay, André B., "Violence against American Indian and Alaska Native Women and Men," National Institute of Justice. June 1, 2016. http://nij.gov/journals/277/Pages/violence-againstamerican-indians-alaska-natives.aspx.

Rose, Dina R., and Todd R. Clear. "Incarceration, Social Capital, and Crime: Implications for Social Disorganization Theory." *Criminology* 36, no. 3 (1998): 441–80.

Rose, Nikolas. "The Biology of Culpability: Pathological Identity and Crime Control in a Biological Culture." In *Governing Risks,* edited by Pat O'Malley, 505–34. London: Routledge, 2021.

Rosenfeld, Richard, and Robert Fornango. "The Relationship between Crime and Stop, Question, and Frisk Rates in New York City Neighborhoods." *Justice Quarterly* 34, no. 6 (2017): 931–51.

Rosino, Michael L., and Matthew W. Hughey. "The War on Drugs, Racial Meanings, and Structural Racism: A Holistic and Reproductive Approach." *American Journal of Economics and Sociology* 77, nos. 3–4 (2018): 849–92.

Ross, Jeffrey Ian, Richard S. Jones, Mike Lenza, and Stephen C. Richards. "Convict Criminology and the Struggle for Inclusion." *Critical Criminology* 24 (2016): 489–501.

Rossman, Shelli. "Criminal Justice Interventions for Offenders with Mental Illness: Evaluation of Mental Health Courts in Bronx and Brooklyn, New York." Office of Justice Programs. 2012. www.ojp.gov/pdffiles1/nij/grants/238265.pdf.

Roth, Abigail. "Anti-Blackness, Abolition, and Criminal Justice: A Conversation with Dr. Emily Wang and Professor Tracey Meares." Yale Medical School. 2020. https://medicine.yale.edu/news-article/anti-blackness-abolition-and-criminal-justice-a-conversation-with-dr-emily-wang-and-professor-tracey-meares/.

Rothwell, Jonathan. "How the War on Drugs Damages Black Social Mobility." Brookings. September 30, 2014. www.brookings.edu/articles/how-the-war-on-drugs-damages-black-social-mobility/.

Rousey, Dennis C. *Policing the Southern City: New Orleans, 1805–1889.* Baton Rouge: Louisiana State University Press, 1996.

Ruback, Barry R., Alison C. Cares, and Stacy N. Hoskins. "Crime Victims' Perceptions of Restitution: The Importance of Payment and Understanding." *Violence and Victims* 23, no. 6 (2008): 697–710.

Ruback, R. Barry, Andrew S. Gladfelter, and Brendan Lantz. "Paying Restitution: Experimental Analysis of the Effects of Information and Rationale." *Criminology and Public Policy* 13, no. 3 (2014): 405-36.

Ruback, R. Barry, and Kim S. Menard. "Rural-Urban Differences in Sexual Victimization and Reporting: Analyses Using UCR and Crisis Center Data." *Criminal Justice and Behavior* 28, no. 2 (2001): 131-55.

Rushin, Kate. "The Bridge Poem." Kate Rushin: Poet, Educator. Accessed January 10, 2025. https://katerushinpoet.com/index.php/the-bridge-poem/.

Russell, Diana E. H. *Femicide: The Politics of Woman Killing*. New York: Twayne, 1992.

Russell, Diana E. H., and Roberta A. Harmes. "Defining Femicide and Related Concepts." In *Femicide in Global Perspective*, edited by Diana Russell, 12-28. New York: Teacher's College Press, 2001.

Russell, Robert T. "Veterans Treatment Courts." *Touro Law Review* 31 (2014): 385-402.

Saleh-Hanna, Viviane, Jason M. Williams, and Michael J. Coyle. *Abolish Criminology*. London: Routledge, 2023.

Sampson, Robert J., John H. Laub, and Christopher Wimer. "Does Marriage Reduce Crime? A Counterfactual Approach to Within-Individual Causal Effects." *Criminology* 44, no. 3 (2006): 465-508.

Sawyer, Wendy, and Peter Wagner. "Mass Incarceration: The Whole Pie, 2024." Prison Policy Institute. March 14, 2023. www.prisonpolicy.org/reports/pie2023.html.

Schauer, Edward J., and Elizabeth M. Wheaton. "Sex Trafficking into the United States: A Literature Review." *Criminal Justice Review* 31, no. 2 (2006): 146-69.

Schur, Edwin M. *Labeling Women Deviant: Gender, Stigma, and Social Control*. New York: Random House, 1984.

Schweik, Susan M. *The Ugly Laws: Disability in Public*. New York: New York University Press, 2009.

Seal, Lizzie, and Maggie O'Neill. *Imaginative Criminology: Of Spaces Past, Present and Future*. Bristol: Bristol University Press, 2021.

Seigel, Micol. "The Dilemma of 'Racial Profiling': An Abolitionist Police History." *Contemporary Justice Review* 20, no. 4 (2017): 474-90.

Selman, Kaitlyn J., and Molly Dunn. "Western Feminist Criminologies: Critiquing 'Malestream' Criminology and Beyond." In *The Handbook of the History and Philosophy of Criminology*, edited by Ruth Ann Triplett, 255-71. Hoboken, NJ: Wiley. 2017.

Semenza, Daniel C., and Jessica M. Grosholz. "Mental and Physical Health in Prison: How Co-occurring Conditions Influence Inmate Misconduct." *Health and Justice* 7, no. 1 (2019): 1-12.

Sengstock, Mary C. "The Culpable Victim in Mendelsonncs Typology." Paper presented at the Annual Meeting of the Midwest Sociological Society, Saint Louis, April 21–24, 1976.

Shaffer, Rachel M., Jenna E. Forsyth, Greg Ferraro, Christine Till, Laura M. Carlson, Kirstin Hester, Amanda Haddock, et al. "Lead Exposure and Antisocial Behavior: A Systemic Review Protocol." *Environment International* 168 (2022): 2–11.

Sharp, Susan F., Dennis Brewster, and Sharon RedHawk Love. "Disentangling Strain, Personal Attributes, Affective Response and Deviance: A Gendered Analysis." *Deviant Behavior* 26, no. 2 (2005): 133–57.

Sharp, Susan F., Toni L. Terling-Watt, Leslie A. Atkins, Jay Trace Gilliam, and Anna Sanders. "Purging Behavior in a Sample of College Females: A Research Note on General Strain Theory and Female Deviance." *Deviant Behavior* 22, no. 2 (2001): 171–88.

Shaw, Clifford Robe, and Henry Donald McKay. *Juvenile Delinquency and Urban Areas*. Chicago: University of Chicago Press, 1942.

Shaw, Jessica, Rebecca Campbell, Debi Cain, and Hannah Feeney. "Beyond Surveys and Scales: How Rape Myths Manifest in Sexual Assault Police Records." *Psychology of Violence* 7, no. 4 (2017): 602–14.

Sheppard, Keller G., and Jacob I. Stowell. "Police Fatal Force and Crime Reporting: A Test of Community Responses to Fatal Police-Civilian Encounters." *Journal of Interpersonal Violence* 37, nos. 21–22 (2022): 19730–58.

Shimei, Nour. "'Though We Are Often Invisible, We Are Always Taking Care of Each Other': Mutual Aid among Sex Workers." In *Sex Work, Labour and Relations: New Directions and Reflections*, edited by Teela Sanders, Kathryn McGarry, and Paul Ryan, 291–314. Cham: Springer International, 2022.

Shohat, Ella. *Talking Visions: Multicultural Feminism in a Transnational Age*. Vol. 5. Cambridge, MA: MIT Press, 2001.

Shover, Neal. *Great Pretenders: Pursuits and Careers of Persistent Thieves*. Boulder, CO: Westview, 1996.

Simpson, Sally S., Mariel Alper, Laura Dugan, Julie Horney, Candace Kruttschnitt, and Rosemary Gartner. "Age-Graded Pathways into Crime: Evidence from a Multi-site Retrospective Study of Incarcerated Women." *Journal of Developmental and Life-Course Criminology* 2 (2016): 296–320.

Slavich, George M. "Social Safety Theory: A Biologically Based Evolutionary Perspective on Life Stress, Health, and Behavior." *Annual Review of Clinical Psychology* 16, no. 1 (2020): 265–95.

Smart, Carol. *Women, Crime and Criminology: A Feminist Critique*. London: Routledge and Kegan Paul, 1976.

Smith, Christopher E. "Blue Lives Matter versus Black Lives Matter: Beneficial Social Policies as the Path Away from Punitive Rhetoric and Harm." *Vermont Law Review* 44 (2019): 463–92.

Smith, Olivia, and Tina Skinner. "Observing Court Responses to Victims of Rape and Sexual Assault." *Feminist Criminology* 7, no. 4 (2012): 298–326.

Snow, Margaret Ellis, Carol Nagy Jacklin, and Eleanor E. Maccoby. "Sex-of-Child Differences in Father-Child Interaction at One Year of Age." *Child Development* 54, no. 1 (1983): 227–32.

Sohoni, Tracy, and Melissa Rorie. "The Whiteness of White-Collar Crime in the United States: Examining the Role of Race in a Culture of Elite White-Collar Offending." *Theoretical Criminology* 25, no. 1 (2021): 66–87.

Sohrabi, Sadaf. "The Criminal Gene: The Link between MAOA and Aggression." *BioMed Central* 9, no. 1 (2015): A49.

Sollund, Ragnhild. "Animal Trafficking and Trade: Abuse and Species Injustice." In *Emerging Issues in Green Criminology: Exploring Power, Justice and Harm*, edited by Dian Westerhuis, Reece Walters, and Tanya Wyatt, 72–92. London: Palgrave Macmillan UK, 2013.

Sommers, Ira, Deborah R. Baskin, and Jeffrey Fagan. "Getting Out of the Life: Crime Desistance by Female Street Offenders." *Deviant Behavior* 15 (1994): 125–51.

Sorokin, David J., and Warren R. Muir. "Too Little Toxic-Waste Data." *New York Times*, October 7, 1985. www.nytimes.com/1985/10/07/opinion/too-little-toxicwaste-data.html.

Southall, Ashley. "'Negligent and Sexist': Why Rape Survivors Asked Feds to Probe N.Y.P.D." *New York Times*, July 28, 2022. www.nytimes.com/2022/07/28/nyregion/nypd-doj-special-victims-investigation.html.

Spade, Dean. "Biography." Seattle University School of Law. Accessed January 2, 2025. https://law.seattleu.edu/faculty/directory/profiles/spade-dean.html.

Spencer, Dale, Alexa Dodge, Rose Ricciardelli, and Dale Ballucci. "'I Think It's Re-victimizing Victims Almost Every Time': Police Perceptions of Criminal Justice Responses to Sexual Violence." *Critical Criminology* 26 (2018): 189–209.

Spitzberg, Brian H., and William R. Cupach. "The State of the Art of Stalking: Taking Stock of the Emerging Literature." *Aggression and Violent Behavior* 12, no. 1 (2007): 64–86.

Sportsman, Kelsey. "Upholding White Supremacy Next Door: Online Neighborhood Social Networking in the Suburbs." PhD diss., California State University San Marcos, 2019.

Springer, Kimberly. "Third Wave Black Feminism?" *Signs: Journal of Women in Culture and Society* 27, no. 4 (2002): 1059–82.

Stanley, Liz, and Sue Wise. "Method, Methodology and Epistemology in Feminist Research Processes." *Feminist Praxis: Research, Theory and Epistemology in Feminist Sociology*, edited by Liz Stanley, 20–60. London: Routledge, 2013.

Stark, Rodney. "Deviant Places: A Theory of the Ecology of Crime." *Criminology* 25, no. 4 (1987): 893–910.

Starr, Chelsea. "When Culture Matters: Frame Resonance and Protests against Femicide in Ciudad Juarez, Mexico." *Qualitative Report* 22, no. 5 (2017): 1359–78.

Steffensmeier, Darrell, and Emilie Allan. "Gender and Crime: Toward a Gendered Theory of Female Offending." *Annual Review of Sociology* 22, no. 1 (1996): 459–87.

Steffensmeier, Darrell, Casey T. Harris, and Noah Painter-Davis. "Gender and Arrests for Larceny, Fraud, Forgery, and Embezzlement: Conventional or Occupational Property Crime Offenders?" *Journal of Criminal Justice* 43, no. 3 (2015): 205–17.

Steffensmeier, Darrell J., Jennifer Schwartz, and Michael Roche. "Gender and Twenty-First-Century Corporate Crime: Female Involvement and the Gender Gap in Enron-Era Corporate Frauds." *American Sociological Review* 78, no. 3 (2013): 448–76.

Steffensmeier, Darrell, Jeffery Ulmer, and John Kramer. "The Interaction of Race, Gender, and Age in Criminal Sentencing: The Punishment Cost of Being Young, Black, and Male." *Criminology* 36, no. 4 (1998): 763–98.

Steiker, Carol S., and Jordan M. Steiker. "The American Death Penalty and the (In)Visibility of Race." *University of Chicago Law Review* 82, no. 1 (2015): 243–94.

Steinmetz, Katy. "She Coined the Term 'Intersectionality' over 30 Years Ago. Here's What It Means to Her Today." *Time Magazine*, February 20, 2020. https://time.com/5786710/kimberle-crenshaw-intersectionality/.

St-Georges, Simon, Vincent Arel-Bundock, André Blais, and Marco Mendoza Aviña. "Jobs and Punishment: Public Opinion on Leniency for White-Collar Crime." *Political Research Quarterly* 76, no. 4 (2023): 1751–63.

Stoliker, Bryce Evan, and Phillip M. Galli. "An Examination of Mental Health and Psychiatric Care among Older Prisoners in the United States." *Victims and Offenders* 14, no. 4 (2019): 480–509.

Strauss, David H., Sarah A. White, and Barbara E. Bierer. "Justice, Diversity, and Research Ethics Review." *Science* 371, no. 6535 (2021): 1209–11.

Strazdins, Lyndall, and Dorothy H. Broom. "Acts of Love (and Work) Gender Imbalance in Emotional Work and Women's Psychological Distress." *Journal of Family Issues* 25, no. 3 (2004): 356–78.

Strohmayer, Angelika, Jenn Clamen, and Mary Laing. "Technologies for Social Justice: Lessons from Sex Workers on the Front Lines." Paper presented at the CHI Conference on Human Factors in Computing Systems Proceedings, Glasgow, Scotland, May 4–9, 2019.

Struckman-Johnson, Cindy, and David Struckman-Johnson. "A Comparison of Sexual Coercion Experiences Reported by Men and Women in Prison." *Journal of Interpersonal Violence* 21, no. 12 (2006): 1591–615.

Stults, Brian J., Jorge Luis Hernandez, and Carter Hay. "Low Self-Control, Peer Delinquency, and Crime: Considering Gendered Pathways." *Journal of Research in Crime and Delinquency* 58, no. 6 (2021): 666–709.

St. Vil, Noelle M., Bushra Sabri, Vania Nwokolo, Kamila A. Alexander, and Jacquelyn C. Campbell. "A Qualitative Study of Survival Strategies Used by Low-Income Black Women Who Experience Intimate Partner Violence." *Social Work* 62, no. 1 (2017): 63–71.

Suarez, Eliana, and Tahany M. Gadalla. "Stop Blaming the Victim: A Meta-analysis on Rape Myths." *Journal of Interpersonal Violence* 25, no. 11 (2010): 2010–35.

Subramanian, Ram, Ruth Delaney, Stephen Roberts, Nancy Fishman, and Peggy McGarry. *Incarceration's Front Door: The Misuse of Jail in America*. New York: Vera Institute of Justice, 2015.

"Success in the Community: A Matrix for Thinking about the Needs of Criminal Justice Involved Women." Women's Prison Association. 2008. www.fedcure.org/information/USSC-Symposium-0708/dir_08/Lerner_WPASuccess_in_the_Community_Matrix.pdf.

Sudbury, Julia. "Celling Black Bodies: Black Women in the Global Prison Industrial Complex." *Feminist Review* 70, no. 1 (2002): 57–74.

Sue, Derald Wing, Christina M. Capodilupo, Gina C. Torino, Jennifer M. Bucceri, Aisha Holder, Kevin L. Nadal, and Marta Esquilin. "Racial Microaggressions in Everyday Life: Implications for Clinical Practice." *American Psychologist* 62, no. 4 (2007): 271–86.

Sullivan, Christopher M., and Zachary P. O'Keeffe. "Evidence That Curtailing Proactive Policing Can Reduce Major Crime." *Nature Human Behaviour* 1, no. 10 (2017): 730–37.

Sultan, Reina, and Micah Herskind. "What Is Abolition, and Why Do We Need It?" *Vogue Magazine*, July 23, 2020. www.vogue.com/article/what-is-abolition-and-why-do-we-need-it.

Surrell, April, and Ida M. Johnson. "An Examination of Women's Experiences with Reporting Sexual Victimization behind Prison Walls." *Prison Journal* 100, no. 5 (2020): 559–80.

Sutherland, Edwin H. *White Collar Crime: The Uncut Version*. New Haven: Yale University Press, 1983.

Sutherland, Edwin H. "White-Collar Criminality." *American Sociological Review* 5, no. 1 (1940): 1–12.

Sutherland, Edwin Hardin. *Criminology*. Philadelphia: Lippincott, 1924.

Swope, Carolyn B., Diana Hernández, and Lara J. Cushing. "The Relationship of Historical Redlining with Present-Day Neighborhood Environmental and

Health Outcomes: A Scoping Review and Conceptual Model." *Journal of Urban Health* 99, no. 6 (2022): 959–83.

"A Tale of Two Countries: Racially Targeted Arrests in the Era of Marijuana Reform." American Civil Liberties Union. Accessed October 23, 2024. www.aclu.org/report/tale-two-countries-racially-targeted-arrests-era-marijuana-reform.

Taniguchi, Nancy J. "California's Anti-Okie Law: An Interpretive Biography." *Western Legal History* 8 (1995): 273–90.

Tasca, Cecilia, Mariangela Rapetti, Mauro Giovanni Carta, and Bianca Fadda. "Women and Hysteria in the History of Mental Health." *Clinical Practice and Epidemiology in Mental Health* 8 (2012): 110–19.

Terry, Geraldine. "No Climate Justice without Gender Justice: An Overview of the Issues." *Gender and Development* 17, no. 1 (2009): 5–18.

Terwiel, Anna. "What Is Carceral Feminism?" *Political Theory* 48, no. 4 (2020): 421–42.

Tewksbury, Richard, and Elizabeth Ehrhardt Mustaine. "Lifestyle Factors Associated with the Sexual Assault of Men: A Routine Activity Theory Analysis." *Journal of Men's Studies* 9, no. 2 (2001): 153–82.

Teye, Simisola O., Jeff D. Yanosky, Yendelela Cuffee, Xingran Weng, Raffy Luquis, Elana Farace, and Li Wang. "Exploring Persistent Racial/Ethnic Disparities in Lead Exposure among American Children Aged 1–5 Years: Results from NHANES, 1999–2016." *International Archives of Occupational and Environmental Health* 94 (2021): 723–30.

Thompson, Alexandra, and Susannah N. Tapp. "Criminal Victimization, 2021." Bureau of Justice Statistics. September 2022. https://bjs.ojp.gov/content/pub/pdf/cv21.pdf.

Thorne, Barrie, and Zella Luria. "Sexuality and Gender in Children's Daily Worlds." *Social Problems* 33, no. 3 (1986): 176–90.

Tjaden, Patricia, and Nancy Thoennes. "Prevalence and Consequences of Male-to-Female and Female-to-Male Intimate Partner Violence as Measured by the National Violence against Women Survey." *Violence against Women* 6, no. 2 (2000): 142–61.

Tjaden, Patricia Godeke, and Nancy Thoennes. "Extent, Nature, and Consequences of Rape Victimization: Findings from the National Violence against Women Survey." National Institute of Justice. January 2006. https://nij.ojp.gov/library/publications/extent-nature-and-consequences-rape-victimization-findings-national-violence.

Tjaden, Patricia Godeke, and Nancy Thoennes. *Stalking in America: Findings from the National Violence against Women Survey*. Washington, DC: National Institute of Justice, 1998.

Toch, Hans. *Violent Men: An Inquiry into the Psychology of Violence*. Chicago: Aldine, 1969.

Tofte, Sarah. *"I Used to Think the Law Would Protect Me": Illinois's Failure to Test Rape Kits*. New York: Human Rights Watch, 2010.

Tonry, Michael. "Learning Cross-Nationally from Josine Junger-Tas: How Knowledge about Other Places and Times Helps Us Better Understand Our Own." *European Journal on Criminal Policy and Research* 19 (2013): 85–90.

Torelli, Riccardo, Federica Balluchi, and Arianna Lazzini. "Greenwashing and Environmental Communication: Effects on Stakeholders' Perceptions." *Business Strategy and the Environment* 29, no. 2 (2020): 407–21.

Turanovic, Jillian J., Travis C. Pratt, and Alex R. Piquero. "Structural Constraints, Risky Lifestyles, and Repeat Victimization." *Journal of Quantitative Criminology* 34 (2018): 251–74.

Turchik, Jessica A., and Katie M. Edwards. "Myths about Male Rape: A Literature Review." *Psychology of Men and Masculinity* 13, no. 2 (2012): 211–26.

Turner, R. Jay, J. Blake Turner, and William Beardall Hale. "Social Relationships and Social Support." *Sociology of Mental Health: Selected Topics from Forty Years, 1970s-2010s.* edited by Robert J. Johnson, R. Jay Turner, and Bruce G. Link, 1–20. New York: Springer, 2014.

"Secretary of the Army Announces Missing Soldier Policy, Forms People First Task Force to Implement Fort Hood Independent Review Committee (FHIRC) Recommendations." U.S. Army. December 8, 2020. www.army.mil/article/241490/secretary_of_the_army_announces_missing_soldier_policy_forms_people_first_task_force_to_implement_fort_hood_independent_review_committee_fhirc_recommendations.

"UCR: Uniform Crime Reporting Handbook." Federal Bureau of Investigation. Accessed October 24, 2024. https://ucr.fbi.gov/additional-ucr-publications/ucr_handbook.pdf.

Uggen, Christopher, and Candace Kruttschnitt. "Crime in the Breaking: Gender Differences in Desistance." *Law and Society Review* 32, no. 2 (1998): 339–66.

Umaña-Taylor, Adriana J., and Nancy E. Hill. "Ethnic–Racial Socialization in the Family: A Decade's Advance on Precursors and Outcomes." *Journal of Marriage and Family* 82, no. 1 (2020): 244–71.

Valcore, Jace, Henry F. Fradella, Xavier Guadalupe-Diaz, Matthew J. Ball, Angela Dwyer, Christina DeJong, Allyn Walker, Aimee Wodda, and Meredith G. F. Worthen. "Building an Intersectional and Trans-inclusive Criminology: Responding to the Emergence of 'Gender Critical' Perspectives in Feminist Criminology." *Critical Criminology* 29 (2021): 687–706.

Van de Weijer, Steve. "Intergenerational Continuity of Crime: A Comparison between Children of Discordant Siblings." *Criminal Behaviour and Mental Health* 32, no. 5 (2022): 308–19.

Van Green, Ted. "Americans Overwhelmingly Say Marijuana Should Be Legal for Medical or Recreational Use." Pew Research Center. November 22, 2022. www.pewresearch.org/short-reads/2022/11/22/americans-overwhelmingly-say-marijuana-should-be-legal-for-medical-or-recreational-use/.

Van Wormer, Katherine. "Restorative Justice as Social Justice for Victims of Gendered Violence: A Standpoint Feminist Perspective." *Social Work* 54, no. 2 (2009): 107–16.

Vazsonyi, Alexander T., Jakub Mikuška, and Erin L. Kelley. "It's Time: A Meta-analysis on the Self-Control-Deviance Link." *Journal of Criminal Justice* 48 (2017): 48–63.

Vito, Anthony G., Vanessa Woodward Griffin, Gennaro F. Vito, and George E. Higgins. "'Does Daylight Matter?' An Examination of Racial Bias in Traffic Stops by Police." *Policing: An International Journal* 43, no. 4 (2020): 675–88.

Vito, Anthony, George Higgins, and Gennaro Vito. "Police Stop and Frisk and the Impact of Race: A Focal Concerns Theory Approach." *Social Sciences* 10, no. 6 (2021): 230–43.

"Vulnerable and Other Populations Requiring Additional Protections." National Institutes of Health. Accessed January 10, 2025. https://grants.nih.gov/policy-and-compliance/policy-topics/human-subjects/policies-and-regulations/vulnerable-populations.

Wagner, Bryan. *Disturbing the Peace: Black Culture and the Police Power after Slavery*. Cambridge, MA: Harvard University Press, 2009.

Wahab, Stephanie. "For Their Own Good: Sex Work, Social Control and Social Workers, a Historical Perspective." *Journal of Sociology and Social Welfare* 29 (2002): 39–58.

Walfield, Scott M. "'Men Cannot Be Raped': Correlates of Male Rape Myth Acceptance." *Journal of Interpersonal Violence* 36, nos. 13–14 (2021): 6391–417.

Walker, Allyn, Amanda M. Petersen, Aimee Wodda, and Ash Stephens. "Why Don't We Center Abolition in Queer Criminology?" *Crime and Delinquency* 70, no. 5 (2022): 1443–61.

Warren, Patricia, Ted Chiricos, and William Bales. "The Imprisonment Penalty for Young Black and Hispanic Males: A Crime-Specific Analysis." *Journal of Research in Crime and Delinquency* 49, no. 1 (2012): 56–80.

Weisburd, David, Alese Wooditch, Sarit Weisburd, and Sue-Ming Yang. "Do Stop, Question, and Frisk Practices Deter Crime? Evidence at Microunits of Space and Time." *Criminology and Public Policy* 15, no. 1 (2016): 31–56.

Weiss, Karen G. "Neutralizing Sexual Victimization: A Typology of Victims' Non-reporting Accounts." *Theoretical Criminology* 15, no. 4 (2011): 445–67.

Weiss, Karen G. "Too Ashamed to Report: Deconstructing the Shame of Sexual Victimization." *Feminist Criminology* 5, no. 3 (2010): 286–310.

Weitzer, Ronald. "The Campaign against Sex Work in the United States: A Successful Moral Crusade." *Sexuality Research and Social Policy* 17, no. 3 (2020): 399–414.

Wertz, Jasmin, Avshalom Caspi, Daniel W. Belsky, Amber L. Beckley, Louise Arseneault, James Christopher Barnes, David L. Corcoran, et al. "Genetics and Crime: Integrating New Genomic Discoveries into Psychological Research about Antisocial Behavior." *Psychological Science* 29, no. 5 (2018): 791–803.

West, Desirée A., and Bronwen Lichtenstein. "Andrea Yates and the Criminalization of the Filicidal Maternal Body." *Feminist Criminology* 1, no. 3 (2006): 173–87.

"What Is Mutual Aid?" Big Door Brigade. Accessed October 24, 2024. http://bigdoorbrigade.com/what-is-mutual-aid/.

"What Is the PIC? What Is Abolition?" Critical Resistance. Accessed October 24, 2024. https://criticalresistance.org/mission-vision/not-so-common-language/.

White, Amina, Christine Grady, Margaret Little, Kristen Sullivan, Katie Clark, Monalisa Ngwu, and Anne Drapkin Lyerly. "IRB Decision-Making about Minimal Risk Research with Pregnant Participants." *Ethics and Human Research* 43, no. 5 (2021): 2–17.

Whitman, James Q. *Harsh Justice: Criminal Punishment and the Widening Divide between America and Europe.* New York: Oxford University Press, 2003.

Wilcox, Pamela, and Brooke Miller Gialopsos. "Crime-Event Criminology: An Overview." *Journal of Contemporary Criminal Justice* 31, no. 1 (2015): 4–11.

Wildeman, Christopher, Hedwig Lee, and Megan Comfort. "A New Vulnerable Population? The Health of Female Partners of Men Recently Released from Prison." *Women's Health Issues* 23, no. 6 (2013): e335–340.

Wilkins, Natalie, Benita Tsao, Marci Hertz, Rachel Davis, and Joanne Klevens. *Connecting the Dots: An Overview of the Links among Multiple Forms of Violence.* Atlanta, GA: Centers for Disease Control; Oakland, CA: Prevention Institute, 2014. www.cdc.gov/violence-prevention/about/connecting_the_dots-a.pdf.

Williams, Clive Kenneth. "Stealing a Car to Be a Man: The Importance of Cars and Driving in the Gender Identity of Adolescent Males." PhD diss., Queensland University of Technology, 2005.

Williams, Jason M., Zoe Spencer, and Sean K. Wilson. "I Am Not Your Felon: Decoding the Trauma, Resilience, and Recovering Mothering of Formerly Incarcerated Black Women." *Crime and Delinquency* 67, no. 8 (2021): 1103–36.

Wilson, Laura C. "The Prevalence of Military Sexual Trauma: A Meta-analysis." *Trauma, Violence, and Abuse* 19, no. 5 (2018): 584–97.

Winfree, L. Thomas, Jr., and Frances P. Bernat. "Social Learning, Self-Control, and Substance Abuse by Eighth-Grade Students: A Tale of Two Cities." *Journal of Drug Issues* 28, no. 2 (1998): 539–58.

Winlow, Simon. "Masculinities and Crime." *Criminal Justice Matters* 55, no. 1 (2004): 18–19.

Wonders, Nancy A. "Postmodern Feminist Criminology and Social Justice." *Social Justice, Criminal Justice* (1999): 109–28.

Woods, Cindy J. P. "Gender Differences in Moral Development and Acquisition: A Review of Kohlberg's and Gilligan's Models of Justice and Care." *Social Behavior and Personality: An International Journal* 24, no. 4 (1996): 375–83.

Young, Jemimah, and Donald Easton-Brooks. "Present but Unaccounted For: Practical Considerations for the Recruitment and Retention of Black Women Teachers." *Theory into Practice* 59, no. 4 (2020): 389–99.

Young, Jock. *The Criminological Imagination*. Cambridge: Polity, 2011.

Young, Jock. "The Failure of Criminology: The Need for a Radical Realism." In *Confronting Crime*, edited by Roger Matthews and Jock Young, 4–30. London: Sage, 1986.

Young, Jock. "Voodoo Criminology and the Numbers Game." In *Cultural Criminology Unleashed*, edited by Jeff Ferrell, Keith Hayward, Wayne Morrison, and Mike Presdee, 27–42. London: Routledge-Cavendish, 2016.

Zaykowski, Heather, Ross Kleinstuber, and Caitlin McDonough. "Judicial Narratives of Ideal and Deviant Victims in Judges' Capital Sentencing Decisions." *American Journal of Criminal Justice* 39 (2014): 716–31.

Zeidman, Lawrence A. *Brain Science under the Swastika: Ethical Violations, Resistance, and Victimization of Neuroscientists in Nazi Europe*. Oxford: Oxford University Press, 2020.

Zhong, Shaoling, Morwenna Senior, Rongqin Yu, Amanda Perry, Keith Hawton, Jenny Shaw, and Seena Fazel. "Risk Factors for Suicide in Prisons: A Systematic Review and Meta-analysis." *Lancet Public Health* 6, no. 3 (2021): e164–174.

Zinn, Howard. *A People's History of the United States*. New York: New Press, 1998.

Index

abolition, 191; of algorithms in the criminal legal system, 63; of the death penalty, 37; prison, 63, 107; and reform, 212–14; sex trafficking and sex work, 182–83
abolitionist feminism, 183, 215–16
Absolute Standards, 192
academic integrity, 101
adaptive technology, 110
Adler, Freda, 146, 159–60
adult labor, 183
Adverse Childhood Experiences (ACE) project, 51
African American Policy Forum, 196
African American Redress Network (AARN), 89
aggression, 59–60
Agnew, Robert, 91, 92
Aichorn, August, 57
Akers, Ronald, 67
Akins, Scott, 149
alcohol and intimate partner violence, 141
Alexander, Marissa, 222–23
Alexander, Michelle, 210
algorithmic risk assessment, 63–64
All of Us or None, 88
alternative courts, 205–6
altruistic mothers, 61–62
Amber Alerts, 107–8

American Civil Liberties Union, 143
American Indian/Alaskan Native people, drug usage among, 177, 179
American Society of Criminology, 122, 125–26
Amir, Menachem, 101
anger, 92, 93–94
anomie, 84
anti-homelessness laws, 173–74
Anti-Okie and vagrancy laws, 172
Anti-Police-Terror Project (APTP), 221
anxiety, 92
Anzaldúa, Gloria E., 10
Archer, Dane, 37
Arford, Tammi, 45
arrest, 150
Arrigo, Bruce, 118, 167
arson, 151–52
Aspers, Patrik, 21
assistive technology, 110
Association of Certified Fraud Examiners, 146
astructural approaches, 40
attachments, 70, 71, 75

Backpage website, 184
bail bond commercials, 204
Baker, Helen, 160–61

291

Balluchi, Federica, 168
Ban the Box campaign, 88
Barber, William J., Dr., Rev., 165–66
Baskin, Deborah, 76
battered women, 82
Baum, Dan, 206–7
Bay Area Transformative Justice Collective, 219
BAYSWAN (Bay Area Sex Worker Advocacy Network), 181
Beccaria, Cesare, 31, 32
Becker, Sarah, 98
Bei Bei Shuai case, 142–43
Beirne, Piers, 167
beliefs, 71
Belly of the Beast: The Politics of Anti-fatness as Anti-blackness (Harrison), 46
Ben-Moshe, Liat, 64
Bentham, Jeremy, 31
Berg, Mark, 108, 109
Bernard, Thomas, 118
Bernstein, Elizabeth, 182
bias/biases: crimes, 123; in decision making, 63; and ethnic-racial socialization (ERS) framework, 70, 71; police, 195; racial, 19–20, 96, 153, 210; in the sentencing of women and men, 119; socioeconomic status, 156. *See also* gender bias
Biden, Joe, 114–15
biological and positivist theories: biology and crime, 50–52; biology and social construction of gender, 47–48; biology of race, 44–46; body mass index, race, and crime, 46; gender bias in scientific language, 48; genetics and crime, 48–49; policy implications of, 53–54; XYY syndrome, 50
biological determinism, debunking, 47–48
Black criminology faculty, 27
Black feminist criminology, 94–95, 122–23
Black feminist theory, 120
Black Lives Matter movement, 196, 199
Black men: aged 15–34, violence against, 133–34; likelihood of arrest of, 39; mental health of, 137; prison sentences for, 203; sexual assault of, 141; and strain, 93
Black-on-Black crime, 135
Black people, drug usage among, 177, 179
Black racial identity development, 58–59
Black researchers, 27
Black students, 92
Black women: fluid identity of, 95; likelihood of arrest of, 149, 196–97; racial oppression of, 122; reentry process, applying CRT framework to, 24–25; stereotypes attributed to, 120; and strain, 92–93
blameworthiness, 95
Bland, Sandra, 196
Blasdell, Raleigh, 40
Bliton, Chloe, 60
blue lives matter bill, 199
blue lives matter movement, 195
body mass index, 46
Bonnes, Stephanie, 114
boundary crossing in criminology, 9
Bowman, Jamaal, Rep., 198
Braz, Rose, 214
BREATHE Act, 198
Broidy, Lisa, 78, 92
broken-windows policing, 35–36, 173, 175
brown, adrienne maree, 224–25
brownfield, 165
Bundy, Ted, 136
Burack, Cynthia, 22, 72, 73
Burgess, Robert, 67
Burke, Tarana, 142
Burkeman, Oliver, 131
Buzawa, Eva Schlesinger, 106

Campaign Zero, 197
Campo-Engelstein, Lisa, 48
Cancer Alley, 165–66
Caputi, Jane, 138
Caputo, Gail, 148
carceral feminism, 182, 215
car insurance companies, 20
Cauffman, Elizabeth, 78, 79–80
causal effect, 49
Causes of Delinquency (Hirschi), 70
Cernkovich, Stephen, 76
Chappell, Bill, 54
Chavis, Benjamin, Dr., Rev., 164–65
Chesney-Lind, Meda, 8
childhood trauma, biological impacts of, 52
childhood victimization and crime, 92
children and women's desistance, 80
children as research subjects, 29
"chivalry thesis," 121
Cho, Sumi, 27
Christ, Carol, 149
Clarke, Ronald, 37–38
class conflict, 117
classical and neo-classical theories: crime-event criminology, 42–43; death penalty, 37; deterrence, 32–37; introduction, 31–32; rational choice theory, 37–40;

routine activities theory and lifestyle approach, 40–42
Clear, Todd, 87
climate change, 166–67
Clinard, Marshall, 159
Clinton, Bill, 207
Cloward, Richard, 98
Cobbina-Dungy, Jennifer, 196
cognition, 56
Collective Action for Safe Spaces (CASS), 221
collective efficacy, 85
collective grief work, 104
collective liberation, 182
collective motherwork, 86
colonial policing, 194
Colorado Chance to Compete Act, 88
commitment, 71
common-law property crimes, 147
common sense, 123
community involvement and intimate partner violence, 140
Community Response Initiative to Strengthen Emergency Systems (CRISES Act), 221
community values, 84
companion animals, crimes against, 167
complicit masculinities, 69
conformity and gender, 39–40
Connell, Raewyn, 68, 123–24
consciousness raising, 139
content notifications, 100–101
conventional morality, 57, 58–59
Cook, Kimberly, 8, 125
cooperation by victims, 97
Copeny, Mari, 163–64
Core Civic, 209
Cornish, Derek, 37–38
corporate crimes, 143, 158
corporate frauds, 160
corporate-level greenwashing, 168
corrections: death penalty, 209–10; difference between prisons and jails, 208–9; reforming prisons, 210–11; War on Drugs, 206–8
Corrections Corporation of America, 209
Corte, Ugo, 21
Cortina, Lilia, 101–2
Coster, Stacy De, 67–68
costs: of cooperation, 97; of punishment, 38
Council of State Governments Justice Center, 192
COUP Act, 198
courts, 202–6
Covington, Stephanie, 81

Cox, Alison, 126
Craigslist website, 184
Crenshaw, Kimberlé, 10, 27, 120, 196
Crime Act of 1994, 207
crime-event criminology, 42–43
crimes against people: corporate crimes as violent crimes, 143; criminalization of pregnant women, 142–43; crisis of masculinity, 135–36; domestic violence, 139–41; femicide, 138–39; intimate partner violence, 139–41; racial disparities in violent victimization, 133–34; rape as men's issue, 141–42; role of patriarchy, 135–36; state violence, 142; trends from victimization data, 132–33; true crime shows, 131–32; vulnerable people, 136–38; white-on-white crime, 134–35
crimes against property: amateur and professional approaches to, 147; arson, 151–52; crime drop and fear of crime, 152–53; larceny and theft, 145–46; motor vehicle theft, 150–51; role of capitalism and patriarchy, 148–49; segregation and property crime, 149–50; structured action and doing gender, 147–48
criminalization: of poverty, 87–88, 171–75; of pregnant women, 142–43; of sex work, 137, 184; of women's reproductive autonomy, 149
criminogenic, 91
criminology: categories of theories, 7; centering marginalized perspectives, 10–11; crime-event, 42–43; defined, 7; intersectionality in, 10. See also critical criminology
Crisis Intervention Teams, 199
crisis motherwork, 86
critical criminology: about, 116–17; Black feminist criminology, 122–23; cultural criminology, 118–19; feminist criminology, 119–22; left realist criminology, 117–18; masculinities and crime, 123–24; need for, 41–42, 43; on patterns of drug-related crime, 179; peacemaking criminology, 124–25; postmodern criminology, 118; queer criminology, 123; radical criminology, 117; social justice perspective on drug use, 180; survivor and convict criminology, 125–26
Critical Criminology (journal), 8
Critical Environmental Adaptation Theory, 86

critical race theory (CRT): research methods and methodologies, 23–25; storytelling and counter-storytelling, 25–26
Critical Resistance, 213–15
cultural criminology, 118–19
cultural socialization, 70, 71
cyberbullying and gender, 42
cyberdystopianists, 42
cycle of trauma and revictimization, 133–34

Dalkon Sheild, 161
Daly, Kathleen, 82, 119, 160, 180
dark level greenwashing, 168
data problems in crime research, 17–18
datasaurs, 15
Davis, Angela, 86, 214
Davis, Richard Allen, 108
death penalty, 209–10; as deterrence, 37
Decarcerating Disability: Deinstitutionalization and Prison Abolition (Ben-Moshe), 64–65
De Coster, Stacy, 74–75, 92
decriminalization of sex work, 185
"Deferred Prosecution Agreements," 161
deinstitutionalization of mental health hospitals, 64–65
DeKeseredy, Walter, 19
depression: and crime, 93–94; and stress exposure, 75
desistance: and crime, 75–76; and employment and job stability, 80; and marriage, 81
"Desistance Emotional Work," 79
deterrence: and crime causation, 33; and punishment, 32–33, 34; rational choice theory, 37–40; and "stop, question, and frisk" (SQF) practice, 36–37; understanding, 33–34; and War on Drugs, 34–36
deviant behavior: and gender, 75; and parental supervision, 72–73; and stress exposure, 74–75
deviant places theory, 103
de Weijer, Steve Van, 49
diethylstilbestrol, 161
differential association and social learning theory, 66–68
differential opportunity and crime, 98
digital redlining, 89
digital spaces reproducing inequality, 42
disabled people and victimization, 110–11
Dodge, Mary, 146
domestic violence, 59, 139–41. *See also* intimate partner violence (IPV)

dopamine, 48–49
Dow Corning breast implants, 161
Drug Policy Alliance, 176
drugs: crimes, 176–80; drug-related crime and critical criminology, 179; overdose mortality, 180; usage and intimate partner violence, 140–41
Du Bois, W. E. B., 85
Durkheim, Émile, 84

early childhood programs, 109
early-onset crime, 80
Earth Guardians organization, 164
eating disorders, 93
eco-pornography, 168–69
education and criminal involvement, 60, 80
egalitarianism, 70
Egger, Steven, 137
Ehrenreich, Barbara, 119–20, 171–72, 175
Ehrlichman, John, 206–7
Eight Can't Wait, 197–200
#8toAbolition, 217–19
emotional labor and relational dynamics, 79
emotion regulation/dysregulation, 59–60
emphasized femininity, 68
empiricus abstractus, 15
employment and women's desistance, 80
End the Exception campaign, 217
environmental constraints, 38
environmental crimes: climate change and intersectionality, 166–67; Environmental Justice Movement, 163; environmental racism and health, 164–66; green criminology, 167–68; greenwashing, 168–69; outsourcing of law enforcement in, 162; young climate activists fighting environmental injustices, 163–64
environmental criminology, 42–43
environmental factors and gene expression, 49
environmental injustice, 163
Environmental Justice Movement, 163
Environmental Protection Agency (EPA), 165, 166
environmental racism, 163
epistemology, 21
Eterno, John, 17, 18
ethics of a research, 28–29
ethnic-racial socialization (ERS), 70, 71
eugenics, 45, 46, 52, 53
exclusion in research, 29
Expanding First Response Commission, 192

Fagan, Jeffrey, 76
family-based research designs, 49
fear: and crime, 92; of the criminal legal process, 16
Federal Housing Administration (FHA), 89
female. *See* women
femicide, 138–39
"Feminism for the Mainstream Criminologist: An Invitation" (Flavin), 8
feminist criminology, 94–95, 119–23, 125
feminist critique of scientific knowledge, 48
feminist empiricism, 22
feminist epistemologies, 22
feminist expansions of carceral developments, 9
feminist pathways theory, 92
feminist perspectives to research methods, 22–23
feminist postmodernism, 22
feminist reflexivity, 23
feminist researchers, 21–22
feminist standpoint theories, 22
Feminist Theory: From Margin to Center (hooks), 224
Ferguson, Melissa, 61
Fight Online Sex Trafficking Act (FOSTA), 184
filicide, 61
financial aspects of the criminal legal system, 216–17
Fine, Michelle, 26–27
Fishman, Mark, 104
Five Hundred Delinquent Women (Laub and Sampson), 78
Flavin, Jeanne, 8, 13, 22, 73, 149
focal concerns theory, 95–97
Frederique, Kassandra, 199
Freud, Sigmund, 56–57, 62
Friedman, Joseph, 180
Fuentes, Kimberly, 181–82
Fyfe, James, 197

Gabbidon, Shaun, 85
Gall, Franz Joseph, 45
Garland, David, 63–64
Gartner, Rosemary, 37
gender: biology of, 47; and crimes against property, 147–48; crossing, 148; defined, 47; and deviance, 75; essentialism, critique of, 47; fluidity, 148; gap, 8; and peer impacts, 74–75; and power, centrality of, 26; ratio problem, 92; and role-taking, 75; and self-control, 74–75; and social bonding, 71; social construction of, 47–48; and socialization, 68–70, 71, 73, 74–75, 93, 136; as a social structure, 68
Gender and Power (Connell), 68
gender bias, 20, 96, 119; in criminological theory, 78–79; in scientific language, 48
gender differences: and crime, 38–40; in expression of emotions, 93–94; and strain, 92
gender discrimination: and climate justice, 166–67; and femicide, 138; institutionalizing, 193; in wages, 184
gendered blame mechanism, 73–74
gendered crimes, restorative justice for, 106
gendered patterns of victimization, 40–42
Gendered Pharma-Harms, 161
gendered stereotypes and narratives, 48
general deterrence, 32, 35
general strain theory (GST), 91–94
general theory of crime (GTC), 72–74
genetics and crime, 48–49
genocidal ideology, 53
gentrification, 172–74
GEO Group, 209
Gerodimos, Roman, 58
"get tough" policy agenda, 33
Gillibrand, Kirsten, 114
Gilligan, Carol, 58, 68
Gilmore, Ruth, 214
Giordano, Peggy, 76
girls' delinquency, 71
Gladfelter, Andrew, 105
global and postcolonial feminisms, 120–21
Glueck, Eleanor, 77
Glueck, Sheldon, 77
Gottfredson, Denise, 201
Gottfredson, Michael, 72, 73–74, 109
Gove, Walter, 75
government housing program and racism, 88–89
Grace, Anita, 80
green criminology, 167–68
greenwashing, 168–69
Grindal, Matthew, 71
guardianship, 40, 43
guidelines-conforming sentence, 96
Guillen, Vanessa, 114
Gurusami, Susila, 86

Haley, Sarah, 167
Hall, Lauren, 79
Hallett, Michael, 86
Han, Edwin J., 53

Hansen, Helena, 180
Hardship Duty: Women's Experiences with Sexual Harassment, Sexual Assault, and Discrimination in the US Military (Bonnes), 114
Harlot, Scarlet, 181
Harris, Casey, 162
Harris, Lyndsey, 79
Harrisburg-Manchester neighborhood, 165
Harrison, Da'Shaun, 46
harsh justice, 33
hate crimes, 17
healing, 106
hegemonic masculinity, 68–69, 123–24, 135
Heidensohn, Frances, 121
Henson, Abigail, 9–10, 33–34, 73, 85–86, 116
Herskind, Micah, 217–18
Hickey, Eric, 137
Hierarchy Rule, 14
Hill, Nancy, 70
Hindelang, Michael, 110
Hippocrates, 62
hiring policies, 88
Hirschi, Travis, 70, 71, 72, 73–74
Hirsi, Isra, 164
historical trauma, 51
Hitler, Adolf, 53
Holland, Kathryn, 102
Holtfreter, Kristy, 80
homelessness, 171–75
Home Owners' Loan Corporation (HOLC), 88–89
hooks, bell, 224
Horney, Karen, 56, 57
hospital-based violence intervention programs, 134
Hotaling, Gerald, 106
household composition, 85
Housing First approach, 174
housing the unhoused, 174–75
human agency and language, 118
human capital, 87
human fetuses as research subjects, 29
human trafficking, victims of, 183–84
The Hunger Games, 220
hypervigilant motherwork, 86
hysteria, 62

I Am Vanessa Guillén Act, 115
"ideal" victim, 107–8
identity/identities: of Black women, 95; change, 75, 76; construction, 76; and criminal legal system, 8; transformation reinforcement, 76
imaginative criminology, 126
Imaginative Criminology: Of Spaces Past, Present and Future (Seal and O'Neill), 220
immersion-emersion racial identity, 59
immigrant concentrations, 85
Immigration and Customs Enforcement detention centers, 54
impulsivity, 38
In a Different Voice (Gilligan), 58
incarcerated women: with children, 81, 224; and desistance and employment, 80; employment for formerly, 80; and marriage, 81; sexual victimization among, 111–12; and strain, 94
Incarcerated Workers Organizing Committee, 219
INCITE! Women of Color against Violence, 223
Indigenous and Alaska Native women, crimes against, 134
individual circumstances, 35
individualism, 58–59
Inform, 166
inner-directed strain, 93
Inside/Out college program, 211
insider knowledge, value of, 27–28
Institutional Review Board (IRB), 28–29
institutional rule violations, 112
interdependence, 84
intergenerational continuity of crime, 49
International Union of Sex Workers, United Kingdom, 186
intersectional feminism, 120
intersectionality, 23, 27; and climate change, 166–67; of gender with social inequalities, 68–69; and general theory of crime, 73; of race and strain, 91–92; as term, 120; in victimization, 41–42; in violence against women, 134
Intersectionality and Criminology: Disrupting and Revolutionizing Studies of Crime (Potter), 13
intervention approaches against violence, 134
intimate partner sexual assault, 96
intimate partner violence (IPV), 60, 139–41; cases, stereotypical views on, 96–97; perspective, 74. *See also* domestic violence
Investigation Discovery (true crime show), 131
involvement, 71

INDEX 297

Jacobi, Tonja, 206
Jasinski, Jana, 42
Jim Crow laws, 172
Jock Young, 117–18
Johnson, Nadia, 48
Jones, Nikki, 85
Jones-Brown, Delores, 196
Jordan-Young, Rebecca, 47–48
Juarez, Mexico, femicides in, 139
judicial discretion, 35
Junger-Tas, Josine, 225
Justice in Policing Act of 2020, 198

Kaba, Mariame, 107, 220
Kaiser, Kimberly, 97
Karkazis, Katrina, 47–48
Kelling, George, 35
King, Anna, 148
Kingsnorth, Rodney, 97
Klaas, Polly, 108
knowledge creation, 9
Kohlberg, Lawrence, 58, 59
Kojola, Erik, 163
Kraska, Peter, 195
Kruttschnitt, Candace, 80

labeling theory, 75–77
Laguardia, Francesca, 25
Lantz, Brendan, 105
larceny, fraud, forgery, and embezzlement (LFFE), 146
larceny and theft, 145–46
LaSalle Corrections, 209
Latinx people, drug usage among, 177
Laub, John, 9, 77–79, 109, 193
Laurencin, Cato, 36
Lauritsen, Janet, 109
Law, Victoria, 215
Law Enforcement Assistance Administration (LEAA), 104
law violation and stress exposure, 75
Lazzini, Arianna, 168
Leach, Mark, 58, 59
lead and crime, 50–51
left realist criminology, 117–18
legalization of sex work, 185
Leigh, Carol, 181
León, Kenneth Sebastian, 117
Lewin, Kurt, 26
LGBTQIA+ people, 123; victimization of, 111
liberal feminism, 119
Lichtenstein, Bronwen, 61–62

life course theory, 77–78
lifestyle choices and victimization, 42
lifestyle theories, 40–42, 109–10
life without parole (LWOP) sentences, 204
likelihood of conviction as focal concern, 97
Liu, Lin, 121
Lombroso, Cesare, 45, 47
London Metropolitan Police, 194
López, María Encarnación, 139
Lorde, Audre, 191
Lum, Cynthia, 197
Lynch, Michael, 167–68

Macintosh, Randall, 97
Madfis, Eric, 45
Maher, Lisa, 119, 180
male. *See* men
Malkin, Michelle, 126
Management and Training Corporation, 209
managerial crime control techniques, 63–64
mandatory-minimum sentences, 35
mandatory minimum statutes, 207
manhood, 148–49, 151. *See also* masculinity
Mapp v. Ohio, 197
marginalized communities and violent crimes, 136–38
marginalized masculinities, 69
Margolin, Jamie, 164
marriage: equality movement, 85; and women's desistance, 81
Martin, Emily, 48
Martinez, Xiuhtezcatl, 164
Maruna, Shadd, 75, 76
masculinity, 68–69; and criminal choices, 38, 39–40, 123–24; crisis of, and violence crimes, 135–36; marginalized, 69; mental health professionals reinforcing stereotypes, 138; and motor vehicle theft, 150; stereotypes, 138; trait of, 93. *See also* manhood
mass media, crime presented in, 118–19
maternal surveillance, 24–25
matriarchal societies, 149
Mayson, Sandra, 63–64
McCall, Leslie, 27
McCorkel, Jill, 98
McCulloch, Jude, 195
McEvoy, Kieran, 124
McKay, Henry Donald, 85
Mckesson, DeRay, 199
mechanical solidarity, 84
media-driven fear vs. statistical reality, 133–34

media portrayal of Black and Brown communities, 180
Megan's Law, 107–8
Meloy, Michelle, 102
men: approach to morality, 68; rape, 141; violence, 58. *See also* Black men
Menard, Kim, 103
Mendelsohn, Benjamin, 101
men's desistance and women, 78–79
mental health: and pregnant women, 142–43; professionals reinforcing masculinity stereotypes, 138; struggles and prisons, 64–65; treatment, 137–38; and women's desistance, 79
Mental Health First, 220–21
Merton, Robert K., 85, 90
Messerschmidt, James, 68–69, 124, 147–48
#MeToo movement, 142
Michalowski, Raymond, 158
Michel, Cedric, 159
Middlemiss, Wendy, 95
migrant women, 184
Milano, Alyssa, 142
Military Justice Improvement and Increasing Prevention Act, 114
military victimization, 113–15
Miller, Jody, 147–48
Miller, Susan, 22, 72, 73, 102
Miller, Walter B., 95–96
minimal risk, 28–29
Miranda v. Arizona, 197
misogyny, 102
mistrust of other ethnic-racial groups, 70
mitigating factors, 35
Moms 4 Housing, 221
Monahan, Kathryn, 79–80
Mondé, Geniece Crawford, 25–26
monoamine oxidase A (MAOA), 48–49
Moraga, Cherríe, 10
moral codes and crime, 39
moral cynicism, 103
moral development theory, 57–59
moral reasoning, 58–59
Morash, Merry, 8, 80
Moreland, Cheryl, 58, 59
motivated offenders, 40, 43
motor vehicle theft, 150–51
Muir, Warren, 166
Mulford, Carrie, 108
multicultural feminism, 120
Musto, Jennifer, 8–9
mutual aid, 223–24

Naffine, Ngaire, 71
Nagin, Daniel, 197
National Advocates for Pregnant Women (now Pregnancy Justice), 143
National Association for the Advancement of Colored People (NAACP), 164–65
National Coalition against Domestic Violence, 105
National Coalition against Sexual Assault, 105
National Crime Victimization Survey (NCVS), 18–19, 20–21, 111, 132, 140
National Defense Authorization Act, 115
National Incident-Based Reporting System (NIBRS), 13–18, 132–33, 157
National Law Center on Homelessness and Poverty, 173, 174
National Organization for Victim Assistance (NOVA), 105
National Violence against Women Survey, 97
Navarro, Jordana, 42
negative stereotypes, 53
Neissl, Katharina, 39
neo-classical criminology, 31–32
neonates as research subjects, 29
Newark Community Street Team (NCST), 221, 222
The New Jim Crow: Mass Incarceration in the Age of Colorblindness (Alexander), 210
New York Police Department (NYPD), 16, 18
Nextdoor (app), 153
Nguyen, Thuy-Trinh, 9–10, 33–34
NIBRS. *See* National Incident-Based Reporting System (NIBRS)
Nixon, Richard, 34, 176, 206–7
noradrenaline, 49
Nuevelle, Taylar, 93

Obama, Barack, 163
occupational crime, 159
Ohlin, Lloyd, 98
Olaghere, Ajima, 9–10, 33–34
older people, incarcerated, 64
Omar, Ilhan, 164
On Crimes and Punishment (Beccaria), 32
O'Neal, Eryn Nicole, 96–97
O'Neill, Maggie, 220
1033 program, 195
ordinances against the publicly poor, examples of, 175
organic solidarity, 84
Ortner, Sherry, 148–49
O'Sullivan, Julie, 161–62

the "other," 84
outer-directed strain, 93
over-policing, 175

Pacific Colony, 53–54
Packnett, Brittany, 199
Painter-Davis, Noah, 162
Paltrow, Lynn, 149
Pappenheim, Bertha, 62
parental supervision: and deviant behavior, 72–73; and women's desistance, 80
parenting and self-control, 72–74
participatory action research (PAR), 26–27
pathways theory, 81–82
patriarchal control, 74, 122–23
patriarchal societies, 149
patriarchy, 58, 102, 119; and intersecting forms of oppression, 148–49; legitimacy of, 68; and violence crimes, 135–36
peacemaking criminology, 124–25
peer: impacts and gender, 74–75; review, 20; role and crime, 39–40
Pellow, David, 163
penis envy, 56–57
pentobarbital for executions, 192
Pepinsky, Hal, 124
perceptions of police legitimacy, 17
phenomenological criminology, 75
The Philadelphia Negro (Du Bois), 85
phrenology, 45
Pickett, Justin, 132
Piliavin, Irving, 39
Piquero, Alex, 33, 41
Piquero, Nicole, 93
police legitimacy, perceptions of, 17
police militarization, 196
policing: beginning of U.S., 194–95; Eight Can't Wait campaign, 197–200; marching on, 195–96; Say Her Name campaign, 196–97; school resource officers (SROs), 201–2; Second Rape, 200–201; of women's bodies, 149
policy implications of biological theories of crime, 53–54
political economy of prisons, 86–87
Poly Implant Prothese breast implants, 161
positivist criminology, 45
post-conventional morality, 57
postmodern criminology, 118
postmodern feminist theory, 120
post-partum psychosis, 60–62
post-traumatic stress disorder (PTSD), 51–52

post-traumatic stress symptoms, 134
Potter, Hillary, 8, 13, 40, 85
poverty: and crime, 35–36; criminalization of, 87–88, 171–75; impact on women, 146; and intimate partner violence, 140; and women's recidivism, 80
power dynamics in research, 22
Pratt, Travis, 32–33, 41
pre-conventional morality, 57
pregnant people, exclusion of, 29
pre-trial detention, 62–63
prisons: abolition and victims' rights, 107; as mental health providers, 64–65; and mental health struggles, 64–65; phone calls, 217; political economy of, 86–87; staff, victimization by, 112–13
prisoners as research subjects, 29
prison industrial complex (PIC), 89–90; abolition, 215
Prison Rape Elimination Act, 113
private prisons, 209
proactive policing, 199–200
product level greenwashing, 169
prosocial identity, 75, 76
prosocial values, 75–76
protected populations in research, 29
protest masculinities, 69
psychodynamics, 56
psychological impacts of violent victimization, 134
psychological theories: algorithms and risk, 62–64; emotional dysregulation, 59–60; moral development theory, 57–59; penis envy and womb envy, 56–57; post-partum psychosis, 60–62; prisons as mental health providers, 64–65
psychological trauma, 51–52
public attitudes towards sex work, 185–86
public health and racial profiling, 36–37
public order crimes: disrupting the public order, 170–71; drug "crimes," 176–80; homelessness and the criminalization of poverty, 171–75; sex work, 181–87
public safety and punishments, 33
punishment, 32–33, 38
Puppies behind Bars, 211

quality of life, 35
quantitative research, 20–21
queer criminology, 123
Quinet, Kenna, 137
Quinney, Richard, 124, 159

Rabelo, Verónica Caridad, 101-2
race: biology of, 44-46; and crime, 46; and ethnicity as risk factors, 40-42; and moral development theory, 58-59
racial bias, 210; and fear of crime, 153; in traffic stops, 19-20
racial categories, 44-45
racial discrimination, 70, 85, 92, 172
racial disparities and drug usage, 177
racial identity development, 58-59
racial microaggressions, 91-92
racial profiling, 20, 36-37
racial segregation, 172
racism and War on Drugs, 35
radical criminology, 117
radical feminism, 119
rape, 74; as men's issue, 141-42; myths, 16; and routine activities theory, 40. *See also* sexual assault
rational choice theory, 37-40
Reagan, Ronald, 34, 105
recidivism: and employment, 80; rates, 34
reconciliation, 106
redlining, 88-89
reflexivity, 124
reforming prisons, 210-11
Reisig, Michael, 80
relative deprivation, 49, 85
Rentschler, Carrie, 103, 104
repeat offender laws, 34-35
repeat offender statutes, 207
repeat violent victimization, 134
replacement discourses, 118
reporting of crime, 15, 17-18; and #8CantWait campaign, 197, 198; in prisons, 112; of sexual assaults, 103, 112, 136, 186
reproductive injustice and climate change, 167
reproductive justice, 143
researcher diversity, 27
researcher neutrality, 22
research hierarchies, traditional, 26
research methods: critical race research methods and methodologies, 23-25; ethics and Institutional Review Boards, 28-29; feminist researchers, 21-23; National Crime Victimization Survey (NCVS), 18-19; peer-reviewed articles, 19; power and participatory action research, 26-28; storytelling and counter-storytelling, 25-26; UCR AND NIBRS, 13-18; Veil of Darkness (VOD) hypothesis, 19-21

research with action, 26-27
residential burglary, 152
resource distribution, 117
restorative justice, 219; and victims, 106-7
Rethink Masculinity program, 221
"reverse deterrent" effect, 36-37
revictimization and trauma, cycle of, 133-34
The Revolution Will Not Be Funded: Beyond the Non-profit Industrial Complex, 223
"revolving door" of incarceration, 173-74
rewards' perception and gender differences, 39
Reyns, Bradford, 41
Rich, Karen, 200
Ridgway, Gary Leon, 137
Ring Neighbors (app), 153
Rippon, Gina, 47
risk assessment in justice system, 62-64
Ritchie, Andrea, 196-97
Robinson, Aaron David, 114
Roesler, Shannon, 163
role-taking and gender, 75
Rorie, Melissa, 162
Rose, Dina, 55, 87
routine activities theory, 40-42, 109-10
Ruback, Barry, 103, 105
Rudolph, Jennifer, 76
Rushin, Kate, 10
Russell, Diana, 138

safe consumption sites, 180
safety, sense of, 35
"salvageability," 96
Sampson, Robert, 77-79, 109
sanctions and women, 39
Scherer, Heidi, 41
school resource officers (SROs), 201-2
school-to-prison pipeline, 201
Schreck, Christopher, 109
Schweers, Dylan, 206
Schweik, Susan, 172
scientific language, gender bias in, 48
Seal, Lizzie, 220
secondary victimization, 16
Securus, 217
segregation and property crime, 149-50
self-control, 38; and criminal behavior, 72-74; and gender, 74-75
self-harm, 93, 94
self-image, 75
self-interest, 68
self-medication, 51
Sentencing Project, 204, 209

Serial podcast, 131
serotonin, 48–49
Service Women's Action Network, 115
sex: defined, 47; trafficking and sex work, 183–84
sexual assault: cases, stereotypical views on, 96–97; in the military, 114. *See also* rape
sexual harassment at workplace, 102
sexual victimization among incarcerated women, 111
sexual violence analysis, 73–74
sex work: criminalization and decriminalization of, 184–86; sex trafficking, 182–84; and solidarity, 186; whorearchy, 181–82; working toward liberation, 186–87
Sex Worker Film and Arts Festival, 181
sex workers, violent crimes against, 137
shame: and crime, 16, 58, 92; and respect, 38
shared identity, 59
Shaw, Clifford Robe, 85
Sheppard, Keller, 17
shoplifting, 145, 146, 147, 148
Shover, Neal, 75
Signs (feminist journal), 48
Silverman, Eli, 17, 18
Sisters in Crime: The Rise of the New Female Criminal (Adler), 159–60
Smart, Carol, 72
social bonding theory, 70–71
social bonds, 84
social capital, 80, 87
social construction of gender, 47–48
social control, 34, 78
social development theories, 80; gender bias in criminological theory, 78–79; life course theory, 77–78; women's desistance, 79–81
socialist feminism, 119–20
socialization and gender, 68–70
socialized gender roles, 60
social learning and gender, 75
social media surveillance, 153
social process theories: differential association and social learning theory, 66–68; gender and socialization, 68–70; general theory of crime (GTC), 72–74; labeling theory, 75–77; life course theory, 77–78; peer impacts and gender, 74–75; self-control and gender, 74–75; social bonding theory, 70–71; social development theories, 77–81
social relationships and gender, 75

social structural theories: Black feminist criminology, 94–95; Durkheim's sociological approach to crime, 84; introduction, 83–84; social disorganization theory, 85–90; strain theory, 90–94; subcultural theories of crime, 95–98
social structures, contrasting, 149
social ties, 85
societal expectations of women, 94
socio-economic deprivation, 117
sociological origins of crime analysis, 83–84
socio-structural induction theory, 73
Sohoni, Tracy, 162
solidarity: and deviant activity, 84; and sex work, 186
Sommers, Ira, 76
Sorokin, David, 166
Spade, Dean, 212
specific deterrence, 32, 35
Speck, Richard, 50
Spencer, Zoe, 24, 27
Spohn, Cassia, 96–97
Stark, Rodney, 103
state violence, 65, 142
Steffensmeier, Darrell, 162
Stella (peer-led sex worker organization), 186
stereotypes: attributed to bisexual people, 17; attributed to Black women, 120; gendered stereotypes and narratives, 48; negative, 53; views of crimes, 96; views on intimate partner violence (IPV) cases, 96–97
sterilization, 53–54
"stop, question, and frisk" (SQF) practice, 36–37
Stop Enabling Sex Traffickers Act (SESTA), 184
storytelling and counter-storytelling, 25–26
Stowell, Jacob, 17
strain, 34
strain theory, 90–94
strategic-level greenwashing, 168
street crimes, 33, 73, 159
street offenders, female, 76, 82
stress exposure, 74–75
structural approach to understanding crime, 83–84
structural factors to crime, 135
structural inequality, 40
structural positions and law violation, 74–75
structured action and gender, 147–48
subcultural theories of crime, 95–98
subordinated masculinities, 69

Substance Abuse and Mental Health Services Administration, 177
substance abuse treatment, 76
Sudbury, Julia, 214
suicidal ideation in prison, 64
Sultan, Reina, 216, 217–18
supervision of girls, 71
Survived and Punished (S&P), 221, 222–23
survivors: and convict criminology, 125–26; credibility, 17
Sutherland, Edwin, 7, 66, 155–56, 158
Swedish model of legal choice for sex work, 185
Sylvia Rivera Law Project, 212

target hardening, 151
Tefler, Mary, 50
Terry, Geraldine, 166–67
thalidomide, 161
theriocide, 167
Thirteenth Amendment, 214, 217
This Bridge Called My Back: Writings by Radical Women of Color (Moraga and Anzaldúa), 10
Thoennes, Nancy, 97
Thomas, April Gile, 79–80
Thompson, Maxine, 92
three-strikes laws you're out law, 35, 108, 207
Tjaden, Patricia Godeke, 97
Toby, Jackson, 33
Tonry, Michael, 225
Torelli, Riccardo, 168
toxic masculinity, 135–36, 137–38
Toxic Release Inventory (TRI), 166
transformative justice, 219
Transform Harm, 220–21
trans frameworks, applying, 8–9
transgender and gender diverse (TGD) people, victimization of, 112–13
translational criminology, 9, 193
trans women, 122
trauma: biological impacts of childhood, 51–52; and revictimization, cycle of, 133–34; and victimization in prison, 112
trauma-informed approaches in policing, 200–201
Travis, Jeremy, 35
trigger warning, 100–101
Truth-in-Sentencing Incentive Grants Program, 207
truth-in-sentencing laws, 35, 207
Turanovic, Jillian, 41

UCR. *See* Uniform Crime Reports (UCR)
Uggen, Christopher, 80
The Ugly Laws (Schweik), 172
Umaña-Taylor, Adriana, 70
underage nonsexual labor, 183
underage prostitution, 183
unemployment: and arson rates, 152; as barrier to mental health treatment, 138; and criminal behavior, 80; and intimate partner violence, 141; and strain, 91
Uniform Code of Military Justice, 114, 115
Uniform Crime Reports (UCR), 13–14, 20–21, 132–33
Urban Indian Health Institute, 134
U.S. Youth Climate Strike, 164

Valcore, Jace, 121–22
Veil of Darkness (VOD) hypothesis, 19–20
Vera Institute of Justice, 203
Verma, Arvind, 17, 18
Veterans Treatment Court, 205
victim blaming, 17; in male-on-female violence, 102; in sex work, 137; and structural violence, 79
victim compensation and restitution programs, 105–6
victim cooperation as focal concern, 97
victim decision making, 97
victimization: and disabled people, 110–11; of people in prison, 111–13; of people in the military, 113–15; and queer people, 111; racial disparities in violent, 133–34; and traffic accidents, 109
victim-offender overlap, 108–9; in prisons, 112
victimology: deviant places theory, 103; ideal victim, 107–8; prison abolition and victims' rights, 107; restorative justice and victims, 106–7; routine activities and lifestyle theories, 109–10; trigger warning, 100–101; victim compensation and restitution programs, 105–6; victimization and disabled people, 110–11; victimization and queer people, 111; victimization of people in prison, 111–13; victimization of people in the military, 113–15; victim-offender overlap, 108–9; victim precipitation theory, 101–2; victims' rights movement and punishment, 103–5
victim precipitated forcible rape, 101
victim precipitation theory, 101–2
victims' rights movement and punishment, 103–5

Victim Witness Protection Act of 1982, 105
Violence against Women Act of 1994, 215
Violent Crime Control and Law Enforcement Act of 1994, 207
violent victimization and mental health, 137
von Hentig, Hans, 101

Wagner, Bryan, 195
Walker, Dominique, 222
Walker, Joanne, 36
War on Drugs, 34–36, 176–77, 206–8
Wedgewood, 222
Weinstein, Harvey, 142
Weisburd, David, 36
Weiss, Karen, 16, 19
well-being, sense of, 35
Wertz, Jasmin, 49, 55
West, Desirée, 61–62
Weston Morrow, Michael White, and Henry Fradella, 36
White, Amina, 29
white-collar crimes, 33, 72, 146; absence of laws, 161–62; concept of, 155–56; and corporate crime, 159; definition of, 156–57; Enron case, 157; and gender, 159–60; gendered corporate harm victimization, 160–61; wage theft, 157–59; and women, 159–60
white-male-centered theory, 59
white-on-white crime, 134–35
white people, drug usage among, 177, 179
white racial hatred, 152–53
white supremacy, 198
white women: in early (first- and second-wave) feminism, 120; middle-class, 94; and violent victimization, 41
whorearchy, 181–82

whorephobia and criminalization, 182
Who Speaks for Me? project, 93
Wikersham and Knapp Commissions, 197
Wildeman, John, 159
Williams, Clive Kenneth, 151
Williams, Jason, 24, 27
Williams, Jerry Dewayne, 207
Wilson, James, 35
Wilson, Sean, 24, 27
womb envy, 56, 57
women: approach to morality, 68; desistance, 79–81; and differential opportunities, 98; drug users, 180; emotion dysregulation in, 60; employment and desistance, 80–81; flexibility and agency and crime, 148; and gender-specific strain, 92–94; Lombroso on criminality in, 47; marriage and desistance, 81; and motor vehicle theft, 151; offenders, leniency towards, 121; parenthood and desistance, 81; poverty and recidivism, 80; rational choice theorists on, 38–40; stereotypical behavior, 121; street offenders, 76, 82; and white-collar crime, 159–60; in workforce and crime, 145–46. *See also* Black women; incarcerated women; white women
workplace mistreatment, 102
Worth Rises, 192, 217

XYY syndrome, 50

Yates, Andrea, case, 60–62
Young, Jock, 15
young adult delinquency, 71

Zero Hour, 164

Founded in 1893,
UNIVERSITY OF CALIFORNIA PRESS
publishes bold, progressive books and journals
on topics in the arts, humanities, social sciences,
and natural sciences—with a focus on social
justice issues—that inspire thought and action
among readers worldwide.

The UC PRESS FOUNDATION
raises funds to uphold the press's vital role
as an independent, nonprofit publisher, and
receives philanthropic support from a wide
range of individuals and institutions—and from
committed readers like you. To learn more, visit
ucpress.edu/supportus.